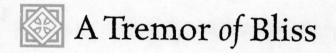

A Tremor of Bliss

A Tremor *of* Bliss

CONTEMPORARY WRITERS ON THE SAINTS

Edited by PAUL ELIE

Introduction by ROBERT COLES

HARCOURT BRACE & COMPANY

NEW YORK   SAN DIEGO   LONDON

Library of Congress Cataloging-in-Publication Data
A tremor of bliss: contemporary writers on the saints/edited by
    Paul Elie.—1st ed.
        p.   cm.
    ISBN 0-15-100101-4
    1. Christian saints—Cult. 2. Christian life—Catholic authors.
    I. Elie, Paul.
    BX2325.T74   1994
    235'.2—dc20   94-22332

Designed by Lydia D'moch
Printed in the United States of America
First edition
A B C D E

Acknowledgments

The editor thanks Alane Salierno Mason, Sue Young Wilson, Celia Wren, and Amanda Urban for their encouragement and support.

I have had a tremor of bliss, a wink of heaven, a whisper,
And I would no longer be denied; all things
Proceed to a joyful consummation.

—Archbishop Thomas Becket,
in *Murder in the Cathedral,*
by T. S. Eliot

CONTENTS

Introduction

ROBERT COLES

THE ESSAYS in this book tell us that the idea and the ideal of sanctity, as it has been lived in certain lives over the centuries, persist in our significantly secular time for these American writers, among others. Not that most of us think of sharing in print our spiritual inclinations or preoccupations, as they find expression in this or that historical figure. Reflection, let alone reflection put forward and shared with others, is surely a privilege— though a curse, too, many authors would also say. In that regard, some who barely can read or write (because

of their age, or the social circumstances of their life)
would eagerly assent—it is a mixed blessing to try to
find one's spiritual bearings. "I wish I wasn't sick," a boy
afflicted with polio told me in 1958, amid a severe epi-
demic of that disease. I was then working on the pedia-
tric ward of a Boston hospital, and was not surprised to
hear those words—they had become a daily chant, spoken plaintively by child after child. But this youngster
had something else in mind for me to hear, to contemplate: "Before I got this [illness] I didn't pray to all those
people, that they should help me out with God." I wasn't
sure what he meant, and I was quite busy, in a hurry. I
was just curious enough, though, to risk a question:
"Which people?" He smiled, volunteered: "All the
saints." His mother, it turned out, had been urging him
to seek help through those who "lived in Heaven," she
put it, and thereby had the ear of God. The boy obliged;
but he wasn't happy to do so: "I don't want to bother
those folks, and besides, they must have so many kids to
worry about." He paused, then added this: "I'd just as
soon they forgot me; and I wish I could go back to my
life before here." He more than implied his desire to forget *them*.

I had no time or inclination, back then, to pursue the
matter with that boy—aim for a bedside colloquy on the
saints as putative, intercessory agents in the lives of
Christ's faithful ones. But many years later, while working as a volunteer teacher in a Boston elementary school

that served a ghetto neighborhood, I found myself remembering that boy and his comments. I was teaching
vocabulary and spelling to a fourth-grade class, nine- and
ten-year-old boys and girls. A girl was spelling the word
"angel," and she stumbled: she wrote "angle" on the
blackboard. Sure she was right, she quickly put the chalk
down and went back to her seat. I waited for objections,
corrections, and soon enough realized that no one had
noticed anything wrong. The children, actually, seemed
bored, noisily indifferent to the entire exercise—no surprise at all. Yet again I prepared myself for a show of
irritation, for an outburst meant to secure attention, interest, compliance. Yet again, I was dragging my feet, praying that somehow, through some miraculous intervention
of luck, someone would say something that would spare
me the necessity of behaving in that manner: raising my
voice high to purchase a fleeting moment of obedience,
silence—all of us, thereby, humiliated, and moments
later all of us once more lost to one another as, inexor-
ably, the sound level would rise and rise. Suddenly, a
boy, a wise guy of a boy, snickered, laughed, and then
spoke: "Hey, that's angle, not angel." Now, a quiet classroom—and then lots of whistling, hooting, slapping of
rulers on desks, cheering. I got annoyed: *Come on*—
enough, more than enough: an overreaction on my part
that had to do, nevertheless, with how little respect for
ordinary classroom civility could be assumed by a
teacher, by any student oddly inclined to be serious.

But I am, too, suddenly moved to take stock. I decide I am too down on these youngsters. I have underestimated their capacity to move from evident playfulness (interpreted by me as the same old disorder and callousness of a failed ghetto school system) to sly, provocative thoughtfulness. Then, I hear: "Well, what's the angle the angels have, I want to know"—a girl musing out loud. Utter quiet, uninterrupted, this time, by any background noise. As if to prompt further introspection, she amplifies: "Everyone has an angle, don't you think?" Nods tell her that she is right on target. A girl sitting right in front of her turns around to offer a conjecture: "The angels are good friends to God, I think. They're good, real good, like God is. They don't go around messing up. They're the ones who are one hundred percent perfect: not like anyone who's here—not like any people, because even the best of people, they'll do wrong as well as good, so there's no one hundred percent from [among] them."

A boy sitting in the last seat of the last row, almost always without comment, though quite observant and quite smart, surprises everyone with his hand raised high, kept there until the teacher acknowledges him, whereupon he gives a pointed disquisition of sorts: "You don't have an angle if you're an angel; that's what I think. The reason is: an angel doesn't exist, the way we do. You see, an angel is a spirit; our priest told us. A saint, that's different. A saint is a person; so I agree, a saint can't be perfect. No one is. A saint will have an angle: he's trying to strike a home run, or she is, if it's a woman who's the saint. [There was Joan of Arc.] Saint Francis, he wanted people to be nicer—that was his angle. He was very nice, and wanted people to be like him, more like him. Our priest says he had 'ambition' for all of the people; and that was his angle, maybe. Do you see what I mean?"

A spell of absolute silence; *he* had hit a home run. Students who had been listening to him had turned to look at him, and continued to do so, while he looked down at his desk. Finally, as others began to stir (and, I speculate, ready themselves with things to say), he looks up, decides he has more to tell: "You could probably guess: a lot of those saints, they would have liked to be angels, but you can't be an angel unless God makes you one. If He makes you a person, then you'll just be here a little while, and you die. I think angels live forever. I'm not sure. That's a difference [between angels and saints]. But the big difference is that if you're a person, you make mistakes; you can't help it. We try to remember the saints because of the good they did; but they didn't always do good. You should remember that."

More of the unusual silence, and then a burst of remarks from other children, the gist of which is a confirmation of the spiritual (if not theological) exegesis just given us. One girl says a lot, summarizes a lot, when she comments upon the "big struggles those saints must have [had] when they were trying to be saints, but they couldn't be, not all the time, that's for sure. Who can be, even one of them?" We all realize, courtesy of this discussion, the real anguish and conflict involved for those men and women, posthumously declared saints by church officials, and by generations of believers, and nonbelievers. It is all too easy to forget the essential humanity of such individuals, as these children, in their charming so-called innocence, were not wont to do—a contrast: their earthy, blunt recognition of that humanity, opposed to the common presentations, in churches, in history books, of so many saints, certainly Saint Francis: a perfection rendered incarnate.

No question the great Danish theologian and essayist Kierkegaard was quite conversant with the point of view those children were proposing when he offered the few who would then be his readers "On the Difference Between a Genius and an Apostle." Again and again he insists that the "difference" has little to do with talent or intelligence; has everything to do with purpose, with a kind of commitment—in his terms, a moral rather than an aesthetic distinction. The apostle, the saint, is "called," but, in consequence, we ought to keep in mind (we who are ever tempted by idolatry of one kind or another) that he or she "does not become more intelligent, does not receive more imagination, a greater acuteness of mind and soul." Rather, the apostle, the saint, makes an appeal to "divine authority," aligns himself or

herself with a specific religious tradition, with its asser-
tions, its convictions, its proclaimed faith. To do so, of
course, has often meant trouble and more trouble; and
the difficulties, the burdens, the pain and suffering have
varied over the centuries: the death meted out by the
Romans, courtesy of animals, or the death (ironically)
meted out by the Church itself in the interest of orthodoxy—or the daily "death" of intellectual or moral scorn
that can take place in, say, modern times when a spiritual
person takes on not so much religious customs and conventions as secular ones.

In all instances, the apostle, the saint, is an antago-
nist, as Kierkegaard keeps insisting, to one or another
kind of "authority," even as he or she speaks in the name
of another kind: that of Jesus. Of course, in that regard
the Roman Catholic Church has claimed, ultimately and
specifically, to be a necessary intermediary, the earthly
institution that names saints, ascribes particular individuals with such a designation. Some would, and do, beg
to differ, though; men and women are called "saints" in
everyday life by those who are witnesses to a particular
life lived, a singular message persistently, ardently con-
veyed, at all costs. Hence the discussion, in this volume,
of Dorothy Day, and maybe a similar discussion has
taken place over the centuries with respect to all the
saints: holiness observed and remembered and treasured
by ordinary people with no special claim to churchly authority.

When I was a college student, I took a course, Classics of the Christian Tradition, offered by Perry Miller, who spent so much of his life trying to fathom the Puritan sensibility of the seventeenth and eighteenth centuries. He was the one who introduced us to Kierkegaard's powerfully affecting, sometimes stunning and haunting essays, to his dramatic virtuosity, his daring raids upon the accepted and the conventional, his moral brilliance, so unnerving and suggestive. We got into a discussion one day about saints (we were a class of about thirty). Miller listened, nodded, asked questions, provoked us to silent contemplation, interrupted, sometimes, by his own gruff, hearty, earthy but thought-laden comments, or, often enough, his outcries of the soul as much as of the head. That day, while names of saints came up, one after the other, as we tried to make sense of their diverse and not rarely difficult, even (seemingly) tormented lives, Miller sat before us in a kind of stoic bemusement, with not a word to say. Finally, we stopped fighting for his attention, stopped fighting with one another. We'd been eagerly, and competitively, offering various explanations and interpretations of sainthood, drawing, of course, on contemporary psychology and sociology, and on history and theology. Miller pushed back his chair, told us he didn't really have a definitive idea or definition of what constitutes sainthood, but he could offer us a "personal surmise." I recall, even now, writing down those two words—so characteristic of this extraordinary professor:

a deliberate tentativeness that certainly approached modesty. We were all ears, and we heard this: "A saint is a sinner, writ large, someone who struggles exceptionally hard to turn a bad thing into a good one." He went on to remind us that rather often such a person has no such explicit or conscious agenda in mind—the conversion of darkness into light, so to speak. Saints, he went on to speculate, are "driven by a moral nature, much in jeopardy," are "ready to take huge risks and chances," because they know well the "terror of hell," or "the loneliness that awaits them in hell."

As he kept learning backward in his chair, we were all hunched, sitting forward, trying to digest a particular offering. Nor were we having an easy time. This was, after all, the second half of the twentieth century, and we were attending a more or less secular American university. We wanted some "psychodynamics," maybe, or some "cultural history," or, if we had to settle for it, some damned original, and of course subtle, theology: no thinly masked pieties from earlier, more "respectful" times in Christendom's past. Yet, we knew not how to spell out our needs, our interests—ourselves, really: who we had already become, what our assumptions were, and, yes, what we found unconvincing, if not utterly unacceptable. At last, one of us broke the spell of nervous quiet with a question: "You don't believe in hell, do you?" Miller laughed; he understood, right away, that as he had been trying to explain the way *saints* thought, *their* reasons for being, for acting as they did, he had spoken as if the hell they dreaded existed for him, too. We wanted him, he realized, to distance himself from that word, to use language, or a mere gesture, a facial expression, to indicate his awareness of ancient superstition! Instead, we were told this: "Hell has lived in minds, driven souls to countless adventures and achievements, inspired great deeds"—a pause, and then the briefest of explications: "Fear or dread as grace."

That last phrase landed on us just as we were summoning what we regarded to be a clever, an adroit psychology, the contemporary mannerisms of the clinic: he is dodging; he is telling us that he believes in the subjective reality of hell as it gets experienced, still, by some, and even gets used "adaptively," that final word meant to be a compliment, though one not without the risks of condescension. But Miller had confused us, as well as given us pause, with his use of the word "grace"—not exactly a word one encounters in today's social-science vocabulary. We wanted to ask about *that*, too: what in the world did "grace" *really* mean? I now realize (I'm sure Miller *then* realized) that we didn't even have the vocabulary that would enable a reasonably polite consideration of the subject matter. We were materialists at heart, and in connection with this discussion we could venture only so far away from our cultural and historical roots—say, toward the metapsychology Freud had bestowed: hell as an assault of the Super-Ego on the Id,

and grace as some "equilibrium" (the "scientific" satis-
factions of such a word!) between Super-Ego and Ego.
Taking stock of us, and looking inward, too, I'm sure,
Miller tried yet again to be of assistance: "How can one
imagine a saint without imagining heaven and hell as utterly imaginable to them?" Once more, he held back
words, just as we craved them, ached for their familiar
solace, no matter their sometimes irritable, or upsetting
challenge. We had learned to wait, though, and did, until
he turned his attention decisively away from those saints,
toward us: "I think if we are to understand saints, we
have to try to follow their lead. Imagine the worlds they
never stopped imagining, reaching for, fleeing with all
their might."

In my notes, with their hurried capture of his remarks, I managed to assert myself with one word he
chose deliberately not to use: the desirability of "empa-
thy"—a caveat to myself, courtesy of the professor, or
so I earnestly believed to be the case. Now I think I
understand the desperation, if not (in the tradition of
Kierkegaard) the resignation, that informed that tutorial
effort. How to speak of angels and devils, of heaven and
hell, of saints and even sinners in such a setting—a reasonably humane (so we hoped) secularism at the peak of
its influence? A professor was both gently and fiercely
suggesting that to comprehend the assumptions of others, we had to give hard scrutiny, first, to our own—
rather than take it upon ourselves to walk, willy-nilly,

into anyone's life with our modern diagnostic strategies, formulations, shoptalk in the expectation that a discovery (always on our terms, in our terms) would be forthcoming. We who claim to understand human feeling more precisely than was possible ever before were being asked to test the range of that understanding, take a big leap into the shoes of others (a bit more, such an effort, I fear, than that of sounding the trumpet of "psycho-historical" theory).

So with these writers here: they try in their several ways to connect with certain saints; to leap across generations, centuries, entire eras, in order to bring alive men and women who are, finally, fellow human beings, at once tempted and tried, hugely given over to spiritual passions, insistently intent on realizing them in word, in deed, no matter the personal consequences. What follows in these essays is a chemistry of bonding, an anthropology of affiliation, of kinship, a psychology of moral imagination raised, given voice. These late-twentieth-century men and women of the industrial West attempt an intimacy of mind, heart, soul with chosen predecessors in the human parade, those who by dint of their daunting, sometimes desperate spirituality continue both to confound and to inspire us. Ordinary souls that we are, we respond to such lives, such lived moments, such brief spells amidst an infinity of time, such utterly transient locations of moral and spiritual struggle in an infinity of space, with what resources we can muster—the biographer's effort at an account, a chronicle; the writer's mix of memory and narrative cogency, urgency. Through these essayists, others long dead or not so long gone come to life yet again, and in turn, the tasks they attempted, the examples they sought to find for themselves and show to others, the passions of faith they tried to affirm, share, encourage, are given the life of a reader's attention, and maybe more, too: a celebration of the miracle of commitment, moment by moment tested and strained by the doubt that not rarely goes under that name of faith.

In their sum, too, these essays attest to the variousness of that faith: the many ways of getting down on one's knees, in the hope (the hope against hope) that there is in this cosmos the listening, the watching, and, not least, the judging, the sorting, which so many of us, for so long have sought, prayed for, spent lives wondering about, waiting for—God in all the mystery of the word, in all the perplexity and frustration that the word can evoke. The saints, maybe, have tried to give their lives over to that mystery, that perplexity and frustration: Here I went, stumbled, but plodded on, and here you are, fellow pilgrim; take my hand, therefore, and walk your given allotment of days with the effort of faith, even if the ending of both of our journeys is known to none of us—but we do pray, Lord, we pray to a world insubstantial, indeed, though real enough right now, right here, for us so tethered to human existence.

Il Poverello

BRUCE BAWER

FOR YEARS, the biggest annual draw at North America's largest cathedral has been a high mass commemorating the feast of Saint Francis. It's called the Missa Gaia, or Earth Mass, and if you show up early enough at New York's Cathedral of Saint John the Divine to squeeze into the teeming nave, you'll witness a procession of animals that includes parrots and turtles, cats and dogs, a horse, a camel, an elephant, even amoebae.

It's an unusual service, but then it honors an unusual saint—indeed, the most popular saint there is. Born late in 1181 or early in 1182, he was baptized Giovanni, for Saint John the Baptist, at the request of his mother, who was named Giovanna but was apparently known as Pica (which may mean that she came from Picardy). His father, Pietro di Bernardone, an Assisi clothing merchant who did business with the French, rejected the boy's baptismal name and replaced it with an unusual one: Francesco. It's tempting to see the contrast between the two appellations—the one Biblical and the other a Francophile neologism perhaps inspired by commercial considerations—as reflecting the tension between a mother who was a good Catholic and a father who was a good businessman. Certainly the history of Francis's early years suggests that the boy was no stranger either to the essence of the Christian message or to the worldview of the medieval mercantile class.

The volumes of saints' lives are crowded with stories of men and women who as children were noted for their piety, self-abnegation, and acts of contrition—and, in many cases, supernatural visions and visitations. Not so with Francis, whose "sudden conversion in the midst of a life of pleasure" H. G. Wells compared with Gautama Buddha's. A worldly youth, he spent his father's money on amusements; perhaps because Bernardone traded in cloth, moreover (Francis is said to have worked in his clothing store), the young man was something of a clotheshorse. He also dreamed of glory in battle. Yet when he was dispatched to the rival town of Perugia with a contingent of armed noblemen, he was promptly captured and imprisoned. Released after a year, he resolved to give war another chance; yet, setting out for the Fifth Crusade, he made it only to Spoleto before he heard a voice telling him to return home. He did.

Soon it was clear: Francis, at twenty-five, had changed. The clothier's son began to dress plainly and to give his good clothes—along with money—to beggars. When it developed that he was also handing out merchandise from his father's store, Bernardone dragged Francis home, beat him, and locked him up. Freed by Pica, he was hauled before the bishop. (Considering himself to be in God's service, Francis refused to face civil authorities.) Ordered to restore his father's possessions, Francis stripped, leaving nothing on his body but that popular medieval penitential aid, a hair shirt. The bishop, impressed by his respectful audacity, released him.

Had Francis stolen from his father? It would seem so. But Francis, stubbornly set on doing good with the wealth he'd been accustomed to spending on himself, may not have realized it. Then again, the Francis–Bernardone relationship does seem awfully like something out of Freudian case study. Whenever their paths crossed after Francis's trial, Bernardone cursed his son. In response, Francis hired an old beggar to follow him around Assisi; if Bernardone began hurling maledictions, the beggar would bless Francis, who would then rebuke his father for *not* blessing him. Was Francis being unfair, using his Heavenly Father as ammunition in an Oedipal rebellion? Or was he, a Biblical literalist, merely observing Christ's injunction that his followers must hate their parents? Was Christ, after all, being unfair to Mary when he refused to see her, saying, "My mother and my brothers are those who hear the word of God and act upon it"?

For that is what Francis was about: he sought to lead a Christlike life, and not to do it by halves. The first lesson of his story is that living like Christ is not just a matter of being vaguely nice and inoffensive; at times one may find it necessary to behave in ways that seem obstinate, self-righteous, even uncharitable. The second lesson is that the path to Christ can be bumpy and meandering. Before discovering how best to serve God with the gifts at one's disposal, one can make some terribly wrong turns and misguided choices. It's said, for instance, that when Francis first became a beggar he frankly sought glory as a "knight of God" in the same way he'd aspired to military glory—hardly an example of proper Christian humility. Did he continue to think this way, or did humility come gradually?

Whatever the case, Francis found his way to God's service by stages. The first stage involved a dilapidated San Damiano church. Convinced that God had commanded him to "repair my house," Francis—a literalist not only Biblically but also, apparently, in the matter of heavenly voices—set about restoring the structure. Pres-

ently, in a wood near Assisi, he discovered a small Benedictine chapel, Our Lady of the Angels, later Our Lady
of the Portiuncula, which would become the hub of Franciscan activity; this, too, he repaired.

At first mocked and stoned in Assisi, Francis came to
be tolerated, then esteemed. Like Christ, he began to
draw disciples to his side, a development that wasn't part
of his original intent. The Franciscan order just *happened*.
Why? Part of the reason for it—and for Francis's popu-
larity down to the present—lies in his simplicity of life,
thought, and expression. His "Canticle of the Sun" (now
considered the first great poem in Italian), his letters, and
the rules he wrote for his order reflect a firm and uncomplicated conviction that human beings are put on earth
to praise, serve, and rejoice. As Hans Küng has noted,
Francis is of all medieval figures the one with whose
view of Christ today's Christians can most readily identify. No intellectual giant, no maker of systematic doctrine, he appeals to most Christians' antipathy for
abstruse formulations. His warning that knowledge could
be self-destructive—a warning motivated by his belief
that theological discourse had severed the clergy from
God's pure message of love and from the laypeople
they were called to serve—speaks loudly to the anti-
intellectualism of the average man or woman in the
average pew. For scholars, this aspect of Francis can be
troubling. Yet even bookish Christians will acknowledge
that a simple hymn can help one to achieve a sense of

spiritual communion that an entire theological library may not. That's the essence of Francis's ministry, then and now: his simple, perhaps overly literal, and (to some) even ingenuous obedience to Christ's charge to serve the poor—his willingness to be "God's fool"— confronts us all with the degree to which our own Christianity is a matter of speech more than of action, a belief intellectualized rather than passionately lived.

One aspect of Francis's simplicity was his strong sense of attachment to and brotherhood with animals— most famously, his preaching to birds. Yet, although this side of Francis may appeal to the sentimentally inclined and theologically shaky—those who dwell on such questions as "Will my dog go to heaven?"—one need not fall into that category to find positive meaning in Francis's avian homiletics. As a smart preacher once observed, the proper Christian question is not "Will my dog go to heaven?" but "Will I bring heaven to my dog?" In other words, "Does my faith manifest itself in such a way that not only my fellow human beings but animals as well can tell the difference?" This is the proper light, I think, in which to regard Francis's preaching to birds—as the manifestation of a love of God so powerful that he felt compelled to share it with all of God's creation.

Francis even saw the heathen as his brothers—a novel idea in thirteenth-century Europe, where high-profile Crusaders were routinely canonized for slaughtering infidels. Traveling in 1219 to Egypt, he determined to make a Christian of the Egyptian sultan, Malek el-Kamil, and bravely crossed the Crusaders' battle lines to meet him. The sultan proved to be a sophisticated man, far more interested in cultural and spiritual matters—and far more tolerant, too—than most European royals. After a friendly theological conversation with Francis, he reportedly said, "I would convert to your religion, which is a beautiful one, but I cannot: Both of us would be massacred." Remarkably, it is recorded that Francis accompanied the sultan's nephew to a mosque and prayed there, saying: "God is everywhere." Today, when stories about Francis meeting Christ don't convince, and when even the Roman Catholic Church recognizes the stigmata as psychosomatic, Francis's sojourn with the sultan stands out as the most impressive event of his life. As Julian Green writes, he "was and still remains the man who transcends our sad theological barriers," rising above the intense sectarian antagonisms of his time—and ours— as an emblem of religious tolerance, interfaith ventures, and ecumenical bridge-building.

For his contemporaries, Francis's simple existence— and his decision to call himself the Little Pauper (the "Poverello") and his society the Order of Friars Minor— contrasted strikingly with the lives of the many priests and monks who kept concubines and lived in luxury. His humility, to be sure, did not prevent him from preaching a sermon to the Pope and several cardinals chiding them for their vanity and dissipation. Yet this archetypal rebel remained a loyal, obedient Catholic. He was also, in some ways, much like other medieval saints. He recoiled from sex, for instance, avoiding women and enjoining his brothers to do the same; when forced into mixed company, he was taciturn, even rude. An early biographer notes that his antipathy for the opposite sex was so powerful that "one would have thought it was fear or disgust rather than prudence." "Don't canonize me too soon," Francis once said. "I am still perfectly capable of fathering children." He shared, then, the tendency often encouraged by the Roman Catholic Church to see physical intimacy, even in marriage, as inconsistent with virtue. Given this severe posture, the introduction into his life of a young woman named Clare seems almost like a plot device out of some old movie—a medieval version, say, of *The Bells of Saint Mary's*. A biographer of Francis has written that Saint Clare "brought to the Franciscan movement a consistency, a strength and a tenacious intuition of elemental issues which it might otherwise have lacked." She also brought women. Pressing herself on Francis, imploring him to allow her into his fold, Clare forced him to accept the fact of female spirituality and to permit her to form an associate order, the Poor Clares. Yet he continued to have misgivings, saying to one of his brothers that "it is the Lord who has preserved us from taking wives, but who knows whether it is not the Devil who has sent us sisters?"

Francis wasn't above the superstitions of his day. It had been decreed that those who died on the Crusades would go straight to Heaven; claiming that Christ had told him to make the request, Francis asked that those who confessed at La Portiuncula be accorded the same benefit. Pope Honorius III agreed, but stipulated that complete absolution would be granted only one day a year. That was enough for Francis, who proclaimed: "I shall send them all to paradise!" The apparent egoism of this remark can give one pause, as can Francis's eagerness to believe that souls might be purchased in such fashion—a view that militates against our sense of him as being, in many ways, our contemporary. And what of his stigmata? The Middle Ages loved them; they figure prominently in most paintings of him, and for centuries had their own feast day. Today, however, these once seemingly miraculous episodes serve only to underscore Francis's similarities to lesser, more ordinary saints.

It's not miracles that mark Francis as extraordinary; it's the fullness of his humanity. Some saints are celebrated for their lives in the world, their practical service to humankind; others are venerated for having been mystics, hermits, visionaries—people who renounced society to be closer to God. Most saints (martyrs aside) fall squarely into one category or the other. Francis straddled them; at once inner- and outer-directed, a man of contemplation as well as action, he adhered with equal ardor to Christ's commandments to love God and one's neighbor. Indeed, it's tempting to see a reflection of this mixture of spirituality and earthiness in his two names: Giovanni, for the Baptist, who marked people as citizens of Heaven, and Francis, for France, a portion of the earth.

This isn't to suggest that the most popular saint was necessarily the most saintly of men, any more than the most celebrated film star is the finest of actors. Like a film star, a great saint is someone whose life can be reduced to a strong, uncomplicated image. Francis's is such a life. Yet he remains, for us, very real. "I want to hear a saint converse," John Henry Newman wrote. "I am not content to look at him as a statue." Countless artists have depicted Francis, but to view their works is not only to be confronted with an image of holiness but also to be reminded of a singular life, to feel a personality's presence, and, yes, to hear a voice. There is no danger that those artworks will be rendered mute any time soon; all it takes is a glance at one of them for Francis to come alive in our minds as do few other Christian figures aside from Christ Himself.

Indeed, in a time when not only Protestants but more than a few Catholics rebel at the idea of sainthood, Francis speaks to us as few men or women of his time do— and as few saints do, medieval or otherwise. What, many Christians wonder with good reason, do hermits, cults of suffering, and supposed posthumous miracles have to do with the gospel message that lies at the heart of the faith?

Why, they ask, must we feel obliged to continue celebrating certain historical figures for what may not, to our
eyes, look like Christian virtue? Especially in an Age of
Celebrity, how can we justify heaping additional praise
onto a life already amply glorified when honor might instead be paid to a virtuous unknown?

The Church canonizes men and women so that they
may be emulated, not prayed to. Yet people being what
they are, canonization has always carried with it the danger of replacing the ideal of a Christlike life with a fetish-
ism about relics and a tendency to pray to saints rather
than to God. Francis defies that sort of vulgarization: the
plain, powerful story of his life keeps forcing us back to
his earthly example even as it reveals to us the startling
light of Christ, that breakthrough of the kingdom into
the darkness of this world. Unlike many saints, who in
medieval paintings look remote and severe, there's nothing forbidding about him. He reminds us that when we
speak of the "communion of saints," we are talking not
just about those famous figures enshrined in the pages of
Alban Butler, but about "the Church in earth and
heaven"—about the people who sit every week around
us in church, and about unsung men and women who
led ordinary lives with faith and goodness. Precisely because the Christlike pattern of his life remains a potent
fact in Christians' minds, Francis is in no danger of being
reduced to a mere name invoked in prayer or an iconic
image set up over an altar—and thus, paradoxically, in

no danger of being magnified beyond his remarkable humanness into a substitute, in some minds, for God.

Time and again, in fact, Francis is paraded in order to defend sainthood itself. When the Catholic Worker founder Dorothy Day was posthumously proposed for canonization, her friends and family protested because in their view sainthood encourages veneration rather than imitation (a fascinating commentary, by the way, on the institution's present state in the Roman Catholic Church). Observes Kenneth L. Woodward: "Who could doubt that Day herself would prefer imitation to veneration? But then again St. Francis of Assisi, surely no lover of pomp and puffery, had survived the rigors of official sainthood; might not Dorothy Day do the same?"

Yet in the very potency of Francis's life there is also a danger. For he's proven to be an easily secularized, or least de-Christianized, saint. His biography and prayers lend themselves to misinterpretation by New Age nature-worshipers who in claiming him as one of their own ignore the Christian context of his earth-love, and by iconoclasts who see him as a comrade-in-arms without recognizing his deep respect for the institutional Church, his appreciation of the proper tension between continuity and Christ's insistence on *dis*continuity. Some modern liturgical celebrations of Francis can be dismaying to serious Christians. Take the Earth Mass I've mentioned: in addition to the parade of animals, it features recorded

whale and seal calls, leotard-clad dancers gyrating eroti-
cally in the pulpit, and reserved seating. During the service, many people take flash pictures and hold crystals
aloft in their open palms. The casual atmosphere is presumably a tribute to Francis's own spartan way of life;
but how to explain the incessant talking, the children
who are urged to shriek and scamper about, and the parents who hoist tots on their shoulders? Most of those in
attendance are content to honor Francis's radicalism, in
short, but have learned nothing from his piety and self-
discipline. John Andrew, rector of New York's Saint
Thomas Church, once noted in a sermon on Francis that
"the world's generation of hippies could have had him as
their special patron saint if only they could have appreciated what led him to do the things they thought they
were doing and to live the life they thought they were
living. But sadly few got it, and got it right."

That's the ultimate point about Francis's life: that he
got it, and got it right. He didn't accomplish everything
he set out to do, and may not always have made wise
choices; as Colin Morris has written, "It is hard to imagine any more improbable founder of an order, for Francis
had a talent for disorganization and was reluctant even
to produce a rule." Yet more than anyone else in his
time, Francis understood the gospel message and acted
on it, dedicating his work and wealth and wisdom to
living out Christ's commandments to love God and his

fellow human beings. Francis recognized the intercon-
nectedness of these two commandments—recognized
that they are, in reality, one. He was a mystic without
being a hermit (though he had periods of solitude), a
servant of his fellow human beings but not just a social
worker. More than any other saint, he continues in the
Age of the Information Highway to do what saints are
supposed to do—namely, to figure in countless lives as
an inspiration to the spiritually torpid and a rebuke to
the pietistic.

I've criticized the annual Earth Mass at Saint John the
Divine. Yet for all its misguidedness, there is in that service enough of Francis to speak powerfully to those who
have ears to hear. The friend (now my companion) who
first took me to the Earth Mass several years ago had
been raised as a Christian, and so had I—he as a Sev-
enth-day Adventist, I as a hybrid Protestant—but we
had long since lapsed. In retrospect, it's clear that the
example of Francis's lively faith and tireless service, as
communicated (however contortedly) in the cathedral's
commemoration of his feast, awakened something that
had been lying dormant in both of us; our attendance at
that service proved to be the first step along the road
to active Episcopal Church membership—though not
(it must be admitted) to a life of single-minded self-
abnegation.

This leads to what is, for all of us, the ultimate question about the Christian life: Does it make us irredeem-

able hypocrites that we honor Francis without even trying to live as he did? I don't think Francis would have said so. "In whatever way you think you will best please our Lord God and follow in His footprints and in His poverty," he wrote to one of his companions, "take that way with the Lord God's blessing." The lesson of Francis is not that one must feel obliged to live as radically abstemious a life as he did, but that one must listen as acutely as he did for the still, small voice in the windstorm and must strive conscientiously to commit one's gifts, whatever they may be, as selflessly to God.

Catherine Means Pure

KATHRYN HARRISON

for Janet

MY MOTHER DIED of breast cancer when I was twenty-four. I took care of her while she died. I gave her her morphine, her Halcion, her Darvocet, Percocet, Demerol, Zantac, and Prednisone. I bathed her and I dressed her bedsores. Though I had to force myself into such communion with disease, I kissed her each morning when she woke and each evening as she fell asleep. Then I went into the bathroom, took a cotton pad soaked with rubbing alcohol, and scrubbed my lips with it until they burned and bled. Sometimes as I did this I thought of

Saint Catherine of Siena, who, in 1373, collected into a bowl the pus from a woman's open breast cancer lesions. The woman was Andrea, an older member of the Mantellate lay order to which Catherine belonged. Previously, Andrea had caused Catherine much trouble and public censure when she had implied that the saint's infamous raptures and fasts were a pretense rather than any manifestation of holiness. The bowl's foul contents stank and made Catherine retch, and both in penance for her disgust and in determination to love her enemy, Catherine drank the old nun's pus. "Daughter! Daughter!" cried Andrea, tears of contrition wetting her cheeks. "Do not kill yourself!"

That night, Catherine had a vision of Christ. Her Holy Bridegroom bade her to his side, and she drank the blood of life that flowed from his wounds.

"You were named for saints and queens," my mother told me, when I was young enough that a halo and a crown seemed interchangeable. We were not Catholics yet. Judaism was our birthright, but we had early strayed and now we were members of the First Church of Christ, Scientist. Above my bed was a plaque bearing these words from its founder, Mary Baker Eddy: "Father-Mother Good, lovingly thee I seek, patient, meek. In the way thou hast, be it slow or fast, up to thee." The little prayer, which I was taught to recite as I fell asleep, worried me. I did not want to die fast. I had asthma, and each attack seemed capable of killing me, so when I was not thinking of my mother, whom I loved without measure, I thought of death and of God. They made my first trinity: Mother, Death, God.

I might have remained immune to the mind-over-matter doctrines of Mrs. Eddy, and to the subsequent seduction of the saints, had I not, when I was five, suffered an accident which occasioned a visit to a Christian Science "practitioner," or healer. The circumstances were these: My mother, divorced when I was not yet a year old, and when she was not yet twenty, had recently moved out of her parents' house in Los Angeles, a house where I continued to live, as an only child with my grandparents. It was the first of my mother's attempts to make a separate life for herself—a life which did not seem possible to her unless motherhood was left behind—and so now it was my grandfather who drove me to school each day. The egocentric logic of the small child damned me to a belief that my mother had left me with her parents because of my unworthiness. I knew already that my birth had interrupted her education; now I learned that my continued existence somehow distracted her from her paralegal job and, worse, chased off romantic prospects. The shiny, pink stretch marks which pregnancy had traced over her stomach seemed emblematic of the greater damage I had done, and each time my mother undressed before me, my eyes were drawn to this record of my first transgression. Each afternoon, I sat in the closet of her old room, inhaling her perfume from what dresses remained; each morning I woke newly disappointed at the sight of her empty bed in the room next to mine. So, despite my grandfather's determined cheer, it was a glum ride to school that was interrupted, dramatically, the day the old Lincoln's brakes failed.

Pumping the useless pedal, my grandfather turned off the road in order to avoid rear-ending the car ahead of us. We went down a short embankment, picked up speed, crossed a ditch, and hit one of the stately eucalyptus trees that form the boundary between Sunset Boulevard and the UCLA campus. On impact, the glove compartment popped open; and, not wearing my seat belt, I sailed forward and split my chin on its lock mechanism, cracking my jawbone.

My grandfather was not hurt. He got me out of the wrecked, smoking car and pressed a folded handkerchief to my face. Blood was pouring out of my mouth and chin, and I started to cry, from fear more than pain. I was struggling against the makeshift compress when, by a strange coincidence, my mother, en route to work, saw us from the street and pulled over. Her sudden materialization, the way she sprang nimbly out of her blue car, seemed to me angelic, magical, an impression enhanced by the dress she was wearing that morning, one with a tight bodice and a full crimson skirt embroidered all over with music notes. Whenever she wore this dress I was unable to resist touching the fabric of the skirt. I found the notes evocative, mysterious; and if she let me, I would trace my finger over the spiral of a treble clef or feel the stitched dots of the notes, as if they represented a different code, like that of Braille or Morse, a message that I might in time decipher.

My mother was unusually patient and gentle as she helped me into her car. We left my grandfather waiting for a tow truck and drove to UCLA's nearby medical center, where I was X-rayed and prepared for suturing. I lay under a light so bright that it almost forced me to close my eyes, while a blue, disposable cloth with a hole cut out for my chin descended over my face like a shroud, blocking my view of my mother. I held her hand tightly, too tightly perhaps, for after a moment she pried my fingers off and lay my hand on the side of the gurney. She had to make a phone call, she said; she had to explain why she hadn't shown up at work.

I tried to be brave, but when I heard my mother's heels clicking away from me on the floor, I succumbed to an animal terror and tried to kick and claw my way after her. All I had understood of what she said was that she was leaving me again—this time with strangers—and it took both the doctor and his nurse to restrain me. Once they had, I was tranquilized before I was stitched and then finally taken home asleep.

Later that afternoon, I woke up screaming, in a panic which had been interrupted, not assuaged, by the drug. My mother, soon exhausted by my relentless crying and clinging to her neck, her legs, her fingers—to whatever she would let me hold—took me to a practitioner, whose name she picked at random from the First Church of Christ, Scientist's directory.

The practitioner was a woman with gray hair and a woolly, nubby sweater which I touched as she prayed over me, my head in her lap and one of her hands on my forehead, the other over my heart. Under those hands, which I remember as cool and calm, even sparing in their movements, I felt my fear drain away. Then, the top of my skull seemed to be opened by a sudden, revelatory blow, and a searing light filled me. Mysteriously, unexpectedly, this stranger had ushered me into an experience of something I cannot help but call rapture. I felt myself separated from my flesh, and from all earthly things. I felt myself no more corporeal than the tremble in the air over a fire. I had no words for what happened—I have few now, almost thirty years later—and in astonishment I stopped crying. My mother sighed in relief; and I learned, at five, a truth dangerous to someone so young and lovelorn. I saw that transcendence was possible: that spirit could conquer matter, and that therefore I could overcome whatever obstacles prevented my mother's loving me. I could overcome myself.

In the years following the accident I became increasingly determined to return to whatever it was I had visited in the practitioner's lap, and I thought the path to this place might be discovered in Sunday school. Around the wood laminate table I was the only child who had done the previous week's assignment, who had marked my white vinyl-covered Bible with the special blue-chalk pencil and had read the corresponding snippet from Mary Baker Eddy's *Science and Health, with Key to the Scriptures.* The other children lolled and dozed in clip-on neckties and pastel sashed dresses while I sat up straight. The teacher had barely finished asking a question before my hand, in its white cotton glove buttoned tight at the wrist, shot up. Sometimes I would see the teacher looking at me with what seemed, even then, like consternation. The lassitude of the other children, their carelessly incorrect answers, which proceeded from lips still bearing traces of hastily consumed cold cereal, were clearly what she expected. What was disconcerting was my fierce recital of verses, my vigilant posture on the edge of the red plastic kindergarten chair.

The arena of faith was the only one in which I had a chance of securing my mother's attention. Since she was not around during the week to answer to more grubby requirements, and because she was always someone who preferred the choice morsel, it was to my mother rather than to my grandparents that the guidance of my soul had been entrusted. On Sundays, we went to church in Westwood and afterward to a nearby patio restaurant, where we sat in curlicued wrought-iron chairs and reviewed my Sunday-school lesson while eating club sandwiches held together with fancy toothpicks. The waiters flirted with my mother, and men at neighboring tables smiled in her direction. They looked at her left hand without any ring; they seemed to share my helpless longing. Through the awful calculus of mortal love, my mother—who already embodied for me the beauty of youth, who had the shiny-haired, smooth-cheeked vitality my grandparents did not, who could do backbends and cartwheels, and owned high-heeled shoes in fifteen colors—became ever more precious for her elusiveness, her withholding absence.

In order to reexperience the ecstatic rise that had for an instant made me an attractive child and that had come through the experience of pain, I began secretly—and long before I had the example of any saint—to practice the mortification of my flesh. At my grandfather's workbench I turned his vise on my finger joints. When my grandmother brought home ice cream from Baskin-Robbins and discarded the dry ice with which it was packed, I used the salad tongs to retrieve the small smoking slab from the trash can. In the privacy of the upstairs bathroom I touched my tongue to the dry ice's surface and left a little of its skin there. I looked in the mirror at the blood coming out of my mouth, at the same magic flow that had once summoned my mother from the impossibly wide world of grown-ups and traffic and delivered her to my side. Now I was fully ensnared in the wishful, initiating mistake that was to confuse and pervert my spiritual growth: from the beginning I viewed whatever power God represented as a means toward my mother's love. Through those transformations made possible by faith, I would become worthy of her loving me. Either that, or faith would make me feel no more pain from my mother's rejection than I had from my jaw while lying in the practitioner's lap. So I looked in the mirror at my tongue, I tasted my blood, and I practiced not hurting.

My mother converted to Catholicism when I was ten, and I followed in her wake, seeking her even as she sought whatever it was that she had not found in Christian Science. We had failed at even the most basic of Mrs. Eddy's tenets, for by then we routinely sought the care of medical doctors. At first we went only for emergencies like the accident to my chin, but then my mother developed an ulcer, and I, never inoculated, got tetanus from a scrape, physical collapses both stubbornly unaffected by our attempts to disbelieve in them.

In preparation for my first Communion, I was catechized by a priest named Father Dove. Despite this felicitous name, Father Dove was not the Holy Spirit incarnate: he chain-smoked and his face over his white collar had a worldly, sanguine hue. Worse, I suspected that my mother was in love with him. She fell in love easily. One Saturday, I made my first confession (that I had been rude to my grandmother and had taken three dollars from her purse), and the next day, I took Com-

munion with eleven other little girls dressed in white;
and from that time forward I attended church in a marble
sanctuary filled with gilt angels, rather than in a gray-
and-blue auditorium. Light came through the stained-
glass windows and splashed colors over everything. A
red circle fell on my mother's white throat. Incense roiled
around us, and I looked down to compare the shiny toes
of my black patent-leather shoes to those of hers. When
we left, lining up to shake Father Dove's hand, I was
able to study the faces around me and confirm that my
mother's wide hazel eyes, her long nose, and high, white
forehead indeed made hers more beautiful than anyone
else's.

For Christmas the following year I received, in my
stocking, a boxed set of four volumes of *Lives of the
Saints,* intended for children. There were two volumes
of male saints, which I read once, flipping through the
onionskin pages, and then left in my dresser drawer, and
two of female saints, which I studied and slept with. The
books contained color plates, illustrations adapted from
works of the masters. Blinded Lucy. Maimed Agatha, her
breasts on a platter. Beheaded Agnes. Margaret pressed
to death under a door piled high with stones. Perpetua
and Felicity mauled by beasts. Well-born Clare, barefoot
and wearing rags. Maria Maddalena de' Pazzi lying on
the bed of splinters she made for herself in the wood-
shed. Veronica washing the floors with her tongue, and

Angela drinking water used to bathe a leper's sores. I saw that there were those who were tortured, and those who needed no persecutors—they were enemies to their own flesh.

Saint Catherine of Siena began by saying Hail Marys on every step she climbed. Soon she slept on a board, with a brick for a pillow. She did not like her hair shirt because it smelled, so she took to wearing a little belt of nails that bit into her waist. As Catherine's *Dialogues* (dictated years later, while she was in a sustained ecstasy, which lasted weeks, even months) make clear, she believed earthly suffering was the only way to correct the intrinsic baseness of mankind.

My mother, also, held forth an ideal of perfection, an ideal for which she would suffer, but hers was beauty. For beauty she endured the small tortures of plucking and peel-off face masks, of girdles and pinched toes, of sleep sacrificed to hair rollers and meals reduced to cottage cheese. I knew, from my mother's enthusiastic response to certain pictures in magazines, to particular waifs in the movies, that the child who would best complement her vanity was dark-haired and slender and balanced on point shoes. I was blond, robust, and given to tree-climbing. By the time I was thirteen, all of what was wrong with me—the very fact of me, my presence—settled in an unavoidably obvious issue between my mother and me: how much I weighed. How much there was of me. As my conception had been accidental, as I ought not to have been there at all, it must have struck my mother as an act of defiance that I was so large a child, taller and sturdier than any other girl in my class.

I wished myself smaller. I began to dream at night of Beyond-the-Looking-Glass potions, little bottles bearing draughts that shrank me to nothing; the bit of mushroom which let me disappear between grass blades. I began, too, to dread Sunday lunches taken with my mother, who fastidiously observed my fork in its ascension to my mouth.

Saint Catherine was fourteen when her older sister Bonaventura died in childbirth. Bonaventura was the only member of Catherine's family with whom she shared any real sympathy, and Catherine blamed herself for her sister's death. She believed God had punished her and Bonaventura because Catherine had let her big sister tempt her into using cosmetics and curling her hair. She had let Bonaventura's example convince her, briefly, that a woman could embrace both heavenly and earthly desires.

Whatever buoyancy, whatever youthful resilience Saint Catherine had had, disappeared when she lost her sister. She became uncompromising in turning away from all worldly things: from food, from sleep, from men. Their mother, Lapa, a volatile woman whose choleric screams were reputedly so loud that they frightened passersby on Siena's Via dei Tintori, redoubled her efforts to marry off her uncooperative twenty-fourth child.

Some accounts hold that Catherine's intended groom was Bonaventura's widowed husband, a foul-tongued and occasionally brutish man. Catherine refused; she had long ago promised herself to Christ. She cut off her hair and she fasted, eating only bread and uncooked vegetables. She began to experience ecstasies, and it is recorded that when she did, she suffered a tetanic rigor in her limbs. Then Lapa would take her daughter up from the floor where she'd fallen and almost break her bones as she tried to bend the girl's stiff arms and legs.

Though it had been ten years since my mother moved out, she had yet to find a place that suited her for any length of time, and so she received her mail at the more permanent address of her parents, and would stop by after work to pick it up. She came in the back door, cool and perfumed and impeccably dressed, and she drifted into the kitchen to find me in my rumpled school uniform, standing before the open refrigerator. One day, I turned around with a cold chicken leg in my hand. My mother had tossed her unopened bills on the counter and was slowly rereading the message inside a greeting card decorated with a drawing of two lovesick rabbits locked in a dizzy embrace. She smiled slightly—a small and self-consciously mysterious smile—and kept the content of the card averted from my eyes. When she had had her fill of it, she looked up at me. She said nothing but let her eyes rest for a moment on the meat in my hand; then she looked away, from it, from me. She did not need to speak to tell me of her disapproval, and by now my habitual response to my mother had become one of despair: muffled, mute, and stumbling. But in that moment when she looked away from me, hopelessness gave way before a sudden, visionary elation. I dropped the drumstick into the garbage can. The mouthful I had swallowed stopped in its descent, and I felt it, gelid and vile inside me as I washed the sheen of grease from my fingers. At dinnertime, after my mother had left for her apartment, I pleaded too much homework to allow time to eat at the table, and I took my plate from the kitchen to my bedroom and opened the window, dropping the food into the dark foliage of the bushes below.

Among saints, Catherine is remarkable for her will more than for her humility. One of the two women in all of history named a Doctor of the Church (the other is Saint Teresa of Ávila), she, too, confused crowns with halos, and presumed to direct the affairs of popes and kings. Even in her reports of self-flagellation, readers find the pride of the absolutist. No one believed more firmly in Catherine's baseness than did Catherine. Determined that she be the least among mortals, so also—by the topsy-turvy logic of Christian salvation—would she be assured of being the greatest. In her visions of Christ, it is Catherine alone who stands beside Him as His bride.

To earn that place was exhausting beyond mortal ability. Even as the saint tirelessly cared for plague victims, even as she exhorted thousands to convert and lobbied effectively for the return of the papacy from Avignon to Rome, she criticized, scourged, and starved herself. She allowed herself not one mortal pleasure: not food or rest, not beauty, not wealth, not marriage or children. Categorically, she rejected the very things that a mother hopes a daughter's life will hold. And reading accounts of her life, one senses how Catherine enjoyed thwarting her mother, Lapa, enjoyed refusing the life her mother gave her. Biographers record that Catherine tried to eat—she wanted to do so in order to dispel accusations of demonic possession—but vomited if so much as a mouthful remained in her stomach. "She lived for years on one lettuce leaf!" was how my mother introduced me to Saint Catherine, as if she were revealing the teachings of a new diet guru.

Holiness. The idea of being consecrated, set apart. And of being whole, pure, untainted by anything. There are different kinds of purity, just as there are many reasons for rejecting life. But, no matter the motive, to the ascetic the rejection always looks the same: like salvation. Catherine would guide me to the salvation I sought. Inhumanly, she had triumphed over mortal limitations, over hunger, fatigue, and despair. She had seen demons and fought them off. And I would use her to fashion my solitary and sinful faith. Sin. A term long ago borrowed from archery: to miss the mark.

During the celebration of the Eucharist, the priest

would place the Communion wafer on my tongue. I withdrew it into my mouth carefully, making the sign of the cross over myself. Back in the pew I kneeled and lay my head in my arms in a semblance of devotion, stuck out my tongue, and pushed the damp wafer into my sleeve. I was a little afraid of going to hell, very afraid of swallowing bread. My rules had grown more inexorable than the Church's; they alone could save me. But the host was the host, and I could not bring myself to throw it away. So I kept it in my sock drawer with my other relics: a small fetish of my mother's hair, stolen strand by strand from the hairbrush she kept in her purse. An eye pencil from that same source. Two tiny cookies from a Christmas stocking long past, a gingerbread boy and girl, no taller than an inch. A red leather collar from my cat which had died. The trinity in my sock drawer: Mother, Death, and God in the form of weeks' worth of accumulated bits of the body of Christ which I would not eat. Despite Christian Science's early announcements to me, despite mind over matter, I remained enslaved to the material world. In my confused struggle with corporeality I clung to these bits of rubbish, a collection that would look more at home in a trash can than in a drawer, and resisted what might better save me: food.

I still had my little books of the female saints. I looked at them before bed some nights, stared at their little portraits, at bleeding hands and feet, at exultant faces tipped up to heaven. But I read longer hagiographies now, grown-up ones. When Catherine was twenty-four she experienced a mystical death. "My soul was loosed from the body for those four hours," she told her confessor, who recorded that her heart stopped beating for that long. Though she did not want to return to her flesh, Jesus bade her go back. But henceforth, she was not as other mortals; her flesh was changed and unfit for worldly living. From that time forward she swallowed nothing she did not vomit. Her happiness was so intense that she laughed in her fits of ecstasy, she wept and laughed at the same time.

As I lost weight I watched with exultation as my bones emerged, believing that what I saw would irresistibly lure my mother's love. By the time they had failed to do that—those unlovely angles and hollows—I had so thoroughly confused the sight of them with the happiness I had hoped they would bring that I had created a satisfying, if perverse, system of rewards, one that did not require my mother's participation. I had replaced her with the bait I had hoped would entice her. I loved my transformed self. I could not look at myself enough, and I never went into the bathroom that I did not find myself helplessly undressing before the mirror. I touched myself, too. At night I lay in bed and felt each jutting rib, felt sternum and hipbone, felt my sharp jaw, and with my finger traced the orbit of my eye. Like Catherine's, mine was not a happiness that others understood, for it was the joy of power, of a private, inhuman triumph. Of a universe—my body—utterly subjugated to my will.

My life was solitary, as befits a religious. Too much of human fellowship was dictated by hunger, by taking meals in company, and what I did and did not consume separated me from others. Since I had not yet weaned myself completely from human needs, I drank coffee, tea, and Tab. I ate raw vegetables, multivitamins, No-Doz, and, when I felt very weak, tuna canned in water. When I climbed stairs, I saw stars. And when forced to eat with my grandparents, I did so, but the mask of compliance was temporary, and upstairs in my bathroom, I vomited what I had eaten. Afterward, I would lift my shirt and examine my ribs in the mirror, wanting to be sure that there was no evidence of my brief defilement.

After meals, Catherine drank cold water and gagged herself with a stalk of fennel or a quill pen. It hurt her, and she was glad. She wanted to do all her suffering on earth so that she would be spared purgatory. *This will make you pure,* I used to think when I made myself throw up. I used ipecac, the emetic kept in first-aid kits, a poison to be taken against poisons. It was worse than using my finger, perhaps even worse than a quill; at least that had to have been quick in its mechanical approach. Ipecac was suffering; it seemed to take forever and caused a reeling, sweaty nausea that made me wish I were dead. The retching was violent, but then, I intended it to be punishment.

My grandmother and grandfather, sixty-two and seventy-one at my birth, were now so old that their failing senses granted me freedom unusual for a teenager. Going blind, they did not see my thinness. Deaf, they never heard me in my bathroom. By the time I was sixteen, they depended on my driver's license for their groceries; and en route to the supermarket, I would stop at the mall. "Where did you go, Kalamazoo?" my grandmother would ask when I returned, trying to understand why I was hours late. Sometimes she accused me of secretly meeting boys; she used the word "assignation." But I had always spent my time alone. In the department stores and I went from rack to rack, garment to garment: size two, size two, size two. Each like a rosary bead: another recitation, another confirmation of my size, one more turn of the key in the lock of safety.

Having conquered hunger, I began on sleep, and one night, in my room, very late, and in the delusional frenzy of having remained awake for nearly seventy-three hours, I began to weep with what I thought was joy. It seemed to me that I had almost gotten there: my flesh was almost utterly turned to spirit. Soon I would not be mortal, soon I would be as invulnerable as someone who could drink pus and see God. The next day, however, I fainted and suffered a seizure that left me unable for a day to move the fingers on my right hand. In the same hospital where I had long ago attacked the ER nurse with my fingernails, I had an electroencephalogram and a number of other tests which proved inconclusive. A different nurse, a different doctor, a different wing of the hospital. But nothing had changed: my mother was making a phone call in the corridor, and I lay on a table trying not to scream, far less able to articulate the danger I sensed than when I was five.

When college gave me the opportunity to leave home, I recovered partially. At heart, I wanted to believe in a different life, and I stopped going to mass and gained a little weight—not too much, because I began taking speed and still made myself throw up sometimes. I wore my mother's clothing, castoffs and whatever I could steal from her, articles that filled the reliquary of my peculiar faith. I zipped and buttoned myself into her garments as if they could cloak me with the love I wanted from her. Like miracle seekers who would tear hair, fingers— whatever they could—from a holy person's body, I was desperate, and one September I took my mother's favorite skirt from under the dry-cleaning bag hanging in the back seat of her car. It was purple, long and narrow. I packed it in my suitcase and took it to school with me. She called me on the phone a week later. "Send it back," she said. I denied having taken it. "You're lying," she said.

Lapa did not want Catherine to scourge herself, so, although her daughter was a grown woman, Lapa took away her private bedroom and forced Catherine to sleep in bed with her. Not to be denied the mortification of her flesh, the saint dragged a plank into the bed after Lapa had fallen asleep, and she laid it between her mother's body and her own. On Lapa's side was smooth wood; on Catherine's, spikes.

I wore the skirt twice, and when it fell from the hanger, I let it remain on the dark, dirty floor of my closet. When my mother called me again, I decided to return it, but there was a stain on the waistband that the dry cleaner could not remove. For an hour I sat on my dorm bed with the skirt in my lap, considering. Finally I washed it with Woolite, and ruined it. I returned the skirt to my mother's closet when invited, during spring break, for dinner at her apartment. *Please,* I begged silently, tucking it between two other skirts. *Please don't say anything more about it. Please.* When she called me late that night at my grandparents' house, I hung up on her. Then I went into the bathroom and I sat on the floor and wept: too late, too many hours past the dinner she had fed me to make myself throw up.

Kathryn, Katherine, Catherine. All the spellings proceed from the Greek, *Katharos,* or "pure one."

Did Lapa know who her daughter would be? Did my mother know me before she named me? Did we announce ourselves to our mothers in the intimacy of the womb, flesh whispering to flesh?

Or did they make us to fit our names?

I still believe in purity, and I believe that suffering

must at least prepare the way for redemption. I believe, too, in love's ability to conquer. I believe in every kiss I gave my mother, even those I scrubbed away in fear. At the end of her life, I waited for my mother to tell me how much she loved me and how good a daughter I had always been. I had faith that my mother was waiting until the end to tell me that all along she had known I had performed impossible feats of self-alchemy.

She did not, but, as faith admits no end, mine continued beyond her death. After the funeral, I packed up her apartment and looked through all her papers for a note, a letter left for me and sealed in an envelope. I closed my eyes and saw it: a meticulous, fountain-pen rendition of *Kathryn* on creamy stationery. When I didn't find that, I looked for clues to her affection. I read what correspondence she had saved. I reviewed check registers dating back ten years. I learned how much she had spent on dry cleaning her clothes, on her cats' flea baths, and on having her car radio repaired.

The death of my mother left me with a complex religious apparatus that now lacked its object, and I expected, then, to become an atheist. I frankly looked forward to the sterile sanity of it, to what relief it would bring. But I could not do it; I could not not believe. The habit of faith, though long focused misguidedly on a mortal object, persisted; and after a few years, I found myself returning to the Church. Sporadically, helplessly, I attended mass. Having relearned to eat earthly food, now I practiced swallowing the Eucharist. Often I found myself crying out of a happiness I did not understand and which mysteriously accompanied the sense that my heart was breaking.

Rapture, too, returned. Long after I had stopped expecting it, it overcame me on a number of otherwise unnoteworthy occasions. I excused this as a fancy born of longing, as an endorphin effect brought on by exercise or pain, as craziness, pure and simple. But none of these described the experience, that same searing, light-filled, ecstatic rise, neither pleasant nor unpleasant, for no human measure applied to what I felt: transcendence.

My prayers, too, were helpless. I mouthed them in spite of myself. *Make me good. Love me. Please make me good and please love me.* For the first time, I entrusted my spiritual evolution to some power outside my self and my will; I entrusted it to God's grace. If I were going to reach any new plane, my enlightenment, it would have to be God who transported me.

In the last months of her life, Catherine lost the use of her legs. Her biographers record that for years she had lived on little more than water and what sustenance she got from chewing, not swallowing, bitter herbs. In church one night, when she was too weak to approach the altar, the Communion bread came to her. Witnesses saw bread move through the air unassisted. Catherine saw it carried by the hand of Christ.

She died at thirty-three, the same age as her Bridegroom at his death. She died in Rome, and her body was venerated from behind an iron grille in a chapel of the Church of the Minerva, so that the throngs who came would not tear her to bits, each trying to secure a wonder-working relic.

All I have left of my mother are a box of books, a china dog, two cashmere sweaters with holes in the elbows, a few photographs, and her medical records. Among the last of these is her final chest X ray, and just over the shadow of her heart is the bright white circle cast by the saint's medal she wore on a thin gold chain. No matter how many times the technicians asked her to remove it, she would not. Not long ago, I unpacked the box of medical records, and retrieved the X ray. I held it before a light once more, trying to see the image more clearly, but of course I could make out nothing. Just a small, white circle of brightest light. A circle blocking the view of the chambers of her heart. A circle too bright to allow any vision.

I will never know, but I have decided that the medal, now with my mother in her coffin, bears a likeness of Saint Jude. I have given my mother to this saint—the patron of lost causes, the patron of last resort—just as long ago she gave me to the saint of her choosing.

A Friend to the Godless

PAUL WATKINS

MY GREAT-GRANDFATHER returned from the Somme in the winter of 1916. He was an officer in a Welsh Guards regiment. He had been gassed and shot and had seen his platoon numerically wiped out and replaced more than three times since he first took command of it. He had used his side arm, a Webley revolver, so much that the barrel was pitted into uselessness. I heard a story about one of his advances across no-man's-land in which he set out with a full company and by the

time he arrived at the German wire was one of only two
men left alive.

Until that time, this branch of my family had been
Calvinistic Methodists, teetotaling, high-minded, and
convinced, as one member of my family phrased it, that
everyone was going to hell except them.

But when he returned from the war, my great-grandfather had seen enough to change his mind. He gathered
the family together and banned religion in his house.
"Either God is a bastard," he said, "or God isn't there
at all."

Since then, religious faith has crept back into
my family, but to me it still feels burdened by my
great-grandfather's pronouncement. Holidays are still
celebrated—Christmas for example—but with more attention paid to the tree than to the birth of Jesus.

The one festival I do remember seeing celebrated
without the aegis of my great-grandfather's proclamation
to muffle it into insignificance is Saint David's day,
March 1.

In writing about Saint David here, I have for the first
time explored why the day of the saint, whose name (my
middle name) has echoed through my family for generations, survived untarnished, even after the war that cata-
pulted my great-grandfather into the ranks of unbelievers.

The first mention of Saint David, and it is only a mention, comes in an Irish manuscript called the "Catalogue

of the Saints of Ireland," which was written in A.D. 730. In it, David is acknowledged as a "Holy Man of Britain." In fact, there is in existence only one original and reliable document on Saint David. It was written, in Welsh, by a man named Rhygyvarch, around the year 1090, shortly after the Norman invasion of Britain. The best copy of this document is in the British Museum in London, in a dust-choked file marked "Vespasian A xiv" of the famous Cottonian Codex.

Rhygyvarch, a local clergyman in the area, now County Dyfed, where St. David's cathedral now stands, may have written his account in order to draw the Welsh together after the Norman invasion. The once powerful rulers of the Cymri (the Welsh word for themselves) lay either dead or defeated in the wake of William the Conqueror. "Alas!" wrote Rhygyvarch in his *Lament of the Times,* "that life hath led us to such a time as this, wherein a cruel power threatens to oust from their rights those who walk justly. Free necks submit to the yoke. Nothing is too excellent that I may be compelled to surrender it. Things once lofty I despise. Both people and priest are scorned by every motion of the French. They increase our burdens and consume our goods. . . . Art thou hated of God, O British nation, that thou darest not bear the quiver, stretch the bow, carry the sword, vibrate the spear?" Some see this, in conjunction with his *Life of Saint David,* as a call to arms for the divided Welsh.

David, or Dewi to the Welsh, was perhaps the only rallying point that Rhygyvarch could have chosen. David's life had been, by that time, converted almost entirely to myth. His coming was foretold to Saint Patrick by a "truth-telling oracle of angels" thirty years before David's birth. David's father, a local ruler by the name of Sant, also received a vision, in which he was ordered by an angelic voice to go hunting stag near the river Teivi, on the banks of which he would find three gifts, "namely the stag which thou pursuest, a fish and a swarm of bees settled in a tree in the place which is called Llyn Henllan. Of these three, reserve a honeycomb, a part of the fish and of the stag, which send to be kept for a son, who shall be born to thee. . . . The honeycomb shall proclaim his wisdom, for as honey in wax, so shall he be spiritual in mind and body. And the fish declares his aquatic life, for as a fish lives in the water, so he, rejecting wine and beer and everything that can intoxicate, shall lead a blessed life for God on bread and water only. The stag signifies his power over the Old Serpent." Bear in mind that to the Welsh, the Old Serpent was as real a presence as anything else around them. It was not, as psychologists have later palmed it off to be, a symbol of the struggle with the self. It was, the Welsh believed, a real dragon, with claws like scimitars and armored scales and incendiary breath. Y Ddraig Goch, the Welsh called it, and today it is the national emblem of Wales. So to have the forecast of a man who would one day hold power over Y Ddraig Goch was no small prediction.

Even the land over which David was to rule was squared away for him in advance. On a visit to west Wales, Saint Patrick was informed by "an angel of the Lord that God hath not disposed this place for thee, but for a son who is not yet born, nor will he be born until thirty years are past." On hearing this, Patrick was so upset that he announced he would give up the faith "and submit no longer to such toil." The angel, however, quickly pacified him with promises of dominion over all of Ireland, which at that point had not yet been Christianized. "As proof of this," the angel said, "I will show thee the whole of Ireland. Let the mountains be bent; the sea made smooth, the eye bearing forth across all things." And at that moment, from the place where Patrick stood, the whole Emerald Isle unraveled before him from across the stormy Irish Sea. Patrick quickly rushed down to the shore, but unable to find a boatman to ferry him across, he raised from the dead a sailor who had lain buried beneath the beach for a dozen years, a man named Crumther, and the two of them left the Welsh to await the arrival of their saint.

Other portents were presented to the small fishing community of the place now called St. David's. When David's mother, Nonn, still pregnant with David, entered the local church, the preacher there was struck dumb and was unable to continue his sermon until Nonn had left the building. The priest then announced, "The son, who is in the womb of that nun, has grace and power and rank greater than I, because God has given him status and sole rule and primacy over all the saints of Britannia forever." Then, just as Patrick had done before him, the priest packed his bags and left town.

God's clearing of land for the arrival of David meant that the young saint had already attracted enemies by the time of his birth. The evening Nonn delivered was heralded by terrible storms, which ravaged the coastline and scattered cattle with bolts of well-aimed lightning. Through all of this, however, Nonn remained bathed in sunlight, long after nightfall had come. The stone on which she rested while she delivered became impressed with her handprints "as if on wax." This stone was later used as the foundation stone for David's church.

David was raised by a sage named Paulens, "in a manner pleasing to God." David "preserved his flesh pure from the embraces of a wife" and was taught the hymns of God by a bird with a golden beak who hovered around his head and sang to him.

David performed the first of many miracles attributed to him when Paulens was suddenly stricken with blindness. "Holy David," Paulens called to the boy, "examine my eyes, for they pain me greatly." But due to the manners of the day, it was forbidden for a pupil to meet a teacher's glance. Instead, David laid his hand upon the old man's face, at which point "the master received the light which had been removed."

Before his twentieth birthday, David had founded twelve monasteries around Britain. Among these were Glastonbury, Bath (where he first "caused the deadly water to become salutary," thus ensuring the survival of a thriving spa town), Croyland, Repton, Colva, and Glascwm, all of which are still in existence.

Close to his home in the Welsh county of Dyfed, his rise in power provoked the anger of a local warlord named Bywa. The chieftain set out with a band of warriors to kill David, but they were stricken with fever along the way, and by the time they arrived were able to do no more than "blaspheme the Lord and Holy David, for the wish to injure was not wanting, although the power to act was thwarted by the Eternal."

Ridiculing Bywa's failure, the warlord's own wife set out to finish off David. She brought with her a gaggle of handmaidens, who proceeded to parade naked in front of the holy settlement, "making shameless sport, simulating coition and displaying love's alluring embraces." This display, in fact, did considerably more damage than Bywa's own cursing, fever-sweating thugs. " 'Let us fly from this place,' " said David's disciples, " 'because we cannot dwell here owing to the molestation of these spiteful sluts.'" Rather than cajole his own supporters, it seems that David gave Bywa's wife such a tongue-lashing that she and all her naked, frolicking maidens ran off into the trees, "and no one under heaven knows by what death they ended their lives."

David wasn't yet finished with Bywa. It is here that Rhygyvarch's narrative grows cloudy, and becomes more of a sermon than a story. He seems reluctant to admit the truth, which was that David and his followers stormed Bywa's camp and butchered everyone in it. Rhygyvarch contents himself with a vague warning: "For it is meet that destruction should overtake him who threatens the death of a man of God, and he who is pitiless to the servants of God will suffer vengeance without pity."

Following the death of Bywa, David set about building the cathedral, parts of which can still be seen in the valley of St. David's town. The cathedral, the smallest in Britain, was built in a hollow to hide it from Viking raiders who patrolled the coast. They raided churches because in those days the church acted as a repository for all local wealth, safe against Christian attack. But to the Vikings, followers of Odin, some heavy crucifix held up by a monk to ward off evil was nothing more than a convenient weapon, with which to bludgeon the monk to death. Not only was St. David's attacked, but hundreds of other churches as well, until the British agreed to pay the Danes protection money (called Danegeld, literally

"Danish money") to stop them from ravaging the countryside.

In building the cathedral, David was a hard taskmaster, withholding food from those he felt did not work hard enough. Again, Rhygyvarch camouflages all brutality with the severity of the devoted: "For knowing that untroubled rest was the fomenter and mother of vices, David subjected the shoulders of the monks to Divine Fatigues." At table, they were allowed to eat only bread, "not however to excess, for too much, though it be bread only, produces wantonness."

During this time, David increased his congregation, not only due to his cathedral but also due to the need for more labor. He was nothing if not choosy, however. Anyone wishing to become a disciple was forced to wait for ten days at the gates of the settlement "as one rejected, being subjected to reproachful words. But if he stood his ground, duly exercising patience till the tenth day, he was received.... And when he had toiled there for a long time, many antipathies of his soul being broken, he was at length deemed worthy of entering the society of the brethren."

Within the brotherhood, life was both spartan and severe. "No superfluity was allowed, voluntary poverty was loved ... being received naked, as one escaping from shipwreck, he might in no way extol or raise himself above the brethren, or relying on his wealth fail to enter upon equal toil with the brethren."

The miracles continued to surface as construction of the cathedral progressed. David never seemed to be at a loss for enemies, and an attempt to poison him was instigated by a former disciple. Having been informed of the plot, David used the occasion to further his stature by breaking the poisoned bread in three. The first piece he gave to a dog at the settlement gates; "as soon as it had tasted the bit it died a wretched death, for in the twinkling of an eye all its hair fell off, its entrails burst forth and all its skin split all over." Not surprisingly, "all the brethren who saw it were astonished." The second piece David gave to a raven, which was in its nest on one of the settlement gates. The poor creature fared no better and "fell lifeless from the tree as soon as the bread touched its beak." The third piece David ate himself, but he showed no signs of poisoning.

When one of the disciples began to rankle under the punishing work schedule, David scolded him. Overcome with rage, the disciple lifted an axe with which he had been working, determined to split David's skull. But the saint merely lifted his hand, and the disciple's arm withered away.

Once he had finished the cathedral, many reports, including Rhygyvarch's, claim David undertook a pilgrimage to the Holy Land. Although this is greatly disputed and has never been proved, Rhygyvarch and others have used the legend to increase the volume of miracles attributed to David. Predictably, the journey was begun when a holy angel appeared and said to David, "Gird thyself, put on thy shoes. Start to go to Jerusalem." His arrival in the Holy Land was foretold and a welcome prepared in Jerusalem before he had even left Wales.

Along the way, all language barriers were broken, not with Latin, the lingua franca of the day, but "with the gift of tongues bestowed upon David, so that he was never in need of an interpreter."

Rhygyvarch is very brief in his mention of this visit, perhaps because there is so little to back it up. With entire, massively armed crusading armies being thrashed to pieces by the likes of Saladin and Basil the Bulgar Slayer, who took ten thousand prisoners, blinded all but one, and then sent them wandering home, one wonders how much chance a small band of Welshmen reared on bread and water would have had.

By the time he supposedly returned, a new crisis had evolved in Britain. The Pelagian heresy was in full swing, moving through the country "like the venom of a poisonous serpent." Pelagius was a fifth-century monk who denied original sin and the need of grace for salvation. This was as a result of a visit he paid to Rome at the time of Pope Anastasius. He found the city so degenerated in moral fiber that the only escape, Pelagius felt, was to offer a doctrine of free will in which "a person is free if he does what he wishes and avoids what he wishes to avoid."

The British, David included, regarded this as the approach of anarchy, and conducted long debates about how to extinguish the movement. Three times David refused invitations to speak to a synod regarding the movement. "Depart ye in peace," he told them. "Let no one tempt me."

Finally he agreed to speak, and it was here, at the synod of Llandewi-Brefi, that David made a name for himself, not only in the realm of myth but also in substantiated fact. He was instrumental in dismantling the Pelagian movement and restoring the church to its original power over the country. The miracles that attended him at Llandewi are, if not the most dramatic, at least the most often recalled.

With David unable to address the masses because of the lack of a pulpit, his disciples began making a pile of clothing on which he could stand and preach. But while he was waiting, the ground rose up under him to offer him a natural podium. During his speech, a dove came to rest on his shoulder, and remained there until he had finished. As a result, depictions of Saint David in manuscripts or stained glass often show him standing on a mound with a dove perched on his shoulder.

Following this restoration of the faith, David retired to Dyfed, where, Rhygyvarch asserts, he lived to be 147 years old, perhaps his most miraculous feat of all. During those final years, David offered sanctuary to anyone who asked for it, "every ravisher and homicide and sinner and to every evil person flying from place to place."

As he weakened and his death approached, David found that he and his tiny cathedral had become objects of pilgrimage. Thousands of soon-to-be mourners crammed the town. They did not have long to wait. On the day of his death, disciples crowded around to hear his final words. "Take me," he said, "after thee."

Today St. David's is still a point of pilgrimage. The cathedral has been rebuilt several times. Some newer structures bear the scars of looting during the English civil war. There is a strange pair of footprints on a grave outside the windowless cathedral building. They are said to belong to the Devil, who appeared on the earth only to find himself face to face with the spirit of St. David, and vanished forever from the valley.

On Saint David's day, March 1, inevitably under a dreary northern winter sky, the Welsh wear the green and pungent leaves of leeks pinned to their lapels. This tradition dates from a hundred years after the death of Saint David, when a detachment of Welshmen at the Battle of Agincourt, finding themselves so plastered with mud that they could not tell friend from enemy, picked leeks growing in a nearby garden and wore them as insignia. Those translate now into the miniature gold leeks worn on the khaki berets of Welsh Guardsmen today, and by my great-grandfather in 1916.

Why would a man abandon God, but not the saint who proclaimed him? I can only guess, but what appears likely is that, although my great-grandfather became an unbeliever, he did not completely lose his faith. His faith merely shifted, and I believe what he chose to respect was not the God whom he blamed for sending his platoon three times into oblivion, but the men themselves, who carried on in full knowledge of that oblivion. They were just men persevering, and I think my great-grandfather thought of David as just a man persevering. I doubt he believed all the miracles. But the church itself is there as proof of David's other work and of the sanctuary that he offered.

I used to wonder about this idea of sanctuary each morning as I walked into the chapel at Eton, where I was a student for five years. The chapel is a vast, echoing building constructed around 1460. The pale stone steps leading up to its main door are worn concave from centuries of use.

Our names were checked off a list as we filed in, and we were punished if we failed to appear. It was always a hovering, uncertain time of day, with classes stretching ahead in a seemingly endless procession. While the hymns were being sung, you could sometimes look across the rows of singing boys and see a few chanting out their Latin grammar instead, in last-minute preparation for a test. Once, when the Thames had flooded, I heard coffins bumping into each other as they drifted around in the crypt below.

This church was no sanctuary for me. My heart did

not beat quickly when I walked under the arch of the titanic organ, with its pipes racked up like leg-thick javelins above me. It gave me no inspiration to stare up at the stained-glass window. I wasn't the only one who felt this way. I know of no one who was with me at the school who now goes to church more than twice a year. We could not be bullied into reverence.

Instead, we chose different Holy Ground. For some, it was the fields or roads or back alleys of home. For myself, not until I reached the windswept beaches of St. David's did I feel a reverence, which came from the knowledge that my ancestors had lived here for a thousand years. It came from the harsh beauty of the purple heather and yellow gorse, balanced at the edge of cliffs which dropped sheer into the sea, and from the fact that the saint himself must have walked here, gathering driftwood for fires, as people still do today.

For the longest time, I did not tell anyone that I thought of this place as sacred. When at last I did, some of the sacredness disappeared. So I think back to a time of greater innocence, when I would walk the beach with my great-grandfather.

I have a photo from this time of myself with him. It was taken one year before he died. We had just walked from the beach. I am staring at the camera, holding a long trail of seaweed. The seaweed is blurred because the wind was blowing. My great-grandfather is leaning on a walking stick and looking out to sea, as if his attention has been momentarily distracted. I think this was his Holy Ground, as well, although he never said so. It is the only picture I have ever seen of him in which he looks at peace.

Sources

The Black Book of Saint David, tr. J. W. Willis-Bund (1902).

Bonned Y Sant, twelfth-century Welsh document containing part of Rhygyvarch's *Life of Saint David* (Wales: Peniarth Library).

J. G. Evans, trans., *The Text of The Book of Llan Dav* (1893).

J. E. Lloyd, *A History of Wales* (1911).

A. W. Wade-Evans, trans., *Life of Saint David* (New York: Macmillan, 1923).

Hugh Williams, *Christianity in Early Britain* (Oxford: Oxford University Press, 1912).

Called by Name

SUSAN BERGMAN

> Is it a fortunate or an unfortunate thing, to own a life that makes
> you believe in the invisible? I still don't know. Faith can come to a
> person slowly, like a gradual climb up a long stairs, or it can be
> heady and dizzying. Or it can be strong as an iron bannister, never
> reached for or thought of at all. But the propensity for faith is
> inherent, like an organ or a sexual inclination. I always possessed
> the place for religion.
>
> —Mona Simpson, *The Lost Father*

I TOO HAVE a propensity for faith. Mine was a childhood gift that hasn't left me but that I find wandering
from its object, which is God, to various ideas and images that I would inadvertently substitute for God. It's a
common meandering—from the unseen Creator to the
visible creature, or creed, or care—a fascination that becomes a distraction, or merely a mistaken hope. Whether
a detour draws me into the deep woods of hard work
(these spiritual exercises, readings of those martyrs' lives,
a pilgrimage into theology, self-sacrifice, self-discipline),

or across the plains of slackness, I am prone to lose clear sight and need to be reclaimed from a dark path.

So I cling to the promises that if we seek God we will find him, that if we knock the door will be opened. In these words lie powerful incentives to an active life of faith. By faith we can cross the threshold between this world and the unseen place where God dwells, though we must accomplish this faith now, in our bodies and encumbered by the hurts and limitations of our lives and those of the world around us. This is the supreme tension that we endure, believing in God: we live in two worlds, this world, which is no longer home and yet attracts and constrains us, and what Jesus calls the Kingdom of God, which we can't enter fully until death, and yet which has already entered those who believe in the form of God's Spirit.

St. Paul wrestles with this tension, which he put succinctly: "I have been crucified with Christ; and it is no longer I who live but Christ lives in me; and the life which I now live in the flesh I live by faith in the Son of God, who loved me, and delivered Himself up for me."[1] To live by faith, Paul suggests, is to enter a spiritual union with God, an existence that will be fully realized only through putting ourselves spiritually to death. To live is Christ, Paul says elsewhere, and to die is gain. The early Christian martyrs took up this cry, and in the first centuries after Christ's death tens of thousands willingly confessed Christ as Savior and lost their lives.

For early saints and for Christians today, faith sets
up a discontent, a longing for God's Kingdom not only
for personal but also for cultural reasons. The passage
above continues: "For all of you who were baptized into
Christ have clothed yourselves with Christ. There is neither Jew nor Greek, there is neither slave nor free man,
there is neither male nor female; for you are all one in
Christ Jesus."[2] Comparing the potentially radical social
promise of such a statement to actual social practice
makes clear the disparity between the life of the spirit
and the life of the flesh. Paul himself seems not to have
fully understood the implications this statement could
have had within his own culture. Yet he and others with
him had clearly undertaken that uneasy process by which
they began to live the Kingdom of God in their daily
lives. It is to the early Christians and those honored as
saints through history that we turn for a glimpse of the
life of faith of which Paul speaks.

Saints challenge us, writes Garry Wills in a compelling essay on Dorothy Day, by "escaping the boundaries
that hold the rest of us constrained by self-regard, con-
vention and fear."[3] We look to their devotion to stir
ours, to their example to strengthen our ardor so that we
may consecrate our lives to Christ. But there are boundaries of a present existence that even saints don't elude
until they finish living.

In the account of another early saint's life, we find
an inspiring and a troubling portrait of life in two worlds,

a story of a woman so compelling that it has been retold for centuries. In A.D. 202, Perpetua, a twenty-two-year-old woman, with her pregnant attendant, Felicity, is arrested by the Roman authorities because she is a Christian. While in prison she records her spiritual visions and gives an account of prison life. She describes her sorrowful conflict with her unbelieving father, whom she loves. An eyewitness records the events of her martyrdom when, after surviving exposure to wild heifers in the arena, she is killed by the sword of a Roman soldier whose hand she guides to her throat.

Saint Perpetua writes in her prison diary with a constant consciousness of the presence of God, which she feels certain she is about to enter more fully. She also writes with a well-tuned awareness of the physical realities that surround her and influence her well-being and that of her child and her father. Saints live, however exemplary their faith, within the same constraints of body and time and world that we all do. This is the consolation saints offer along with their challenge.

It is this kind of comfort I seek when I turn to the text of Perpetua's prison diary, which begins with these words:

> While I was still with the police authorities my father out of love for me tried to dissuade me from my resolution.

"Father," I said, "do you see here, for example this vase, or pitcher, or whatever it is?"

"I see it," he said.

"Can it be named anything else than what it
really is?" I asked, and he said,

"No."

"So I also cannot be called anything else
than what I am, a Christian."[4]

Her life displays a faith which, instead of wavering when
opposed, strengthens her belief that God is ever present
with her. "You may be sure," Perpetua says to her father, who worries for her, "that we are not left to ourselves but are all in his power."[5] She speaks of her faith,
alive with the unseen world-to-come, in the vital, sen-
sory detail of her experience, which allows us to feel her
hardship and aspire to her fidelity.

Hers is the earliest record I have found of writing by
a woman about spiritual experiences. Perpetua is one of
four known Christian women of the late Roman Empire
whose writing survives.[6] In vigorous language she recounts her capture and torture by Roman authorities in
Northern Africa when she was a new convert to Christianity. Arrested in Carthage with six friends during the
persecutions by Emperor Septimius Severus, she refuses
to fear, defying her tormentors, though not escaping torture, and she records visions more vivid to her than her
own body's pain. Tertullian, a contemporary of Per-

petua's, is thought by some scholars to be the witness and redactor of her death, completing her story when she was unable to continue. The original manuscript's survival, paired with its verification by another prisoner and the testimony of an eyewitness to their deaths, makes it one of the more historically reliable documents within a body of works known for their embellishment.

Written in Latin, Perpetua's manuscript consists of twenty-one sections with four divisions. The unnamed eyewitness provides a simple theological context for what follows. As the narration begins we are told that the purpose of such a record is to honor God and encourage Christians, so that we may be reminded of the glory of God and through the narration "associate [ourselves] with the holy martyrs and, through them, with the Lord Jesus Christ." This account of two martyrs' visions and the deaths of several others manifests "God's continuing work among his people," the narrator tells us, and also signals the "last days," which promise the return of Christ.

Sections three through ten are Perpetua's prison diary, in which she briefly describes her trial, her life in captivity, and her visions while she is imprisoned. Following her diary, another captive, Saturus, depicts his vision, and the narrator concludes with an account of the actual killing of the captives.

In the opening passage of the diary, in which Perpetua asks her father to consider the reason for her public confession, we see that the basis for Perpetua's clear sense of her place, her identity, is her committed identification with Christ. She is a Christian. To claim to be something other than what she is will not change her condition, Perpetua tells her father, a wealthy provincial whose tranquility has been spoiled by his daughter's conversion, and whose sight does not extend with hers beyond his immediate cares. This is a young woman whose faith in Christ has altered the very core of her existence. She bears the name Christian as a testimony to that change. No longer is she merely a Roman citizen willing to offer sacrifice to the emperor as deity; she is now a citizen of Heaven who cannot recant despite the pleas of her aged father or even the pangs of motherhood when, because of her imprisonment, she must depend on others to care for the child to whom she has recently given birth.

Perpetua's spiritual identity causes her to break every cultural and ecclesial code of her day. Writing during the decline of the Roman Empire, in which women were rarely educated, she proclaims Christ the one true God and so contests the Romans' army of deities. When asked by the governing authority to offer a sacrifice for the emperor's welfare, Perpetua refuses, and at her father's plea, while her heart breaks to witness his hurt for her, she reiterates, "I am a Christian." Opposing both the power of Rome and the authority of her father, Perpetua asserts her submission to God alone and so is condemned to die.

Perpetua's faith, which she clearly enacted to comply with the teachings of those in authority in the early Christian community, implicitly amends the limited perceptions of women's value within that community. Among those who have committed themselves to following Christ, she lives within the constraints of an incomplete realization of God's Kingdom. Unable to love as Christ loved, to fully envision the liberation Christ offered, believers of any age will ache with the longing that results from discord between the promise of unity in Christ and our actual circumstances.

A few women are known to have served as deaconesses in the early Christian church, but they were not ordained as elders or priests. Valued as virgins and widows if they committed themselves to the service of the church, these women are the ones who have most often been canonized as saints. The act of martyrdom, however, granted an equality among those who gave their lives for their faith—laity or clergy, male or female. Martyrdom was thought to usher one immediately into Heaven, where communication with God was face to face. To die for Christ offered a distinction impossible for women to realize through any other service. And

perhaps, given women's position, the material world ten-
dered a lesser promise than it might have for a person
with property rights and social or religious standing.

But Perpetua's writing expresses no consciousness of
a desire to die in order to reform the church's governing
structures or to desert her present situation. Her martyrdom does not seem to be consciously political, or escap-
ist. The force of the defiance of her actions is balanced,
in her account, with her wish not to offend and with her
evident consternation when she sees the effects of her
testimony on others. She weights her decision to declare
her faith, despite the risk to her own life, with genuine
compassion for those who surround her, often expressing
more acute feelings for the suffering of others than for
herself.

> In my anxiety for the infant I spoke to my
> mother about him, tried to console my brother,
> and asked that they care for my son. I suffered
> intensely because I sensed their agony on my ac-
> count. These were the trials I had to endure for
> many days. Then I was granted the privilege of
> having my son remain with me in prison. Being
> relieved of my anxiety and concern for the infant,
> I immediately regained my strength. Suddenly
> the prison became my palace, and I loved being
> there rather than any other place.

Her personal woes are mitigated when she is able, from prison, to care for the needs of those she loves. Later, as Perpetua stands before the governor, Hilarion, and testifies that she is a Christian, her father's pleading with her to renounce her faith becomes so incessant that the governor throws him out of the hall and has him beaten with a rod.

> My father's injury hurt me as much as if I myself had been beaten, and I grieved because of his pathetic old age. Then the sentence was passed; all of us were condemned to the beasts. We were overjoyed as we went back to the prison cell. Since I was still nursing my child, who was ordinarily in the cell with me, I quickly sent the deacon Pomponius to my father's house to ask for the baby, but my father refused to give him up. Then God saw to it that my child no longer needed my nursing, nor were my breasts inflamed. After that I was no longer tortured by anxiety about my child or by pain in my breasts.

Overjoyed. The prisoners identify their present suffering with that of Christ and so find reason to celebrate their own earthly condemnation, mixed, again, with care for those who take no pleasure in these temporal losses.

As may be evident in these few passages, the prison

journal documents Perpetua's experience for the encouragement of others. Her private meditations and visions reveal a figure who is mentally preparing herself for whatever it is that her faith will require of her. Rich with anticipation of her imminent death and of a life to come, the prose melds visions of heavenly reward with images of physical endurance. In contrast to her apocalyptic visions, her description of her life as a prisoner is immediate and matter-of-fact. "Never before had I experienced such darkness," Perpetua writes. "What a terrible day!" Calm in crisis, she writes almost clinically about nursing her baby and the premature birth of her slave Felicity's child while in captivity, aspects of experience often passed over or nonexistent in the records of saints' lives.

Married women with children are not often regaled with their spiritual options. The early church fathers directed their writings concerning women to virgins and consecrated celibates, perhaps conscious of their unfamiliarity with a mother's lot, but in effect ignoring mothers. The contemporary church has consistently resisted the freedom for women that Jesus offered. Women's "wrestlings," it has been assumed, are less with aesthetic and spiritual fiends than with the quotidian fevers of necessity.

In Jesus' lifetime we see his loving release of one woman from the socially assigned role she had adopted, that of feeding and nurturing others. He does not criticize

her service, but the way her perception of her duty en-
croached on her ability to know Him. Jesus is staying at
the home of his friends, Mary and Martha, and Lazarus,
who has recently died. Luke gives an account of that
visit. "Martha was distracted with all her preparations;
and she came up to him, and said, 'Lord, do You not
care that my sister has left me to do all the serving alone?
Then tell her to help me.'" To which Jesus replied,
"Martha, Martha, you are worried and bothered about so
many things; but only a few things are necessary, really
only one, for Mary has chosen the good part, which shall
not be taken away from her." Jesus contrasts Martha's
activity, her domestic "preparations," to the quiet devotion of her sister to things eternal.

This invitation to become spiritually complete, to engage with him, which Jesus offers to all in the example
of Mary and Martha, is an opportunity that Perpetua
seems to grasp. Her understanding is shaped, however,
by the young institution of the church, which had not so
fully eluded social norms and restraints for women.
Though Perpetua studied Scripture with other men and
women under the tutelage of a more mature believer, the
teaching passed among early Christians was laced, as we
shall glimpse, with disregard for the character of women.

Because of Perpetua's clear sense of purpose she is
able to release her hold on this world with great joy,
setting her sights on the promise of Heaven. But, as
would be impossible for any person, she can never fully

release herself from the grasp of her culture's ideology. As she records her last vision the day before the games are to take place in the Roman arena, we again see her borrow from and transcend her culture's view of women. In her most poignant writing she describes the struggle she imagines will lead up to her death.

The day before the battle in the arena, in a vision I saw Pomponius the deacon coming to the prison door and knocking very loudly. I went to open the gate for him. He was dressed in a loosely fitting white robe, wearing richly decorated sandals. He said to me, "Perpetua, come. We're waiting for you!" He took my hand and we began to walk over extremely rocky and winding paths. When we finally arrived short of breath, at the arena, he led me to the center, saying, "Don't be frightened! I'll be here to help you." He left me and I stared out over a huge crowd which watched me with apprehension. Because I knew that I had to fight with the beasts, I wondered why they hadn't yet been turned loose in the arena. Coming towards me was some type of Egyptian, horrible to look at, accompanied by fighters who were to help defeat me. Some handsome young men came forward to help and encourage me. I was stripped of my clothing, and suddenly I was a man. My assis-

tants began to rub me with oil as was the custom
before a contest, while the Egyptian was on the
opposite side rolling in the sand. Then a certain
man appeared, so tall that he towered above the
amphitheater. He wore a loose purple robe with
two parallel stripes across the chest; his sandals
were richly decorated with gold and silver. He
carried a rod like that of an athletic trainer, and
a green branch on which were golden apples. He
motioned for silence and said, "If this Egyptian
wins, he will kill her with the sword; but if she
wins, she will receive this branch." Then he
withdrew.

We both stepped forward and began to fight
with our fists. My opponent kept trying to grab
my feet but I repeatedly kicked his face with my
heels. I felt myself being lifted up into the air and
began to strike at him as one who was no longer
earthbound. But when I saw that we were wast-
ing time, I put my two hands together, linked my
fingers, and put his head between them. As he
fell on his face I stepped on his head. Then the
people began to shout and my assistants started
singing victory songs. I walked up to the trainer
and accepted the branch. He kissed me and said,
"Peace be with you, my daughter." And I trium-
phantly headed towards the Sanavivarian Gate.
Then I woke up realizing that I would be

contending not with wild animals but with the
devil himself. I knew, however, that I would win.

In this striking transformation of Scripture into literary
imagery we see a metamorphosing of genders, which
Perpetua envisions as necessary to be able to defeat her
opponents. Not only are her advisers and trainer and assistants male, as we might expect, but she herself takes
on the form of a man as she removes her shirt and is
oiled for battle. This is not an evasion of her femaleness
for the sake of modesty, but an absorption of the teaching prevalent in the church of the first centuries. Clement
of Rome, in his letter to the Corinthians, admonishes the
virgins and widows to fulfill their duties to the church
and, recognizing women who were prophets, praises
"many women invested with power through the grace of
God, [who] have accomplished many a manly deed."[7]
This implied deprecation of women as women repeats a
common strain of thought that virtue is the property of
men but that women whom God favors with a certain
manliness also may be recognized as having the capacity
for valor. Given this climate, it is little wonder that an
estimated seventy-five percent of martyrs in the early
centuries were women.[8] The willing acceptance of a martyr's death was one of the few ways that women's service to God could be recognized within their spiritual
communities. These figures' names and stories, with the

exception of Perpetua and a few others, have long since been forgotten.

To attain victory over her assailant, Perpetua adopts a male form, and the needed characteristics thought to be reserved for men. But as she receives the reward of the golden apples (an image evidently drawn from local mythology) she refigures herself in the form of a woman. Her trainer kisses her and says, "Peace be with you, my daughter." With the incomplete vision offered by the material world, the enemy inside or out taunts that we cannot contribute unless we call ourselves by another name, another gender, unless we busy ourselves with "women's work." This is a trickery to which even Perpetua momentarily fell prey, and then, in her woman's body, in her own dignified way, at the very moment she was called to lose it, she reclaimed the prize of her own life, which belonged to Christ.

The narrator goes on to describe the events in the arena in great detail. Perpetua's tormentors had readied a mad cow to match the sex of the women to be tortured. They stripped Perpetua and Felicity and enmeshed them in nets. "How horrified the people were as they saw that one was a young girl and the other, her breasts dripping with milk, had just recently given birth to a child." So, the indelicacy of the torture being too much even for a bloodthirsty crowd, the women were recalled, dressed in loosely fitted gowns, and led back into the arena:

> Perpetua was tossed first and fell on her back. She sat up, and being more concerned with her sense of modesty than with her pain, covered her thighs with her gown which had been torn down one side. Then finding her hair-clip which had fallen out, she pinned back her loose hair thinking it not proper [the redactor supposes] for a martyr to suffer with dishevelled hair; it might seem that she was mourning in her hour of triumph.

My sense is that she was neatening herself not for appearances' sake, at this point, but so that she could more clearly see the world she was about to leave behind. This last look was not her only hour of triumph. She had, through faith, understood her worth as a person and so been able to stand up to social force. She had recognized the constant presence of Christ in her life and the way in which her identification with him freed her from this world's constraints. These victories, as I read of them, are more significant to me than the triumph of the moment when she finally guides the gladiator's hand to her throat because he is trembling as he tries to strike her. "Perhaps it was that so great a woman, feared as she was by the unclean spirit, could not have been slain had she not herself willed it," the narrator concludes.

Perpetua first promised her life, and then gave it to God. In her culture, that resulted in her martyrdom. Called to no less than the Kingdom of God, we understand that the human battle is not against flesh and blood alone but against spiritual powers, and coercive evil and death. But, as Perpetua's life reminds us, we are Christ's who made us and does not forsake us and calls us each by name into the unity and ultimate triumph of his presence.

NOTES

1. Galatians 2:20, New American Standard Bible.

2. Galatians, 3:27–28.

3. Garry Wills, "The Saint of Mott Street," *The New York Review of Books,* April 21, 1994, 36.

4. Patricia Wilson-Kastner, G. Ronald Kastner, Ann Millin, Rosemary Rader, Jeremiah Reedy, eds. *A Lost Tradition: Women Writers of the Early Church* (Lanham, Maryland: University Press of America, 1981). All quotations from Perpetua's account are taken from translations in this work.

5. Herbert Musurillo, trans., *The Acts of the Christian Martyrs* (Oxford, Oxford University Press, 1973), 106ff.

6. See also the *Cento* by Proba, Egeria's "Account of Her Pilgrimage," and Eudokia's "Life of St. Cyprian of Antioch," in Kastner et al., *A Lost Tradition.*

7. *A Lost Tradition,* ix.

8. Arthur F. Ide, *Martyrdom of Women* (Garland, Texas: Tangelwüld, 1985), introduction.

Nuns, Prophecies, Communists, the Bomb, the Dread of Angels, Reason, Faith, and the *Summa Theologica*

R I C H A R D   B A U S C H

"W E   P R O C E E D *thus to the first article: It seems that the existence of God is self-evident . . .*"

Since Time is a human invention, and since the psyche knows nothing of it, really, I am always at least partly living in the presence, among all the other presences, of two separate days, both sunny and cool, both taking place in late March, at the tag end of winter, when the ground is still mostly gray or winter brown, but when some early blossoms are out, and the air has that fresh, earthy new-grass fragrance of spring.

The first of these days is in 1959. A Saturday morning. I'm sitting in a CCD class—Confraternity of Christian Doctrine—for Catholic children who attend public schools. There's a wall of windows to my left, looking out on the world, the wide fallow field and budding trees of the land bordering the church grounds; the sky is as blue as the idea of blue, and it is impossible to think that the whole of it is threatened.

1959. People are building fallout shelters, and everybody is talking about the Communists, and the Bomb. New tests are being conducted on both sides of the world. We have seen the huge terrible blooms of "smoke" in the newsreels. Scientists are finding something called strontium 90 in the milk we drink. It filters down in the rain, settles in the grass the cows eat, and gets into their bones, into their milk. Thus, the very essence of health and life—so the frowning newsmen on our little General Electric black-and-white television have informed us—now carries this deadly poison in varying amounts. Recently, Father Russell, our pastor, delivered a sermon about the end of the world—we must, as individual souls on our very private separate journeys to God, worry more about the end of our individual worlds, which is certain, than the end of the whole world, which is out of our hands.

It's out there somewhere in the blue, blue sky, and people have been talking about trying to shoot it down.

On television there are ads with musical jingles about ducking when you see the white flash. "Duck . . . and cover," the voices sing. And in my eighth-grade class someone has given me a yellow card with instructions on what to do in case of a nuclear attack: 1. Remove all sharp objects from your pocket; 2. Remove glasses and any jewelry; 3. Seat yourself in a hardback chair; 4. Put your head between your legs; and 5. Kiss your ass good-bye.

Regularly at my public school the teachers conduct drills, which have us all lined up in the halls, crouched with our hands over our heads. It's so much a part of everything that we think nothing of it. I pretend the white flash comes, though I'm unable to imagine what the following shock might really feel like. At an all-school assembly, our assistant principal, a World War II veteran, like all the adult men, talked about how in 1944 and 1945 it took thousands of bombs to cause the destruction of Berlin. "Nowadays," he said, pausing for dramatic effect, "it would take one bomb. Just one bomb." He spoke into a surprisingly long silence for a junior-high-school gymnasium full of teenagers. The Bomb, the one Bomb, has taken on a mythical power, as if it were something alive, with a kind of random will.

Everything is tinged with uncertainty and fear.

My father leads us in the Rosary every night, and I

have begun thinking, as most Catholic boys do at one time or another, of the priesthood. My own whispered prayers, during the cold predawn weekday mornings I walk to the six o'clock Mass and Communion, are addressed to the fading stars, as if I'm already traveling among them. I seem to lose the sense of my own body: I'm all spirit in these moments, and keeping the commandments is easy.

But such passages are brief.

Mostly, all each damned day—to paraphrase John Berryman—I have to fight the battles of the flesh, and, as everyone knows, those battles are always fought, for good or ill, in one's mind. Some buried paragraph of a newspaper article I came upon in the school library said that people who bite their nails or move their legs rhythmically when seated, or perform other unconscious nervous movements when supposedly idle—all of which I do to the point of irritating those around me—are giving off the signs of "a marked mental conflict." I can't believe that others are not subject to the same constant fight. It feels sometimes as if I am nothing less than the battleground between God and the devil, and the devil seems to be winning. Mostly, I feel as if nothing of the faith my family practices is quite possible or true. For all the prayers and rituals, the sacraments and devotions, I am having trouble believing in any of it.

At Christmas, when my mother read to us the account of the angels appearing to the shepherds, how the shepherds were "sore afraid," I couldn't understand the passage at all. Why afraid? To have such visible and undeniable proof of the divine presence, to have the necessity of faith removed by the blinding fact of the angels suspended in the air over our heads? I would have rejoiced at such a vision, would have leapt to my feet shouting, "Look! Look everybody! It's true! It's all true! You don't have to worry about it anymore!"

On this particular Saturday morning in 1959, I am gazing out at the perfect sky, and trying not to think about the satellite hurling through it. Over the past few days, I have been reading some of the more dramatic accounts of the lives of the saints, and there's been talk from the nuns we spend the CCD classes with, about the stigmata—with graphic details, of course. I am trying to imagine the stigmata when abruptly I hear my name called, and realize that my instructor, Sister Theresa, has asked me a question. Because I am half in a daze, I say, "What?"

Calmly, yet quite firmly, she asks everyone to leave the room but me. I watch everyone else file out, some of them glancing at me as they go. The last one to go out is asked to close the door. He does so. The door makes its little clicking sound, and then the room is quiet. I'm sitting there with my sleeves rolled up and my hair combed as much as I can make it like Ricky Nelson's, and for an aching long time it's just the two of us, Sister Theresa and me. She shuffles papers at her desk, and stares out the sunny window, her face perfectly serene, as though she's forgotten me entirely. She's not an attractive woman, Sister Theresa; there's just nothing at all appealing about her: not her face, not her voice, not her personality, not her mind or heart, even—certainly not her manner. "These girls in their sunsuits," she'd said only this morning, having got onto the subject of the approaching summer and what everyone would be wearing. "Well, they aren't sunsuits, they're *sin* suits." This through crooked teeth, with a kind of relishing hatred; it's something she's fed on a long time, apparently.

Now, she rises slowly and comes toward me. Maybe she's learned of my plans for the priesthood (I have recently seen Gregory Peck in *Keys of the Kingdom*, and the plans include my standing on some hilltop with music in the background while I recite the Magnificat to the sun and wind.) She takes my hand and squeezes it. It hurts.

"Ow," I say.

"Do you know what color your soul is when you're born?"

"No," I tell her, though I think I do. And then I remember to say, "Sister."

"This color," she says, and puts my hand against her starched white wimple. "And do you know what color your soul is now?" she asks.

Before I can answer, she puts my hand against the black cloth of her habit. "This color," she says.

I am in full agreement with her. But I say nothing. I

know better than to speak unless asked to. This is not the place for discussion, or anything like reason, and I know this without having a way to express it, quite. I just know that there is no appeal, and nothing to say.

The nuns have a story about something the Blessed Virgin gave to those children at Fátima—a letter, the contents of which are so momentous that the Pope wept upon reading it. And each succeeding Pope has wept to know its frightful contents. These contents are to be revealed to the world in 1960. At Fátima, the nuns have told us, the Virgin prophesied that a country called Russia would rise up and cause trouble in the world, and we know this is all connected to the famous letter, which is stored in some secret vault in the Vatican.

It has been said that during the time of Paul, Christians ever expected the second coming. I expect it because I'm fourteen years old and adults are talking about it. The Russians are playing with their bomb and their space toys on the other side of the world. There are bigger and bigger explosions. Last week, in this same CCD class, we were shown slides depicting, in lurid color and graphic detail, people falling into a flaming canyon. A voice intoned, "Listen to the cries of the damned, falling into the everlasting fires of Hell." And we heard the tumult of a thousand voices, the screams of the punished— mostly, it seemed to me, the screams of women. Then the little dull, echoless bell dinged, and the picture of

Hell was obliterated in the small mechanical clatter of the slide changing, and we saw the drawn throne of God, with an Egyptian-stiff Jesus seated at the right hand (our left) all in glorious light. The light, we were told, of Heaven.

I have no hope of Heaven, sitting in that small room with the nun holding my hand against the black cloth of her habit and staring at me with the eyes of an angry Godliness.

I never think of my religion in terms of reason.

"Now, get out of here," she says, letting go of me at last.

Later, in the evening, remembering the cries of the damned, and worried about falling into Hell, I kneel in the dark of my room, feeling that the end is indeed close at hand—it will be 1960 next year—and I begin to pray, thinking about the stigmata, the miracles and signs, all the hoped-for proofs. Perhaps such a thing might happen to me. I am devout; my soul is troubled if it is not black as a nun's habit; I am the battleground; I invite the moment, in a way, with that part of my mind that seems always to be idly speculating. The room is quiet, and quite dark; and abruptly I have the sense of something hovering near. There is an imminence, it seems, a deep pause in the darkness around me. I have stopped breathing. But it's more than that. Any second, it will happen—some gesture from the power and majesty. I can feel it along my spine; it is here. Here!

I have never moved more swiftly in my life.

I bolt out of the room as though it is on fire, or as if, to paraphrase poor old proscribed Boccaccio, ten thousand devils are after me. I almost collide with my mother, walking through the hallway of the house with a basket of laundry. "What's the matter with you?" she says.

"Nothing," I say.

"Well, look where you're going, honey. Will you?"

"We proceed to the second article: It seems that God is not altogether simple . . ."

The second of my two days takes place more than two decades later, though it is no more present or vivid than the first, since it occupies a place in that same wide, quiet province, the lived life that is behind me. It is another sunny March day, 1982, and I am being honored at a gathering of writers in Charlottesville, Virginia, the second annual PEN/Faulkner Awards. My second novel, *Take Me Back,* is one of the six nominees that year, and my wife, Karen, and I have been spending a lot of time with one of the judges, Walker Percy, and his wife, Bunt. We have toured Monticello, and spent hours walking around the city of Charlottesville. It is Walker who nominated me for the award, and who wrote the citation for it. He says that some time after reading the copy the

PEN/Faulkner people sent him, he discovered a complimentary copy *I* had had my publisher send him, back when the book was published.

"Somehow it got in under some papers on my desk," he says. "There's always a lot of stuff piled up there. Some of it has been there for years."

I had the book sent to him because he is one of the writers I admire most in this world. The fact that he likes my book means more than I can adequately say, and I know enough not to embarrass him by saying this out loud. It is implied.

The night before, we stayed up late, with all the other writers, drinking bourbon and talking, though Walker did very little talking. He rattled the ice in his glass, leaning against the back of a sofa, in this crowded room with dim paintings of nineteenth-century faces on the walls, and debating voices going on around him. He sipped the bourbon, attending to everything. I sensed that some of the other writers were trying to outdo themselves in his presence, performing for him. I could feel it in myself when it was my turn to talk. There was an argument about whether a historical novelist has a responsibility not to alter the facts as he knows them in order to tell his story or make his metaphor about history. Walker seemed amused by this. He smiled, sipped the bourbon, and rattled the ice in the glass.

"Telling the truth used to be a pledge of the whole

self, of the very soul," one of the other writers said. "A
bargain with God. Telling an intentional lie in a circum-
stance of such an implied pledge was considered a violation of divine law. A sure ticket to Hell." This was
spoken in the tone of someone explaining the use of an
antique tool.

Walker yawned, and excused himself. I did, too. Out
in the hallway, he asked what I was working on, and I
told him that I was having trouble writing anything at
all. I couldn't convince myself that the problems of the
characters I'd made up mattered.

"You might listen to a lot less of that stuff in there,"
he said. "It doesn't pay to think too much about that end
of it. Sometimes I think it's a little silly. To be an aging
man, still making up stories. You shouldn't worry too
much about the theoretical end of it, though." He smiled,
then headed off to his room.

This bright Sunday, the four of us are off to find a
place to go to Mass. I am driving. Walker and I are in
the front seat, Karen and Bunt in back. Bunt sees a beautiful blanket of nasturtiums in a field we pass, and she
calls our attention to it. Walker points out another splash
of color on the other side of the road—a bed of tulips.
It seems to me that both of them notice the natural world
more than other people; certainly more than I have
tended to over the years. Karen points out a prodigious
drooping wall of a weeping willow, which seems to
dwarf the mansion whose front lawn it shades. We all

remark on the fine weather, the mountains in the near distance, the blooms of forsythia bordering one fenced lawn. Walker and I talk briefly about writers we like to read. We talk about Henry James.

"I have a complete set of the New York Edition of James," he tells me. "But I haven't looked in them much."

I tell him that I've been reading all the short stories.

"I had a student years ago who got interested in James in a big way," Walker says. "She wanted to read everything he wrote." He looks out the window of the car, pausing, letting out a small sigh. "She disappeared into Henry James without a trace."

We laugh. It is getting late, and we haven't been by any churches yet. I vaguely remember a street with several, though I'm not certain any of them are Catholic. I do not know this city very well, and I am driving aimlessly around, looking for anything that looks like a church. At last, we come over a rise and find a gray edifice with spires and stained-glass windows, and ivy climbing the tall sides. We stop at the crest of the hill across from it, in the striped shade of trees that are about to bloom. Walker and I get out to investigate. As we approach the building, he says, "This one has an Episcopal look about it."

I laugh.

"It's too much like a real church," he says.

We make our way along the shaded walk to the

front. Two men are standing outside, and we see from the big stone plaque at the entrance that this is indeed an Episcopal church.

"Excuse me," I say to one of the men. "Is there a Catholic church nearby?"

"Why, yes," the taller of the two says, squinting at us in the sunlight. "You go on down this road and take your first right, then take the next right, and it's on the left as you go up the hill. Look for a big aluminum statue."

Walker looks at me, and we both laugh. We are for the moment in that state of wordless understanding that nourishes the spirit, even if the object of that understanding is a sort of mutual dismay.

"It's Saint Thomas Aquinas," the young man says. "You can't miss it. Big statue of Saint Thomas right out front."

"Thanks," Walker says to them, and we walk back down to the car, still laughing, quietly. We pile in, and I take us to the church. We see it on the left, coming up still another hill, just as the man said we would—an enormous shining sculpture, flanked by the church, which is oddly suspended on many thin white columns over a deep declension in the ground. It looks a little like a flying saucer on props. And then it reminds me of houses near the ocean, built to withstand high water. A catwalk leads to the door, and to the left of the entrance to the catwalk, sits the big statue of Saint Thomas. He's wearing what I suppose are the robes of a monk, and is indeed made out of something like aluminum—bright metal, at any rate. He resembles no image I've ever seen of a saint. He's sitting or squatting, and the tin folds of the robe fall about him as if they have been arrested in the process of melting. He holds books on one massive arm, and he looks jowly, well-fed, faintly disgruntled, almost goofy. No stigmata for this portly gentleman, and no battles with himself about faith, either.

No, Thomas battled with his family when they tried to keep him from the priesthood, and he battled the ignorance and superstitions of his time, battled them reasonably, with that amazing document, the *Summa Theologica*. I cannot imagine him having any arguments with himself over the matters of ultimate concern. Certainly there are no wavering moments in his famous book.

I began reading it, understanding little, when I was eighteen, and still thinking about entering the priesthood. Having run away in abject terror from the intimation of some more visceral proofs, and having come to the knowledge of how superstitious and atavistic most of my training had been, I found the Aquinas as a form of searching, though I was mostly unaware of its deeper meanings, for some final intellectual explanation of the matters on which my tottering faith might rest.

I was destined to fail in this, of course.

And through the years of my journey away from the superstition and fright of the first day I've described—

which consequently became a journey away from my church—the memory of the calm, reasonable, teacherly passages of Aquinas remained, an anomaly in my experience. And Aquinas himself remained, a voice from the distance, disputing in the pages of his book, which I had kept. The great serene intellectual acumen of those marvelous propositions, with their clearly stated purposes and precisely countered objections, gave me an inexpressible sense of some sure knowledge beyond faith, which I had come to see as a form of superstition. But I never stopped to think about it at all. I went through the book, and then went on to the next. In my late teens, I was finding a kind of nourishment provided by the printed word alone. I hoarded everything, traveling indiscriminately in the world's literature—reading mostly philosophy and history. But I kept going back to Thomas—this medieval saint, who had attempted an explanation of the whole matter of divinity.

And as I entered my twenties, and my concerns were far from anything religious, I kept him in my mind as a hedge, somehow, against all the desperate ravings of the world I moved in, with its assassinations and its hopeless little various wars near and far, its riots and body counts and burning villages and atrocities; its glass-littered streets, and broken houses, its many innocent slaughtered—the wages of all those suppurating hatreds and appalling cowardices, and bigotry of every stripe and kind—the world I was trying to make my way in.

To this day, I know less about him than about his book. I have learned that after he took the habit of the Dominicans, who had recently put together a school of theology at the University of Naples, where he had been a student, he was seized by members of his own family, and it took special pleas from the Pope and from the Dominican order, along with his own resoluteness about his future, to obtain his release. I know that he spent his days, as I am spending mine, teaching and writing, and I know that along with the great *Summa,* he wrote hymns, composed a work attempting to reconcile the Greek and Roman Catholic churches, crafted explications of several works of Aristotle; and produced many, many treatises, on everything from Boethius to Scripture.

For me, over the two decades, drifting far from the church, yet still carrying the two sides of it—the atavistic and the reasonable—inside, still praying out of something like superstition, and still fighting the urge to give in to all on those terms, wanting to come to my religion without fear, if I could, and without all the hysterical and narrow voodoo of the nuns—I still thought of Thomas, with his questions, articles, objections, and replies. Thomas stood in my mind as a principle of sorts: the one who reasoned his way to God.

And so on this particular early spring day in 1982, kneeling beside Walker Percy in the discouragingly modernistic building that is the Church of St. Thomas Aquinas Church in Charlottesville, Virginia, I find that I am aware of this terrible modernism as against the monk perched on his bench outside, and, as happens often when I am at Mass, I'm vaguely troubled, unpleasantly and somehow reprehensibly detached—feeling that perhaps I ought to be elsewhere, that my doubts and my old angers about the ignorance and folly of the earlier time, not to mention my lapsed state, make me an intruder here. I probably would not have come, were it not for Mr. Percy. And there he is, kneeling next to me, that consummate artist and philosopher, a deeply learned man with a scientist's knowledge (Percy, as most people know, was a trained physician), there he is, saying his prayers, head bowed, eyes closed, simply believing. Or, at any rate, believing first, before the complexities. And in that one moment, still thinking about the heavy scholarly figure depicted in the ugly metal statue on the lawn, I have a kind of revelation: for perhaps the first time in my life I think of Thomas not in terms of his great intellect, not in terms of reason at all, but of the faith that could drive an enormous undertaking like the *Summa*. Abruptly, with a shiver, deep, I realize something everyone else must already know: that it all has finally to stop there, in faith. *At* faith. That what I have always felt was the tremendous reasonableness of Aquinas's book is not so much the product of intellect, as it is the most powerful manifestation of his faith. And I remember hearing that the year before he died, he stopped writing or dictating, claiming that what had been revealed to him in a revelation while saying Mass made everything he had written in his life seem "as straw."

Reason wedded to faith, then. But faith is first. The end and the beginning—or, in the exact words of the old prayer: as it *was* in the beginning, is now, and ever shall be, world without end.

Amen.

A Moderate in a Disputatious Age

AVERY DULLES, S.J.

I FIRST came across Robert Bellarmine in the late 1930s, when I was an undergraduate at Harvard, studying the history and literature of the Italian Renaissance. I remember him particularly because of the respectful presentation of his work in Charles H. McIlwain's course on the history of political thought in the West. About the time that I became a Catholic, in my first semester of Harvard Law School, I devoured James Brodrick's two-volume life of Bellarmine and came to admire the saint's many-sided personality and his manifold accomplishments.

Several months later, in the spring of 1941, when I received the sacrament of confirmation at the hands of Bishop Richard J. Cushing (who later became cardinal-archbishop of Boston), I was asked to choose a confirmation name, and I selected without hesitation "Robert." On that occasion the bishop presented me with a fine illustrated volume on Francis of Assisi, one of the saints that Bellarmine most admired. Born on the feast of Saint Francis, October 4, 1542, Bellarmine had been given "Francis" as his second name. He died on September 17, 1622, the feast of the stigmatization of Saint Francis, a feast that he had helped to insert into the calendar. When that feast was suppressed in the reform of the liturgical calendar after Vatican II, the feast of Saint Robert Bellarmine was transferred from May 13 to September 17, where it now stands.

When I entered the Society of Jesus in 1946, after a stint with the Navy in World War II, I was delighted to find that Bellarmine was one of the two Jesuit doctors of the Church and was the patron of all Jesuit theologians. I made him in a special way the patron of my own studies. When I went to Rome to get my doctorate at the Gregorian University, my associations with Bellarmine increased. I said Mass daily in the Church of Sant' Ignazio, where Bellarmine lies buried, as he requested, at the feet of his former penitent, Aloysius Gonzaga, whose marble tomb is a masterpiece of Baroque sculpture.

Since 1973 I have taught three times as a visiting

professor at the Gregorian University. The last time, in the fall of 1993, coincided with the fourth centenary of Bellarmine's rectorship of the university, known in his day as the Roman College (1592–1594). It was here that Bellarmine had studied philosophy (1560–1563), taught theology (1576–1588), and served as spiritual director (1590–1592). The college received its present name in honor of its "second founder," Pope Gregory XIII (1572–1585), who built the new Roman College, with its imposing classical façade, during Bellarmine's tenure.

There is every reason, then, why I should look back to Bellarmine as representing the finest traditions and perhaps the most glorious period of my own Jesuit theological heritage. He was a major actor in one of the most dramatic periods of Church history—the reorganization of the Catholic Church in response to the challenges of the modern age. The sixteenth century had witnessed, in many respects, the birth of modernity. Capitalism was edging out the medieval agrarian economy. Europe was becoming divided into rival principalities or nation-states, often governed by Machiavellian rulers who claimed absolute powers over their subjects. The Holy Roman Empire survived in theory, but it ceased to be a true empire (not to mention its failure to be either holy or Roman, as Voltaire once quipped).

This period also witnessed intellectual and cultural revolutions. Medieval manuscript communication rapidly yielded to the new print culture. Pamphlets and books, including the Bible, were widely circulated in affordable editions, frequently in the vernacular. Under the impetus of classical humanism, scholars were producing new and critical editions of ancient texts, both classical and religious, and were questioning many venerable legends about Christian origins. Critical reason was beginning to assume the upper hand over traditional faith. Dramatic scientific discoveries were being made, including the Copernican theory, which situated the sun rather than the earth at the center of the universe. It was also the great age of discovery, when Europe suddenly became conscious that it was only a fraction of a much larger world, in many parts of which Christianity was still unknown. Thus the medieval world picture, so glowingly immortalized in Dante's *Divine Comedy,* was in many respects superseded.

It was into this volatile situation that Luther, in 1518, issued his urgent call for ecclesiastical reform. His appeal hit upon receptive ears, because everyone recognized that corruptions and abuses were rampant in the Church. Luther's personal doctrines, however, were another question. Pope Leo X wrote him off as simply another German heretic, but he proved to be much more. With the support of several German princes, and the backing of German national feeling, he obtained a large constituency, so that his excommunication by Rome resulted in a major schism. Soon afterward, several other parts of Europe followed suit in seceding from the Catholic allegiance.

By the time Bellarmine reached adulthood, Europe was a checkerboard of different denominations—Lutheran, Calvinist, Zwinglian, Anglican, Anabaptist, and even Unitarian (Socinian). In many cases the religious affiliation of the people depended on that of their sovereigns. Catholics and Protestants therefore vied with one another in seeking to win the patronage of secular princes. Not infrequently the patronage became so vigorous that members of other denominations were tortured and executed. The principle of religious toleration was practically unknown.

The Jesuit order, founded by Saint Ignatius of Loyola in 1540, was immediately caught up in this religious ferment. While Ignatius governed his new Society from his headquarters in Rome, his companions fanned out to all parts of the world. They labored, often at the price of martyrdom, in India, China, Japan, Africa, and the Americas, seeking to spread Catholic Christianity all over the globe. In Western Europe they were involved in the inner reform of the Church, in the education of the clergy, and in turning back the advancing tide of heresy. At the Council of Trent the pope chose several of Ignatius's most brilliant companions to be his personal theologians. That council issued what still stands as the authoritative statement of Catholic doctrine in response to the Reformers. It set the agenda for Bellarmine's generation in much the same way as Vatican II has set the agenda for the late twentieth century.

Bellarmine, like other Jesuit theologians of his day, was first of all a servant of the Church, a defender of orthodoxy in an age when the foundations of Catholicism were being assailed. He taught, preached, and wrote in the Jesuit style, according to the rules laid down by Saint Ignatius. The early Jesuits were Christian humanists, well educated in classical languages and literature, with a high esteem for human nature, reason, and freedom. They kept abreast of the latest developments in scholarship and the sciences. Without being a scientist himself, Bellarmine kept himself informed through friends such as his colleague the great Clavius (Christoph Klau, S. J.), with whom Galileo often exchanged ideas. Clavius is best known as the principal author of the Gregorian Calendar and is also remembered by the "sea" on the moon that bears his name.

Although Bellarmine was by temperament a peaceful and friendly person, his career took him into a series of battles. In 1570, as a young professor at Louvain (in modern Belgium), he began his six-year struggle against Baius (Michel de Bay), whose pessimistic views concerning man's fallen condition resembled those of Calvin. Bellarmine, as a champion of human freedom and dignity, threw himself into the combat with alacrity.

When recalled by superiors to teach at the Roman

College, Bellarmine produced his magnum opus, the *Disputationes de Controversiis Fidei Catholicae adversus huius temporis haereticos,* published in three large folios in 1586, 1588, and 1593. Although never translated as a whole into vernacular languages, this work remained for centuries the standard Catholic response to the Reformation. It also established the main lines of Catholic ecclesiology until the middle of our own century. Many of the Latin apologetics manuals and textbooks published in the intervening years were little more than simplified versions of Bellarmine's masterpiece. While writing overtly as a controversialist, Bellarmine was exceptionally fair and moderate toward his adversaries, at least by the standards of his day. In order to meet the real difficulties, he took pains to state the opponents' arguments at their strongest. On occasion he even defended Protestants against unfair charges, such as Calvin's alleged deviations from the orthodox doctrine of the Trinity. Some Catholics distrusted Bellarmine on the ground that Protestants were using his account of them to find ammunition in their own defense.

Bellarmine's ecclesiology differed in several respects from that of his medieval predecessors. He portrayed the Church not primarily as a mystical communion but rather as a visible society, no less visible, he said, than the Republic of Venice. This society was, moreover, monarchical in structure, governed by a pope who could on occasion speak with infallibility. When the First Vatican

Council was preparing to define the doctrine of papal infallibility in 1869 and 1870, many speakers referred to Bellarmine as an authority.

Bellarmine taught that membership in the Church was absolutely necessary for salvation, but he made an important distinction between belonging to the "body" of the Church and to its "soul." Non-Catholics and non-Christians, if they erred in good faith, could belong to the "soul" of the Church. This distinction was widely accepted among Catholics until the middle of the present century, when different terminology came into use. Vatican II, for example, distinguishes between Catholics, who are "fully incorporated" in the Church, and others who, when separated from the Catholic communion without personal fault, may be secretly "conjoined" or "ordered" to the Church in various ways.

Bellarmine's work is still a valuable resource for ascertaining and criticizing the positions of Reformation thinkers. I experienced this a decade ago, when engaged in a dialogue with Lutheran theologians about the role of the saints in the Christian life. The Catholics and Lutherans managed to achieve a large measure of agreement on several issues: that the saints are to be honored for what God's grace had wrought in them, that their lives inspire us with gratitude and confidence toward God, and that they provide examples for us to imitate. With some hesitation the Lutherans conceded that the saints probably intercede for the Church on earth.

But at one point our ways parted. Was it proper for Christians to invoke the saints in prayer? The Lutherans contended that there was no biblical example or precept for so doing, that we have no way of knowing whether the saints in glory can hear us (even supposing them to be in glory), that consequently the invocation of saints introduces an element of doubt and uncertainty into Christian prayer, and, finally, that prayer to the saints derogates from the trust that should be placed in Christ as the sole and sufficient mediator of all grace.

Hard-pressed by these formidable objections, I made an expedition to the subterranean stacks of Fordham University, located the appropriate passage in Bellarmine's *Controversies*, and found to my delight that he had given an exceptionally lucid exposition of the Catholic doctrine of honoring the saints, in the course of which he dealt with ten objections culled from the Reformers, including all the objections I have listed. A central point in his argument was that, whether we pray to God directly or invoke the intercession of saints, nothing is asked or granted that does not come from God through the mediation of Christ. In the last analysis every prayer is directed to God, the giver of all perfect gifts. From this perspective it may be said that we do not so much pray *to the saints* as seek their solidarity with us as we pray *to God.* Prayer to the saints can never be played off in competition with prayer to God, nor can the intercession of the saints be regarded as detracting from the redemptive mediatorship of Christ alone.

From this example, which I have chosen in view of the theme of the present collection, it should be evident that Bellarmine's old volumes can still be uncommonly useful for theologians today. They should not be allowed to accumulate dust in deserted library stacks.

The Bible, of course, was a major point of contention between Protestants and Catholics, both of whom wanted to prove that their doctrines were consonant with the written word of God. Jesuits such as Bellarmine became expert in the biblical languages. As a young professor he wrote a very popular Hebrew grammar. In 1579, during his Roman professorate, he was called upon to assist Alonso Salmerón, an elderly survivor from Ignatius's original band of companions, in editing his sixteen folio volumes of commentaries on the New Testament. Later Bellarmine composed a large commentary on the Psalms (1611), a piece that is devotional rather than scholarly in character.

More significant for posterity is Bellarmine's role in the revision of the Latin Vulgate. Carrying out a decree of the Council of Trent, Pope Gregory XIII appointed a commission, with Bellarmine as a member, to produce a reliable edition of the ancient Vulgate translation. The commission did its work with great care, and in 1588 presented the results to the temperamental Sixtus V. To general astonishment, he rejected the commission's work and took the revision into his own hands. In 1590, just as his very faulty edition was emerging from the press, the pope suddenly died. Bellarmine was again called in to assist in correcting the errors. A new text was published in 1592 under the name of Pope Sixtus V, although Clement VIII was then reigning. In a preface Bellarmine tried to protect the reputation of the earlier pope by dwelling on the printer's errors in the edition that had begun to be published. The Sixto-Clementine Vulgate (as it is usually called) remained the standard Catholic Bible until the mid-twentieth century, when fresh translations from the original biblical languages were encouraged.

Another debt that the Church of later centuries owes to Bellarmine is for his contribution to the reform of the Breviary. Because of his mastery of ecclesiastical history, he was asked by Clement VIII to serve on a commission for this purpose. He argued for excluding various improbable legends concerning James the Greater, Denis the Areopagite, and Catherine of Alexandria, but his opinions did not always prevail. He composed a beautiful Latin hymn to Mary Magdalen that was included in the office for July 21, at the vespers of her feast.

In the 1590s, under Clement VIII, Bellarmine became heavily involved in a truly epochal struggle within Catholic theology—the controversy between the Dominicans and the Jesuits on the relations between efficacious grace and free will. Bellarmine, as a Jesuit, was inclined to favor the "Molinist" position (devised by Luis de Molina, S. J.) to the effect that God's salvific decree depends upon his eternal knowledge of the use that human beings make of their freedom in response to God's grace. While he did not fully accept Molina's theory, he resisted the opinion of Domingo Bañez, O. P., that God determines human acts by giving an infallible "physical premotion" *(praemotio physica)* to the will. Clement himself was inclined to support the Dominican view and, perhaps for that reason, removed Bellarmine from Rome in 1602, appointing him archbishop of Capua. But after Clement's death, Bellarmine was recalled to Rome, where he labored as a cardinal of the Roman curia. Following Bellarmine's recommendation, Paul V decreed in 1607 that both opinions were to be tolerated. Neither party was to impugn the positions of the other as heretical or temerarious. This decree illustrates the way in which the hierarchical magisterium can on occasion serve to protect the freedom of theologians and their immunity from unjust accusations.

In an age when popes were much given to deposing temporal sovereigns (as Pius V deposed Queen Elizabeth), Bellarmine was required to speak to the question of the pope's temporal power. Some theologians still held to the extreme position that Christ had given Peter "two swords," the spiritual and the temporal, thereby bestowing on the popes universal sovereignty in both spheres. Bellarmine held for the autonomy of the temporal power in secular matters, but he made provision in his theory for the pope to intervene in secular politics where the good of souls was at stake. Bellarmine's moderate doctrine of the "indirect power" of the Holy See did not satisfy the impetuous Sixtus V, who took steps to place the *Controversies* on the Index of Prohibited Books. But here again the death of the pope intervened, preventing him from promulgating this edition of the Index.

The most vehement objections to the theory of the indirect power came not from popes but from secularists who attributed absolute powers to kings. They rejected Bellarmine's contention that the temporal sovereign should be bound by international law to abide by moral principles and respect the human rights of all subjects, including the aborigines in the colonies.

Bellarmine's bad reputation in the English-speaking world is largely due to his polemical exchanges with King James I, undertaken at the direction of Paul V (1605 – 1621). Against the King of England, Bellarmine defended his doctrine of the pope's "indirect power," and attacked the idea that kings rule with absolute power by divine right. Bellarmine held that civil power comes to the ruler not directly from God but through the people, who may set up any kind of regime that serves the common good. Regalists such as William Barclay and Robert Filmer, responding to Bellarmine, characterized him as the ablest defender of the doctrine they were opposing.

John Locke, Thomas Jefferson, and James Madison seem to have been acquainted with Bellarmine, especially through the writings of his adversaries. It has been plausibly argued that in this way Bellarmine exercised an indirect influence upon the American system of government. In any case he belonged to the general movement of thought that favored popular sovereignty.

Yet another of the controversies in which Bellarmine was engaged is the trial of Galileo. As a member of the Holy Office he was asked in 1616 to be a judge when charges were made against the orthodoxy of the new astronomy. Like the other judges, he concluded, after consulting leading experts in the field, that Galileo had not proved his case, and that his theory stood in contradiction to the apparent meaning of several passages in Scripture. He advised Galileo to propose his theory simply as a hypothesis, which would seem to have been a reasonable solution. When Galileo refused, Bellarmine was party to a declaration that the Copernican theory, as received by Galileo, ought not to be held. But at that trial no condemnation was issued, no punishment imposed, nor was Galileo ordered to make any retraction. For the results of the second trial of Galileo, which occurred in 1633, Bellarmine cannot be held responsible, for by that time he had been dead for eleven years.

The Galileo case long continued to be a point of friction between the Church and the scientific community. In 1981 Pope John Paul II set up a papal commission to study the case anew. This commission, in its report of October 31, 1992, gave high praise to Bellarmine for having declared that if it were really demonstrated that the earth revolves about the sun, it would be necessary to reinterpret the biblical passages which seem to say the contrary. The commission also faulted Galileo's judges, who in the trial of 1633 judged that the Copernican theory, not yet definitively proven, was contrary to the teaching of Scripture and Catholic tradition. Pope John Paul II, addressing the Pontifical Academy of Sciences on the same occasion, repeated the commission's praise for Bellarmine. He agreed with its findings that the sentence of 1633 was "not irreformable" and was based on a misconception of the relations between biblical revelation and physical science.

Central though controversies were to the life of Bellarmine, as a theologian in a disputatious age, they do not make up his total achievement. A more positive element of his legacy may be found in the two catechisms he composed in Italian, the first for children (1597), the other for adults (1598). These catechisms, modeled on the Roman Catechism of 1566, remained popular for several centuries. Translated into various languages, they inspired other manuals, such as the famous Baltimore Catechism, widely used in this country until Vatican II. But unlike the Baltimore Catechism, Bellarmine's did not begin by having the child ask the metaphysical questions "Who made us?" and "Who is God?" The first question

is, rather, "Are you a Christian?" to which the child replies, "By the grace of God, I am." Then the catechism
goes on to inquire into the principal mysteries of the
Christian faith, the Trinity, and the Incarnation.

At the First Vatican Council, in 1869, Pius IX announced his intention, with the fathers' approval, to have
a new catechism drawn up on the pattern of Bellarmine's.
Because the council was disrupted by war, it never arrived at a vote on this proposal. The Church had to wait
another century before it would have a new universal
catechism. The new *Catechism of the Catholic Church,* like
Bellarmine's, is based on the Roman Catechism and uses
as its four "pillars" the Apostles' Creed, the Our Father,
the Ten Commandments, and the Seven Sacraments.
Like Bellarmine's, again, it treats the Trinity and the Incarnation as the central mysteries of faith.

I have focused here on Bellarmine's theological writings rather than on his personality and his qualities as a
pastor, spiritual director, and saint. His biographers tell
us that he was serene, joyful, and optimistic. He had a
playful sense of humor and was much addicted to puns.
In spite of his exceptional talents he was always content
to be given the smallest rooms, to wear the oldest
clothes, and eat the poorest fare. As an archbishop and a
cardinal he put his revenues at the disposal of needy families and drew multitudes of beggars to his doorstep.

One of my favorite stories about Bellarmine captures
at once his self-mortification and his theological wit. In

the Roman summers he was pestered, like others, by flies. His companions asked him why he did not brush these nuisances away. He explained with a smile that it would not be fair to trouble the little creatures, since his nose was their Paradise.

In the entire corpus of Bellarmine's writings the spiritual works of his final years are the most accessible in vernacular translations. Although the style of these works reflects the mentality of an earlier age, they vividly illustrate how the piety of the saint can permeate the reflections of the theologian.

The most popular of these spiritual works, *The Mind's Ascent to God* (1614), is comparable in content and structure to Saint Bonaventure's *Journey of the Mind to God*, but in place of Bonaventure's flights of mysticism, Bellarmine pursues a more logical and moralistic course. Yet his prose is not devoid of eloquence. In examining, in the first pages, how we are created in the image of God, he delights in explaining that the mind, as a principle of reason and freedom, distinguishes us from the animals and makes us similar to God. The final chapters celebrate the mercy and justice of God.

The series of small spiritual classics ends with Bellarmine's last work, appropriately named *The Art of Dying Well* (1620). He maintains that "death, as the offspring of sin, is evil, but that by the grace of Christ, who deigned to undergo death for us, it has been rendered for us in many ways useful and salutary, lovable and desirable."

Bellarmine was not remarkable for his originality or speculative genius. He was a practical man, concerned with serving the universal Church as it responded to the crises of the age. By his own intention he stood in firm continuity with the past, confident that the tradition of the Church was sound and valid. Yet, almost in spite of himself, he absorbed the spirit of the new age. As compared with Saint Thomas Aquinas and the medieval Scholastics, he was far more careful in scrutinizing the written sources and ascertaining the history of the questions he treated. Faithful to the precepts of Saint Ignatius, he brought positive and speculative theology into partnership. Breathing the spirit of Renaissance humanism, he adamantly opposed the assaults of neo-Augustinian pessimism.

The stature of Bellarmine is indicated by the enduring influence of his writings. They continued to be a major, even a dominant, source for Catholic doctrine during the next three centuries. Ours, however, is an age with different questions, different assumptions, and a radically changed context. We have passed from a print-dominated culture to one that is electronic. We have passed from a Eurocentric consciousness to one that is global and is verging on the galactic. Catholics are no longer arrayed in battle against Reformation Protestantism. They are seeking ecumenical rapprochement, and are in dialogue with other world religions. In short, theologians are called to do again, in a vastly changed context, something analogous to what Bellarmine did, with remarkable success, for early modern times.

What endures in Bellarmine is his example of loyal service to the Church in a time of confusion and crisis. He is a model of moderation and rationality, open to new developments but deeply attached to the Catholic heritage. He undertook almost nothing on his own initiative, and was content to labor at uncongenial tasks where duty seemed to require. He never raised a finger for the sake of his personal advancement, and perhaps for that reason was generally trusted by his religious and ecclesiastical superiors. Among his many virtues I would single out loyalty as perhaps the greatest. He did what was asked of him; he spoke frankly when consulted, but he never urged his own opinions to the detriment of the Church itself. He was loyal to his religious order, loyal to the Holy See, loyal to the Church, and loyal especially to God, in whom he placed all his trust and confidence.

The Pilgrim

RON HANSEN

MORE THAN two hundred miracles were attributed to Ignatius of Loyola when the judges for the cause of his canonization, the Rota, assembled their sixteen hundred witness statements in 1622.[1] A surgeon held a signature of Ignatius to his head and his headaches and sight problems ended. A Franciscan nun's broken femur was healed when a Spanish priest applied a patch of Ignatius's clothing to her thigh. A Spanish woman held a picture of Ignatius to her hugely swollen stomach and was soon cured of dropsy. Juana Clar, of Manresa, was gradually

losing her sight until she got down on her knees and
permitted a fragment of Ignatius's bones to be touched
to her eyelids. She felt at once such pleasure that it was
as if, she said, she'd seen fresh roses. Within a day her
pain went away and her vision was perfectly restored.
And so on.

Even though I presume those stories are true, I find
myself oddly unaffected by them; it's as if I heard that
Saint Ignatius, like Cool Hand Luke, could eat fifty eggs.
I have read every major biography and book about Ignatius, I have held his shoes in my hands, I have walked
through his freshly restored rooms in the house next to
what is now the Church of the Gesù, and I have next to
me as I write this a nail that was in one of the walls.
Supernatural prodigies have nothing to do with my rapt
and consuming interest in him. I have simply been trying
to figure out how to live my life magnificently, as Ignatius did, who sought in all his works and activities the
greater glory of God.

Iñigo López de Loyola was born in the Loyola castle in
1491, the last son of thirteen children born to a wealthy
and highly esteemed family in Azpeitia, in the Basque
province of Guipúzcoa.[2] His father, Beltrán de Loyola,
died in 1507, but we do not know when his mother, Ma-
rina Sánchez de Licona, died, only that she predeceased
her husband; it's highly probable she died in the child's
infancy, for Iñigo was nursed by María de Garín, a

neighboring blacksmith's wife, who later taught him his prayers and with whose children he played.[3]

Guipúzcoa means "to terrify the enemy"[4] and there was a huge, legendary emphasis on fearlessness and aggressiveness among the region's men. Juan Pérez, the oldest of Iñigo's brothers, joined a ship's escort for Christopher Columbus and finally died heroically in the Spanish conquest of Naples, and another brother, Hernando, gave up his inheritance in order to go to the Americas, where he disappeared in 1510. In fact, of Iñigo's seven older brothers, only one was not a conquistador or fighting man. That brother, Pero López, took holy orders and became rector of the Church of San Sebastián at Azpeitia; and his father may have sought holy orders for Iñigo as well, for he was enrolled in preseminary studies in the arts of reading and writing before he was sent, at the age of thirteen and probably at his own behest, to acquire the skills and manners of a courtier in the household of his father's friend, the chief treasurer of King Ferdinand of Castile.[5]

His fantasies became those of intrigue and gallantry and knightly romance. Of him in his twenties it was written: "He is in the habit of going round in cuirass and coat of mail, wears his hair long to the shoulder, and walks around in a two-colored, slashed doublet with a bright cap."[6] We have evidence that he was cited in court for brawling, and he himself confessed that "he was a man given over to the vanities of the world; with a great and vain desire to win fame he delighted especially in the exercise of arms."[7] We have no evidence from him of his affairs of the heart beyond his furtive confession that he was "fairly free in the love of women" and, later, that he often spent hours "fancying what he would have to do in the service of a certain lady, of the means he would take to reach the country where she was living, of the verses, the promises he would make to her, the deeds of gallantry he would do in her service. He was so enamored with all this that he did not see how impossible it would all be, because the lady was of no ordinary rank";[8] indeed, she seems to have been Doña Catalina, the glamorous sister of Emperor Charles V and future queen of John III of Portugal.[9]

When his employer, the king's treasurer-general, died in 1517, the twenty-six-year-old Iñigo found another friend and benefactor in the Viceroy of Navarre, who hired him as his "gentleman," a kind of factotum or right-hand man. Iñigo de Loyola was a finished hidalgo by then, a haughty Lothario and swashbuckler, famous for his flair and charm and machismo, his fastidiousness and fondness for clothes, his highly educated politeness and chivalry and hot temper, his ferocity of will, his fortitude and loyalty—his Basqueness, as the Spanish would say—and also his acuity and craft in negotiations, his penetrating stare, his photographic memory, his fine penmanship, his reticence and precaution in speech, his love of singing and dancing. Like his Spanish friends, he was religiously naive, and Catholicism seems to have been rather perfunctory for him—high-table rituals without flourish or kisses. "Although very much attached to the faith," a friend and biographer wrote, "he did not live in keeping with his belief, or guard himself from sin: he was particularly careless about gambling, affairs with women, and duelling." [10]

Iñigo was not a professional soldier then, as he'd fancied he'd be, but a public administrator, "a man of great ingenuity and prudence in worldly affairs and very skillful in the handling of men, especially in composing difficulties and discord." [11] But in May 1521, his skillfulness in the handling of men put Iñigo alongside the magistrate of Pamplona in Navarre, defending its fortress in the midst of a huge French offensive in the region along the Pyrenees that the Spanish king had annexed five years earlier. We have no idea how many citizens were with Iñigo, but there could not have been more than a handful holding out against a highly trained French force of three hundred. [12] Late in the nine-hour siege of the fortress, an artillery shot crashed between Iñigo's legs, shattering the right and harming the other. After he fell, the fortress surrendered, and the French made it a point of chivalry to treat Iñigo with such exemplary kindness that it may have seemed a form of sarcasm. Their finest physicians operated on him and graciously hospitalized him for a fortnight in his own Pamplona residence before hauling him forty miles northwest to Azpeitia on a litter.

In his family's castle Iñigo's fever and illness grew worse, and village surgeons decided the skewed bones of his leg would have to be broken again and reset—without anesthetic. Even thirty years later he would describe that agony as "butchery," but he was fiercely determined to give no "sign of pain other than to clench his fists." [13] When finally his right leg healed, Iñigo realized that it was foreshortened and that the fibula had knitted jaggedly so that an ugly jutting was just under his knee. Still thinking of finding fame in royal courts and of striding forth in fashionably tight leggings and knee-high boots, he made himself "a martyr to his own pleasure" [14] and underwent the horrific ordeal of having the offending bone chiseled and shaved away.

And then a change began to occur in him. While lying about and suffering further treatments that failed to lengthen his brutalized leg, he sought books of Medieval chivalry to read. Surprisingly, the only books available in the Loyola house were a four-volume *Vita Jesu Christi* by Ludolph of Saxony and a kind of dictionary of saints called *Flos Sanctorum* by Jacopo da Varazze. [15] With a sigh he read even those. A confidant later overstated the situation by writing of Iñigo that "he had no thought then either of religion or piety," [16] but it can be fairly said that his simple, unreflective, folk Christianity had not forced him to take his life here seriously nor to compare himself to the holy men of the past, whom Ludolph of Saxony called knightly followers of Christ—*caballeros imita-*

dores.[17] Speaking of himself in the third person in his autobiography, Ignatius put it this way:

> As he read [the books] over many times, he became rather fond of what he found written there. Putting his reading aside, he sometimes stopped to think about the things he had read and at other times about the things of the world that he used to think about before. . . . Our Lord assisted him, causing other thoughts that arose from the things he read to follow these. While reading the life of Our Lord and of the saints, he stopped to think, reasoning within himself, "What if I should do what St. Francis did, what St. Dominic did?" So he pondered over many things that he found to be good, always proposing to himself what was difficult and serious, and as he proposed them, they seemed to him easy to accomplish.[18]

We are challenged by Ignatius in much the same way that he was challenged by Francis and Dominic. And that may be the best purpose for books of saints: to have our complacency and mediocrity goaded, and to highlight our lame urge to go forward with the familiar rather than the difficult and serious. We often find tension and unease with the holy lives we read about because there is always an implicit criticism of our habits and weaknesses in greatness and achievement. We know God wants us to be happy, but what is happiness? What is enough? What is the difference between that which is hard to do and that which ought not be done by me? Women are often put off or mystified by this highly masculine saint, but I find so many points of intersection with Iñigo's life that I feel compelled to ask, What if I should do what Ignatius did? And it does not seem to me easy to accomplish.

Iñigo was thirty years old, which was far older then, and yet he found himself wrought up by questions about his purpose on earth that his friends had put a halt to as teenagers. But he was helped in his religious crisis by his discovery of affective patterns to his inner experience, a discovery that would later form the basis for the "Rules for Discernment of Spirits" in his *Spiritual Exercises*.

> When he was thinking about the things of the world, he took much delight in them, but afterwards, when he was tired and put them aside, he found that he was dry and discontented. But when he thought of going to Jerusalem, barefoot and eating nothing but herbs and undergoing all the other rigors that he saw the saints had endured, not only was he consoled when he had these thoughts, but even after putting them aside, he remained content and happy. . . . Little by

little he came to recognize the difference between the spirits that agitated him, one from the demon, the other from God.[19]

Concluding that he ought to change radically, Iñigo chose to give up his former interests and pursuits, and, on a pilgrimage to Jerusalem, undergo the hard penances for his sins that "a generous soul, inflamed by God, usually wants to do."[20] Confirmation of that choice came one August night in his sickroom when he was graced with a clear and tremendously consoling image of Our Lady with the Infant Jesus, "and he was left with such loathing for his whole past life and especially for the things of the flesh, that it seemed that all the fantasies he had previously pictured in his mind were driven from it."[21] Even his family noted the difference in him and, far from thinking him crazy, seemed inspired by his faith and good example. Seeing that Iñigo wanted to go even farther in his religious life, however, Martín García de Loyola took his limping brother from room to room in the grand old house, pointing out the jasper and furnishings and fine tapestries, and appealing to him to "consider what hopes had been placed in him and what he should become . . . all with the purpose of dissuading him from his good intention."[22]

But Iñigo was not budged. He filled three hundred pages of a blank account book with extracts from the

Gospels and his readings, found a picture of Our Lady of Sorrows and a book of hours of Our Lady, fitted himself out like a knight-errant, and finally left the Loyola house in late February 1522. Offering farewells to his sister Magdalena at Anzuola and to his former employer, the Viceroy of Navarre, in Navarrete, he went eastward on his mule another two hundred miles to the Benedictine monastery of Montserrat in Catalonia. After a full, general confession of his past life in writing, which took three days, Iñigo gave up his fine clothes to a tramp, put on a penitential sackcloth tunic and rope-soled sandals, and on the eve of the Annunciation of Our Lady observed a knightly vigil-at-arms at the feet of the Black Madonna, where he vowed perpetual chastity and left his flashing sword and dagger in the shrine. Effectively, his former life was over.

Barcelona was the port of embarkation for Rome where, through agreement with the Turks, pilgrims were given permission to go to the Holy Land by the pope himself at Easter. But Adrian of Utrecht, the new pope-elect, was himself in Spain and on his slow way to the port, and Iñigo was at pains to avoid his old friends in the Navarrese nobility, whom he rightly presumed would be part of Adrian's retinue.[23] So he went from Montserrat to Manresa, a few miles north, with the intention of staying perhaps three days, but the affective experience of God he felt there was so powerful that he stayed in

Manresa almost a year, a period he later thought of as "my primitive Church."

To vanquish his vanity there, Iñigo let his nails go untrimmed and his hair and beard grow full and wild as nests, and as he tilted from door to door for food and alms in his prickly tunic, he found joy and sweetness in the jeering of children who called him *El hombre saco*— Old Man Sack.[24] He helped with the poor and sick in the hospital of Santa Lucia, finding no task offensive, and primarily resided in a Dominican friary, though he often withdrew to a hermit's cave in the hillsides above the river Cardoner. Eating no meat and drinking no wine, fasting until he was little more than skin and skeleton, ill and sleepless much of the time, flagellating himself for his sins, Iñigo was still an Olympian at prayer, attending Matins with the Dominicans, and Mass, Vespers, and Compline in the cathedral where the canons regular chanted the office in Latin, of which he knew not a word. Exhausting as that regimen might have been, he gave a full seven hours more to kneeling at prayer and, if he found a peseta of free time, read to the point of memorization *The Imitation of Christ* by Thomas à Kempis, a book he would later call "the partridge among spiritual books."[25] And yet, as he says in his autobiography,

> Sometimes he found himself so disagreeable that
> he took no joy in prayer or in hearing mass or

in any other prayer he said. At other times exactly the opposite of this came over him so suddenly that he seemed to have thrown off sadness and desolation just as one snatches a cape from another's shoulders. Here he began to be astounded by these changes that he had never experienced before, and he said to himself, "What new life is this that we are now beginning?" [26]

Compared to his former life as a grand hidalgo, it seemed to have no purpose, and he was so further anguished by his infirmities, fasts, mortifications, and scruples that he found it hard to imagine going on as he had and was assailed with the urge to kill himself, fear of offending God being the one thing that held him back. But gradually Iñigo figured out—possibly with the help of his Benedictine confessor—that he'd simply gone too far, and he gently tempered his penances in obedience, he thought, to the promptings of a Holy Being who was treating him, as he said, "just as a schoolmaster treats a child whom he is teaching." [27]

Enlightenment came to him on the foremost aspects of Catholic orthodoxy, of the Holy Trinity functioning like three harmonious notes in a musical chord, of how God created the world from white-hot nothing, of how Christ was really present in the Eucharist; and frequently over the next few years he saw the humanity of Christ and Our Lady, giving him "such strength in his faith that he often thought to himself: if there were no Scriptures to teach us these matters of the faith, he would be resolved to die for them, only because of what he had seen."[28] And one famous day on the banks of the Cardoner, the pilgrim, as he habitually called himself, was graced with an illumination of such great clarity and insight about "spiritual things and matters of faith and learning"[29] that "he seemed to himself to be another person and had an intellect other than he had before."[30] Testimony to the great learning Iñigo seemed to have acquired, as he said, *de arriba,* from above, was provided later by Martial Mazurier, a professor of theology at the Sorbonne, who asserted "that never had he heard any man speak of theological matters with such mastery and power."[31]

Because he often referred to his Cardoner illumination as the foundation of all that he would later do, it has been argued that Iñigo was given foreknowledge then and there of the Society of Jesus that would be formally instituted in 1540, but far more likely was it the origin of Iñigo's shift from a worried, isolated, flesh-despising penitent to a far more tranquil and outgoing man who was less concerned with harsh penances than he was with Christ-like services to others.

Essential elements of his *Spiritual Exercises*—finally

published in 1548—were probably composed in Manresa about this time. Influenced in part by Ludolph of Saxony's *Vita Jesu Christi,* the Abbot of Montserrat's *Ejercitatorio de la vida espiritual,* and *Meditationes vitae Christi* by a fourteen-century Franciscan, the *Spiritual Exercises* fashioned for the first time what is now popularly known as a retreat.[32] The handbook offered spiritual directors a practical and systematic method of having retreatants meditate, in silence and solitude over an intensive four-week span, on God's plan in the creation of human beings, humanity's fall from grace through sin, the gifts of humility and poverty, and the glory of the life, passion, and resurrection of Jesus.[33] Each psychologically astute meditation gently guided a retreatant to choose a fuller Christian life and, as the author himself had done, "to overcome oneself, and to order one's life, without reaching a decision through some disordered affection."[34]

Early in the *Spiritual Exercises* practitioners are told to reflect on themselves and ask: "What have I done for Christ? What am I doing for Christ? What ought I to do for Christ?"[35] Iñigo's own reply to that final question was to complete his long-delayed pilgrimage to Jerusalem. *El hombre saco* was by then affectionately being called *El hombre sancto,* the Holy Man, and when in the hard winter he forsook his tunic and sandals for a family's gift of shoes and beret and two brown doublets, the family preserved his sackcloth as a holy relic.[36] Refusing alms that were offered by friends—possibly because they themselves were in such great want—Iñigo left Manresa on foot in late February 1523, and stayed in Barcelona twenty days, going from door to door to beg for food and provisions for his journey and so impressing Isabel Roser with his talk of God and religion that she paid for his sea passage to Rome and remained his principal benefactor throughout his life.

Whoever met him seems to have liked him; he found no trouble getting an apostolic blessing for his pilgrimage in Rome from Adrian VI, formerly Spain's prime minister, nor finding free passage on ships in Venice and Cyprus, and on September 4, Iñigo walked into the Holy City in the midst of a huge procession of Christians and Egyptian Jews. He hoped never to leave.

Palestine was then fiercely held by Turkish Muslims, whose Christian go-betweens were Franciscan friars. After following a highly regulated program of pilgrimages to the Holy Sepulcher, Bethany, Bethlehem, and the Jordan, Iñigo's fervor was such that he approached a friar and told of his plan to stay on in the city where Jesus had walked, continually venerating the holy sites and helping souls. But he was forbidden that option by the friar's superior, who feared the Spanish crusader would be killed by the Turks. In fact, five hundred Turkish cavalrymen freshly arrived from Damascus were truculently prowling the city, and the panicked governor of Jerusalem was urging pilgrims to leave.[37] After hurried last looks at Christ's footprints on the Mount of Olives, for which he paid the Turkish guards a penknife and scissors, Iñigo obediently left with other pilgrims for Europe, hoping to find his way to Jerusalem again, but preferring, for the time being, to immerse himself in philosophical and theological studies.

To do that he would need Latin. Hence he withstood the hazards of four months of shipboard travel to go back to Spain, where Isabel Roser furnished the little that Iñigo needed while he was taught, gratis, by a professor of Latin grammar at the University of Barcelona. His life there was full of self-imposed hardships: he slept on the plank floor of a friend's garret room, walked about in shoes that had no soles, and begged food for the poor while subsisting himself on plain bread and water.

I feel furthest from Iñigo when he seems to ignore his needs and inflict miseries upon himself. A healthy discipline, chastity, and solidarity with the poor are all honorable desires, of course, but so often he seems to go over the top, to hate and scourge what is wholly natural and, in essence, pure gift. God finds us where we are, however, and God found Iñigo with one foot in the Middle Ages, believing, as the faithful did then, that flesh and spirit were at war and fearing that pleasure was a kind of death to the holy. There was little integration of flesh and spirit then, only rivalry and argument. We have not completely shaken those notions to this day.

After two years in Barcelona, his Latin tutor gave Iñigo permission to go to the University of Alcalá, just east of Madrid, where he studied the physics of Albertus Magnus, the logic of Domingo de Soto, and Peter Lombard's twelfth-century theological treatise *Four Books of Sentences*. And in his free time, he said, "he was busy giving spiritual exercises and teaching Christian doctrine and in so doing brought forth fruit for the glory of God."[38]

In so doing he also brought forth the fruit of the Spanish Inquisition, as officials accused Iñigo and his followers[39] of being heretical *Alumbrados,* or Illuminists, because they wore ankle-length cassocks of cheap *pardillo*[40] that looked like religious habits and because Iñigo was giving high-tension religious instruction whose affect often produced fainting and weeping in his audiences. In Holy Week of the year 1527, Iñigo was jailed, and held in a cell for forty-two days, but he frustrated officials with his frankness and serenity, and depositions from his female admirers only proved how orthodox were his principles: "Weekly confession and Communion, examination of conscience twice a day, the practice of meditation according to the three powers of the soul,"[41] that is, memory, intellect, and will. When Iñigo was finally released in June, he was given as a kind of peace offering a free black cassock and biretta, the fashion for students then, and was forbidden to teach on faith and morals until he completed four years of theology.

For that he went to the prestigious University of Salamanca, but within a fortnight he was dining with

Dominican friars, who heard hints of the Dutch humanism of Desiderius Erasmus in his talk and held him in
their chapel until an inquisitor from Toledo could get
there. Iñigo was again jailed. After twenty-two days of
being shackled to a post in a foul upper room, he was
interrogated by four judges, who found no great error in
his teaching and ruled that he could catechize again, but
only insofar as he did not try to define what were mortal
and what were venial sins. Ethical distinctions in conscience and conduct were so at the heart of his public
talks that Iñigo may have felt that they'd told him to
teach geometry without azimuths. Hamstrung by that
sentence, he thought it was high time to get out of Spain.

After hiking seven hundred miles north, he arrived
in Paris on February 2, 1528, and went to the Sorbonne,
a consortium of fifty colleges that was the greatest international center of learning in Europe. Even in peculiar
times, he was a peculiar student, a frail mystic who knew
no French, was less than fluent in Latin, and was then
in his thirty-seventh year. Because his hasty studies at
Barcelona and Alcalá had left him deficient in fundamen-
tals, Iñigo enrolled in humanities at the Collège de Montaigu and studied Latin with boys of nine and ten.[42]
Habitually heedless of money, he asked a Spanish friend
at Montaigu to hold for safekeeping the princely sum he
had been given for his education, but the friend frittered
it away on wild living, and by Easter Iñigo was forced
to find horrible lodging far away at the hospice of Saint-

Jacques and to go begging again, first among the wealthy Spanish merchants in Bruges and Antwerp in Flanders, and finally in England, garnering enough to enable him to be a magnanimous almsgiver back in France.

In the fall of 1529, Iñigo transferred to the Collège de Sainte-Barbe, "a kind of Portuguese dependency in the University of Paris,"[43] and shared housing with his professor and two highly regarded scholars whose lives he was to change significantly. The first was Pierre Favre of Savoy, a gentle, intelligent, psychologically intuitive twenty-three-year-old whose intent was the Catholic priesthood and who'd recently passed examinations for the licentiate in philosophy. Francisco de Javier—or Francis Xavier, as we know him—was also twenty-three, and a handsome, jubilant, outgoing grandee and fellow Basque from Navarre who wanted to be a famous professor or counselor to princes, as his father had been, and was already a regent in philosophy in the Collège de Beauvais.[44] Each finally fell to Iñigo's flattery and imprecations and agreed to go through a full month of his Spiritual Exercises. Upon finishing them, Favre and Xavier were inflamed "friends in the Lord"[45] with Iñigo, filling their hours with theological studies, religious practices and conversations, and in thinking about a future that still had no firm goal. Allied with them were the Portuguese student Simâo Rodrigues, who was at Sainte-Barbe on a royal burse from King John III; Diego Laínez and Alfonso Salmerón, both Spaniards and former

students at Alcalá; and Nicolás de Bobadilla, a philosopher at Alcalá and theologian at Valladolid before becoming a regent in the Collège de Calvi.

Ignatius de Loyola was given the title Master of Arts
at Easter ceremonies in 1534. We have no certainty
about his change of name. It may be that he mistakenly
thought the far more familiar name Ignacio was a variant
of Iñigo,[46] but it's also possible that in the age of reformation he was inspired by the Syrian prelate Ignatius
of Antioch, who faced the persecutions and theological
disputes of second-century Christianity and whom Emperor Trajan threw to the lions in Rome.

We do know that Ignatius was seeking priesthood
by Easter of 1534, and in preparation for holy orders he
was studying the *Summa Theologica* of Thomas Aquinas
with the highly esteemed Dominican faculty of the Collège de Saint-Jacques.[47] But Pierre Favre was the first
companion ordained, and on August 15, 1534, the feast
of the Assumption of Mary, he celebrated Mass for his
friends on the heights of Montmartre in the shrine of
the martyrdom of Saint Denis and his companions. At
Communion, Ignatius, Xavier, Rodrigues, Laínez, Salmerón, and Bobadilla professed vows to a life of poverty
and to undertake a pilgrimage to Jerusalem or, failing
that, to offer themselves to the Vicar of Christ, the pope,
for whatever mission he wished. Chastity was not vowed
but presumed, for they all intended to receive holy orders. Even Ignatius seems not to have thought that their

profession was the origin of a new religious order, but in hindsight it was.

Within a year, Claude le Jay, a Savoyard friend of Pierre Favre, had completed the Spiritual Exercises and made the same vows, and a year after that, again on August 15, the group was increased by Paschase Broet of Picardy and Jean Codure of Dauphiné. Ignatius missed those ceremonies. Chronic stomach pains that were prompted by gallstones forced him in 1535 to go on horseback to Azpeitia for the familiar weather and air of home that was thought then to heal a host of ills. After some time in Spain, giving news to their families of his "friends in the Lord," he went ahead of them to Venice, where they hoped to find a ship to the Holy Land. While waiting for them to get there, Ignatius studied theology, taught catechism, and helped a Spanish priest named Diego Hoces through the Spiritual Exercises and later welcomed him as another companion. And, it would seem, Ignatius was thinking a good deal about how a religious foundation ought to be organized, for with chagrin and humility he wrote a chiding letter to Gian Pietro Caraffa, a founder of the first order of clerks regular, called the Theatines:

When a man of rank and exalted dignity wears a habit more ornate and lives in a room better furnished than the other religious of his order, I am neither scandalized nor disedified. However, it

would do well to consider how the saints have
conducted themselves, St. Dominic and St. Francis, for example; and it would be good to have
recourse to light from on high; for, after all, a
thing may be licit without being expedient.[48]

Of the Theatines in Venice, who shut themselves in their
houses of prayer and passively filled their needs with
gifts from the faithful, Ignatius wrote that people "will
say that they do not see the purpose of this Order; and
that the saints, without failing in confidence in God,
acted otherwise."[49]

Caraffa, the Italian bishop of Chieti, was a good but
impatient and tempestuous Neapolitan who in December
would be created a cardinal, and he did not take kindly
to faultfinding from a Spaniard, an unfinished theologian,
and a forty-five-year-old mendicant who was not yet
even a priest. We have lost his reply to Ignatius, but we
know his hostility was such that when the companions
from the Sorbonne finally got to Italy in 1537, Ignatius
sent them on to Rome without him so that Cardinal Caraffa would have no punitive reason to foil their Easter
presentation to Pope Paul III.

At that papal audience in Castel Sant' Angelo, the
highly impressive companions told the pope of their
project to go to Jerusalem and begin an apostolate to the
infidel there, and of their further wish to receive holy
orders. Knowing the Turkish fleet was belligerently ply-

ing the Mediterranean, Paul III quietly put it that "I do not think you will reach Jerusalem."[50] And yet not only were their requests granted by the pontiff, but they also were given close to three hundred escudos for the voyage.

In Venice on the feast of Saint John the Baptist, June 24, 1537, Vincenzo Nigusanti, Bishop of Arbe, ordained Ignatius, Bobadilla, Codure, Xavier, Laínez, and Rodrigues under the title of poverty, *ad titulum paupertatis.*[51] Bishop Nigusanti "frequently repeated, later, that no ordination had ever given his soul such pure consolation."[52] In humility, Ignatius put off presiding at his first Mass for a year and a half, so he would be the last of the ten to do so, and so he could perhaps celebrate it at a shrine in Bethlehem. When that proved impossible, he chose to celebrate his first Mass in Rome on Christmas, 1538, at the church of Santa Maria Maggiore, which Christians believed held the true crib of the child Jesus— a worthy substitute, he thought, for Christ's birthplace.

While waiting for a ship to Palestine in the fall of 1537, the new priests preached in the streets and performed works of mercy in hospitals throughout the Republic of Venice, but for the first time in nearly forty years however, hot rumors of war and piracy kept any ship from sailing to the east. Gathering together again in Vicenza that winter, the priests chose to be patient in their hopes of sea passage and to concentrate their preaching in cities with universities, where they might find high-minded students to join them. If anyone asked who they were, they agreed, "it seemed to them most fitting that they should take the name of him whom they had as their head, by calling themselves the 'company of Jesus.' "[53]

Acknowledging at last that their hoped-for pilgrimage to Jerusalem was improbable, Ignatius, Favre, and Laínez walked two hundred and fifty miles south to Rome in order to offer their services to the pope in fulfillment of the vow they had professed on Montmartre. Stopping in the outskirts of Rome, at a place called La Storta, Ignatius and Laínez went into a chapel, where Ignatius prayed that Mary hold him in her heart as she did her son. Then he felt a change in his soul, and later told Laínez that he beheld "Christ with the cross on his shoulder, and next to Him the eternal Father, who said to Him: 'I want you to take this man as your servant,' and Jesus thus took him and said: 'I want you to serve us.' "[54] Ignatius also told Laínez "that it seemed to him as if God the Father had imprinted the following words in his heart: *Ego ero vobis Romae propitius.*"[55] I will be favorable to you in Rome.[56]

Uplifted by the La Storta illumination, Ignatius and his friends went into the city in late November 1537, and were again graciously received by the pontiff. Hearing their offer of service, Paul III gladly assigned Diego Laínez to teach scholastic theology at La Sapienza, a palace that housed the University of Rome. Pierre Favre was to fill an office in positive theology there, giving commentaries on Sacred Scripture. With those surprising papal assignments, the Italian Compagnia di Gesù ever so gradually became a company of teachers, but Ignatius sought to forgo the classroom in favor of giving the Spiritual Exercises in Rome, first to the ambassador of Emperor Charles V, and then to the president of the pontifical commission for reform of the Church, to the ambassador of Siena, to a Spanish physician, and to Francesco de Estrada, a Spanish priest who'd worked for the formidable Cardinal Caraffa in Rome and been fired. Upon completion of the Exercises, Estrada too joined the Company of Jesus, and late in life he would be named the Jesuit provincial of Aragón in Spain.[57]

Rome became Ignatius's and the companions' Jerusalem. After Easter 1538, all of them gathered there and, through the skills of Pietro Codacio, a papal chamberlain and the first Italian companion, got title to the Church of Santa Maria della Strada, Our Lady of the Wayside, chosen by Ignatius because it was on a high-traffic piazza that was handily near the papal court, government offices, a significant Jewish community, palaces of the upper class, houses of prostitutes, and hovels of the poor.[58] Santa Maria della Strada was the first foundation in the Eternal City for a host of what Ignatius called "works of piety"[59]: the Catechumens, a house for the religious instruction of Jewish converts; the Casa Santa Marta, a house of refuge for former prostitutes; the Conservatorio delle Vergini Miserabili, a house for girls who might be attracted to prostitution; homes for children that were supported by the Confraternity of Saint Mary of the Visitation of Orphans; and the Collegio Romano, a high school for grammar, humanities, and Christian doctrine that was free to boys in Rome.[60]

But the foundation of the greatest importance was, of course, that of the Society of Jesus—*societas* being the Latin for company—which was confirmed by Paul III in the papal bull *Regimini Militantis Ecclesiae* on September 27, 1540. Ignatius sketched the "formula" for the institute in five brief chapters that he introduced in this way:

> Whoever desires to serve as a soldier of God beneath the banner of the cross in our Society, which we desire to be designated by the name of Jesus, and in it to serve the Lord alone and his vicar on earth, should, after a solemn vow of chastity, keep what follows in mind. He is a member of a community founded chiefly to strive for the progress of souls in Christian life and doctrine, and for the propagation of the faith by means of the ministry of the word, the Spiritual Exercises, and works of charity. . . .[61]

Upon hearing the "formula" read to him, the aged Paul III had orally given his approval and added, "*Digitus Dei est hic*—" "The finger of God is here."[62] Ignatius and

Jean Codure later expanded "A First Sketch of the Institute of the Society of Jesus" into *Constitutions* of forty-nine points regulating frugality, governance, admission and formation of novices, and housing and other practical matters, but generally offering Jesuits flexibility in their ways of proceeding in order to give room to, as Ignatius put it, "the internal guidance of the Holy Spirit."[63]

In fulfillment of their rules on governance, on April 8, 1541, Ignatius was elected the first superior general of the Society of Jesus, the only ballot against him being his own. Xavier's ballot was probably typical of the others; he voted for "our old leader and true father, Don Ignacio, who, since he brought us together with no little effort, will also with similar effort know how to preserve, govern, and help us advance from good to better."[64]

Ignatius was then fifty and far different from the man he'd fantasized he'd be when he was a page to Spanish royalty, or a pilgrim to the Holy Land, or a philosopher at the Sorbonne. Ever seeking the greater glory of God and the good of souls, Ignatius surely imagined a grander fate than that of fifteen years of grinding office and managerial work in the house for forty professed fathers that he built on Via Aracoeli, or that of having as one of his prime contributions to history his hand-cramping composition of more than seven thousand letters to his scattered Jesuit sons—twelve full volumes in the *Monumenta Historica Societatis Jesu*. We hear no regret in his letters, however, no aching to be elsewhere, only geniality and hunger for news as he writes to the Jesuit *periti* at the Council of Trent; gentle hints as to how a homosexual scholastic could preserve his chastity; tenderness for the many Spanish women for whom he was a spiritual director; sympathy for a priest in Sicily afflicted by scruples, as he had been; fatherly chiding as he orders a house in Portugal to curb its hard penances; affection for his friend Xavier in Japan: "We have rejoiced in the Lord that you have arrived with health and that doors have opened to have the Gospel preached in that region."[65]

His holiness was unmistakable; he practiced self-mastery until there seemed to be no difference between God's will and his own. *"Eres en tu casa"* was his wide-armed greeting to anyone who visited him—You are at home—and all who talked with him left with the impression that he was kindliness itself: Michelangelo was so affected by Ignatius that he offered to build the Church of the Gesù for nothing. Ever a mystic, there were times in the midst of an official transaction when the saint's thoughts would lift up to God and hang there, and his witnesses would shyly shuffle their shoes until he got back to his papers again. But there were also stories of him surprising a melancholic with a jig in order to cheer him up, and his happiness was such that he said he could no longer apply his own rules for discernment of spirits, because he was finding consolation in all things: he once said he saw the Holy Trinity in the leaf of an orange tree.[66] Although children threw apples at him when he first preached in the streets of Rome—probably because of his horrible Italian—he soon was as genuinely beloved as the pope. In fact, he was so highly thought of by prelates that in the 1550 conclave at which Julius III was elected pontiff, Ignatius de Loyola received five votes. And we can get a feeling for the high esteem in which he was held by his fellow Jesuits when we read letters such as this from Frans de Costere, S.J., of Cologne:

> The day before yesterday I saw for the first time, with indescribable joy and eagerness, Reverend Father Ignatius. I could not see enough of him. For his countenance is such that one cannot look upon it long enough. The old man was walking in the garden, leaning on a cane. His face shone with godliness. He is mild, friendly, and amiable so that he speaks with the learned and the unlearned, with important people and little people, all in the same way: a man worthy of all praise and reverence. No one can deny that a great reward is prepared for him in heaven. . . .[67]

But Gian Pietro Caraffa, whom Ignatius insulted in his frank letter about the Theatines, thought of him as a tyrant and a false idol. In fact, the friction between Caraffa and Ignatius was such that when, in 1555, Ignatius heard that Caraffa had been elected pontiff, as Paul IV, Ignatius's face went white, and he falteringly limped into a chapel to pray. But after a while he appeared again and happily said the new pope would be good to them, which he was only to a degree, for after Ignatius died he tried to merge his Theatines with the Jesuits, and briefly forced them to sing the Divine Office in choir and to limit the superior general's term to three years.[68]

Even some of his early companions had difficulties with Ignatius, though. Nicolás de Bobadilla angrily called him "a rascally sophist and a Basque spoiled by flattery,"[69] and Simâo Rodrigues, whose contrariness prompted Ignatius to recall him from Portugal, claimed that the superior general did so out of passion and hate, and with slight regard for his reputation. Juan de Polanco supposedly received hardly one compliment during his nine years as Ignatius's secretary; Jerónimo Nadal was often so harshly criticized that he couldn't hold back his tears; and Diego Laínez, a favorite of his, once objected, "What have I done against the Society that this saint treats me this way?"[70]

An affectionate man who was wary of his *affectus,* Ignatius was probably hard on his friends in accordance with his fundamental principle of *agere contra,* that is, to go against or contradict one's own inclinations if they are not for the honor and glory of God or for the good of others. We see hints of this in the sixteenth annotation to his *Spiritual Exercises,* in which Ignatius wrote: "If by chance the exercitant feels an affection or inclination to something in a disordered way, it is profitable for that person to strive with all possible effort to come over to the opposite of that to which he or she is wrongly attached." [71]

He was harder on himself than on his friends, punishing himself for his sins, getting to bed late and waking up at half past four, hardly ever going outside the house or strolling in the gardens, which he insisted on for his sons, dining on food that he called a penance, holding his gaze on the ground when he did walk in Rome, loving plainchant but forbidding choir for the order.

All of that took its toll. By 1556 his health was failing to such a degree that to his chronic stomach pains were added a hardening of the liver, high fevers, and general exhaustion. He was rarely seen outside his room and ate little more than fish scraps and broths and lettuce prepared with oil. [72] Spells of illness had troubled him so frequently in the past, however, and he'd shown such resilience in healing, that no one was especially upset by his confinement, and physicians often failed even to visit him as they ministered to others in the house who were thought to be far worse off, among them his friend Diego Laínez. But Ignatius knew how far he'd sunk and on the afternoon of July 30, he thought it would be fitting if Juan de Polanco, the secretary of the Society, would go and inform Paul IV that Ignatius "was near the end and almost without hope of temporal life, and that he humbly begged from His Holiness his blessing for himself and for Master Laínez, who was also in danger."[73] Misprizing his superior's condition, Polanco asked if he could put off the walk, because he was trying to finish some letters for Spain before a ship sailed. Ignatius told him, "The sooner you go, the more satisfied I shall be; however, do as you wish."[74]

Brother Tommaso Cannicari, the infirmarian, slept in a cell next to the superior general's quarters, and off and on heard Ignatius praying until, after midnight, he heard only, over and over again, the Spanish sigh *Ay, Dios!*[75] At sunrise the fathers in the house saw that Ignatius was dying, and Cannicari hurried to find the superior general's confessor while Polanco hurried to the papal residence to request the Holy Father's blessing. But it was too late. Two hours after sunrise on Friday morning, July 31, 1556, Ignatius of Loyola died, without having received the quite unnecessary graces of Extreme Unction or Viaticum or papal blessing.

In the first week of the *Spiritual Exercises,* Ignatius had offered this as the "Principle and Foundation" for all the meditations that would follow:

> Human beings are created to praise, reverence, and serve God our Lord, and by means of doing this to save their souls.
> The other things on the face of the earth are

created for the human beings, to help them in the pursuit of the end for which they are created.

From this it follows that we ought to use these things to the extent that they help us toward our end, and free ourselves from them to the extent that they hinder us from it.

To attain this it is necessary to make ourselves indifferent to all created things, in regard to everything which is left to our free will and is not forbidden. Consequently, on our own part we ought not to seek health rather than sickness, wealth rather than poverty, honor rather than dishonor, a long life rather than a short one, and so on in all other matters.

Rather, we ought to desire and choose only that which is more conducive to the end for which we are created.[76]

Saint Irenaeus said that the glory of God is a human being fully alive. But what is it to be fully alive? We are apt to look at Ignatius's life as one of harsh discipline and privation, and find only loss in his giving up family, inheritance, financial security, prestige, luxury, sexual pleasure. But he looked at his life as an offering to the God he called *liberalidad*, freedom,[77] and God blessed that gift a hundredfold in the Society of Jesus. The house of Loyola ended when Doña Magdalena de Loyola y Borgia died childless in 1626,[78] but in that same year there were 15,535 Jesuits in 36 provinces, with 56 seminaries, 44 novitiates, 254 houses, and 443 colleges in Europe and the Baltic States, Japan, India, Macao, the Philippines, and the Americas.[79]

NOTES

1. Paul Dudon, S.J., *St. Ignatius of Loyola,* trans. by William J. Young, S.J. (Milwaukee: The Bruce Publishing Co., 1949), 439.
2. Dudon, 17.
3. W. W. Meissner, S.J., M.D., *Ignatius of Loyola: The Psychology of a Saint* (New Haven: Yale University Press, 1992), 9.
4. Dudon, 13.
5. John W. O'Malley, S.J., *The First Jesuits* (Cambridge, MA: Harvard University Press, 1993), 23.
6. Meissner, 24.
7. Luis Gonçalves da Câmara, S.J., *The Autobiography of St. Ignatius Loyola,* trans. by Joseph F. O'Callaghan, S.J. (New York: Harper & Row, 1974), 21.
8. Meissner, 241.
9. Meissner, 240.
10. Juan de Polanco, S.J., *Chronicon,* quoted in Dudon, 37.
11. Cándido de Dalmases, S.J., *Ignatius of Loyola, Founder of the Jesuits: His Life and Work,* trans. by Jerome Aixalá, S.J. (St. Louis: The Institute of Jesuit Sources, 1985), 38.
12. Dudon, 36.
13. Câmara, 22.
14. Câmara, 22.
15. Dalmases, 43.
16. Jerónimo Nadal, S.J., quoted in Dudon, 37.
17. Hans Wolter, S.J., "Elements of Crusade Spirituality in St. Ignatius," in *Ignatius of Loyola: His Personality and Spiritual Heri-*

tage, 1556–1956, ed. by Friedrich Wulf, S.J. (St. Louis: The Institute of Jesuit Sources, 1977), 126.

18. Câmara, 23.   25. Dudon, 57.
19. Câmara, 24.   26. Câmara, 34.
20. Câmara, 24.   27. Câmara, 37.
21. Câmara, 24.   28. Câmara, 39.
22. Câmara, 26.   29. Câmara, 39.
23. Dalmases, 55.
24. Dudon, 59.
30. Dalmases, 62.
31. Hugo Rahner, S.J., *Ignatius the Theologian,* trans. by Michael Barry (New York: Herder and Herder, 1968), 1.
32. O'Malley, 46, 47.
33. George E. Ganss, S.J., *The Spiritual Exercises of Saint Ignatius* (Chicago: Loyola University Press, 1992), 1–3.
34. Ganss, 31.   37. Dudon, 83.
35. Ganss, 42.   38. Câmara, 61.
36. Dudon, 67.
39. Calixtio de Sa, Lope de Cáceres, Juan de Arteaga, and Juan Reynalde.
40. Dalmases, 97.   43. Dudon, 138.
41. Dudon, 113.   44. Meissner, 151.
42. Meissner, 142.   45. O'Malley, 32.
46. Gabriel María Verd, "De Iñigo a Ignacio: El cambio de nombre en San Ignacio de Loyola," *Archivum Historicum Societatis Jesu* 60 (1991), 113–60, in O'Malley, 29.
47. Dudon, 144.   50. Dudon, 249.
48. Dudon, 234.   51. Câmara, 87.
49. Dudon, 234.   52. Dudon, 238.
53. Juan de Polanco, S.J., *Fontes narrativi de S. Ignatio de Loyola et de Societatis Jesu initiis,* I, 204, quoted in Dalmases, 149.
54. Hugo Rahner, S.J., *The Vision of St. Ignatius in the Chapel of La Storta* (Rome: Centrum Ignatianum Spiritualitatis, 1979), 46.
55. Rahner, 46.
56. The La Storta experience probably inspired the conclusions to

the meditations of the second week of the Spiritual Exercises, wherein practitioners are asked to make a threefold colloquy, first with Mary, then with Christ, and finally with God the Father.

57. Dalmases, 154–55.

58. Thomas M. Lucas, S.J., *Saint, Site, and Sacred Strategy: Ignatius, Rome, and Jesuit Urbanism* (Rome: Biblioteca Apostolica Vaticana, 1990), 30.

59. Câmara, 92.

60. Tuition was free because of a magnificent gift from Francisco Borgia, the Duke of Gandía in Spain, the great-grandson of Pope Alexander VI and King Ferdinand V of Aragón, a father of eight, and, after the death of his wife, a Jesuit and the third superior general. See Dalmases, 186.

61. Lucas, 121.

62. Dalmases, 170.

63. Peter Hebblethwaite, "The Society of Jesus," in *Modern Catholicism: Vatican II and After,* ed. by Adrian Hastings (New York: Oxford University Press, 1991), 256.

64. O'Malley, 375.

65. Lucas, 8.

66. Dalmases, 273.

67. Hubert Becher, S.J., "Ignatius as Seen by His Contemporaries," in Wulf, 86.

68. Dalmases, 286.

69. Wulf, 84.

70. Wulf, 87.

71. Ganss, 26.

72. Dudon, 426.

73. Dalmases, 294.

74. Dudon, 428.

75. Dalmases, 295.

76. Ganss, 32.

77. Rahner, *Ignatius the Theologian,* 4.

78. Dudon, 421.

79. Lucas, 35.

The Ironic Doctor

FRANCINE PROSE

IRONY IS NOT the quality we associate first with the saints.

Seen from this distance, and with the modernist's double vision, their lives appear to us to have been rich in ironic and playful incident and detail. Consider the vegetarian Nicholas of Tolentino, who, on being forced to eat a pigeon stew, caused the cooked birds' feathers to regrow, the sauce to flow like blood in their veins, until the revivified pigeons fluttered their wings and flew out the window; or Saint Datius, who exorcised a haunted house by mocking the devil for making the sounds of ghostly animals in the night. Let us think of Saint Ansovinus, who embarrassed a stingy innkeeper with a miraculous lesson about the ethics of watering the wine, or the gravity-defying Joseph of Cupertino, expelled from a series of monasteries for being unable to stop himself from frightening his brethren by levitating at mealtime or in the midst of saying Mass. Or let us contemplate the famous—and famously ironic—prayer of Saint Augustine, begging God to send him the gift of chastity . . . but not yet.

Even so, the character of the saint and the nature of sainthood may strike us profoundly incompatible with the ironist's perspective. Saints, we feel, are, by definition, impassioned and single-minded, tormented by unruly desires and devious temptations, by demons and doubt—but not by alienation and contradiction. Their apprehension of the world and of God is immediate and cohesive, not fragmented and conflicted. The saint's experience is that of proximity, of presence, of the imminence of grace, not of the world seen through a glass darkly: through the cloudy, fingerprinted lens of ironic distance.

As a Jewish child growing up in New York, I quite naturally longed to be a saint. Like many little girls (and many saints, one imagines), I intuited at a young age that early martyrdom would preemptively circumvent the problems and pressures of adulthood. Perhaps enough has been written (some of it by myself) about the allure of a perfect Bridegroom who promises that He will ask nothing of us but absolute devotion and (in the case of St. Thérèse of Lisieux) a fairly daunting amount of housework. And much has also been said about the appeal of the promise of glory, of an eternity to be spent in a paradise that our imaginations may endow with the pink light and verdant heavenly landscapes of a Sienese religious painting.

For the would-be and future saint, the lives of the saints and martyrs can function as a kind of how-to manual, listing the various obstacles posed and overcome: the pagan background, the stubborn and often violent opposition of parents and of society, one's own troublesome fondness for the pleasures and comforts of the material world. But nowhere in the saints' lives that I devoured with such avidity did I find a single example of a saint who had triumphed over what I sensed early on to be the main stumbling block in my path.

I have heard adults with no knowledge of children claim that irony is an acquired trait, a quality belonging to a later stage of development, like a taste for olives, caviar, or champagne. But some children are born ironists; I know because I was one. Almost from the cradle, I watched the world from a certain remove and with the consciousness of watching; everything seemed to me to have several possible (or opposite) meanings and explanations, and that disjuncture, that ambiguity, struck me, more often than not, as at once disturbing, comforting, marvelous—and funny.

Much of the *Autobiography* of Saint Teresa of Ávila— which I first read in my twenties during the early 1970s—is permeated by that same familiar, ironic, and (to me) intensely sympathetic sensibility. She is funny, edgy, self-mocking, and extremely sympathetic toward the excesses and self-dramatization that goes along with being young.

Who knows how different my life might have been had her book come into my possession earlier.

The opening sentence of Saint Teresa's account of her life is not only one of the great beginnings in religious or secular literature, but it may be one of the most barbed, ironic, and double- (or triple-) edged sentences ever written: "Had I not been so wicked, it would have been a help to me to have such virtuous and pious parents . . ."

So begins the narrative of the complicated, extraordinary life that began in March 1515 in an aristocratic household in Ávila, the walled city that rose out of the harsh, arid landscape of Central Spain. Teresa's father, Don Alonso Sanchez de Cepeda, was a charitable man who taught his daughter to read in an era when literacy was generally not numbered among the requisite feminine virtues, and despite his own disapproval of the distractions of frivolous literature—the chivalric romances that Teresa so loved. ("So completely was I mastered by this passion that I thought I could never be happy without a book.")

The little girl's fascination with courtly romances was shared by her mother, Dona Beatriz, who married at fourteen, bore nine children and, perhaps as a consequence, remained a lifelong invalid until her early death. ("Though extremely beautiful, she was never known to give any reason for supposing that she made the slightest account of her beauty; and, though she died at thirty-three, her dress was already that of a person advanced in years.")

In this large, chaotic household, Teresa's closest ally was her brother Rodrigo, and the most celebrated anecdote of her childhood—clearly the one she most delights in telling—involves their frustrated attempt to run away from home in search of instant martyrdom. Her description of their escapade typifies her irony, her humor, and the compassion—in this case, for her younger self—that (as the paragraph turns and turns) forms a sort of bridge between her gentle, forgiving self-mockery and the deep seriousness of her moral and devotional purpose:

> We used to read the lives of the saints together; and, when I read of the martyrdoms suffered by saintly women for God's sake, I used to think they had purchased the fruition of God very cheaply; and I had a keen desire to die as they

had done, not out of any love for God ... but in order to attain as quickly as possible ... the great blessings which, as I read, were laid up in heaven. I used to discuss with this brother of mine how we could become martyrs. We agreed to go off to the country of the Moors, begging our bread for the love of God, so that they might behead us there; and, even at so tender an age, I believe that the Lord had given us sufficient courage for this ... but out greatest hindrance seemed to be that we had a father and mother. It used to cause us great astonishment when we were told that both pain and glory would last for ever. We would spend long periods talking about this and we liked to repeat again and again, 'For ever—ever—ever!' Through our frequent repetition of these words, it pleased the Lord that in my earliest years I should receive a lasting impression of the way of the truth.

Recognized by an uncle as they were leaving Ávila, the two runaway children were promptly returned home, where, in time, Teresa grew into a handsome, vain, strong-willed and talkative young woman. ("I began to deck myself out and try to attract others by my appearance, taking great troubles with my hands and hair, using perfumes and all the vanities I could get—and there were a good many of them, for I was very fastidious. . . .

I always had the facet of making myself understood only with a torrent of words.")

Then with the onset of early adolescence came a series of personal and health crises that conspired (or, as Teresa would have said, manifested the will of God) to lead and then impel her toward the cloister. The most intriguing and mysterious of these involved a cousin from whom "I learned every kind of evil.... The result of my intercourse with this woman was to change me so much that I lost all my soul's natural inclination to virtue, and was greatly influenced by her, and by another person who indulged in the same kinds of pastime." The normally forthright, ironic Teresa is uncharacteristically elusive, vague, and portentous about the nature of this pastime, but much about her tone inclines one to agree with Vita Sackville-West's rather delicate and tactful assessment of her in *The Eagle and the Dove:* "Since few things are more distasteful than veiled hints, it may also be outspokenly noted that in her own country the name of Teresa has been associated with that of Sappho.... Nobody in their senses ... would dream of comparing the organised orgies of Lesbos with the rudimentary experimental dabblings of adolescent girls.... The point is in any case perhaps not of very much interest, except in so far as every point concerning so complex a character ... is of interest.... Above all, it is not introduced here in any spirit of scandalous disrespect to a wise woman and a great saint."

In flight from the guilts and terrors that this incident evoked in her, Teresa was, at sixteen, at once distressed and greatly relieved to find herself enrolled as a student at the convent of Our Lady of Grace. Her confusion about the religious life (and perhaps about her sexuality) may have led to the first of the many terrifying and near-fatal illnesses that would plague her for the rest of her life. (Like any number of historical figures—Van Gogh and El Greco, among others—Saint Teresa has had the benefit of better diagnostic and medical care after her death than she had during her lifetime: her condition has been variously diagnosed as hyperthyroidism, consumption, epilepsy, and, perhaps needless to add, psychosexual hysteria.)

After a recuperative stay at her sister's house, she stopped for a brief visit at the home of an uncle, to whom she read aloud from holy books. In the process, she began to understand "the truth . . . that all things are nothing, and that the world is vanity and will soon pass away. I began to fear that, if I had died of my illness, I should have gone to hell; and though, even then, I could not incline my will to being a nun, I saw that this was the best and safest state, and so, little by little, I was determined to force myself to embrace it. This conflict lasted for three months. I used to try to convince myself by using the following argument. The trials and distresses of being a nun could not be greater than those of purgatory and I had fully deserved to be in hell. It would not be a great matter to spend my life as though I were in purgatory if afterwards I were to go straight to heaven, which was what I desired. *This decision, then, to enter the religious life seems to have been inspired by servile fear more than by love.*"

The italics are my own, and the reason I've been quoting at such length from Teresa's own version of these critical events is in the hope of conveying a sense of her unsparing honesty, her plainspoken urgency, her self-critical humorous sympathy, and, most strikingly, her immense tolerance for ambivalence and ironic contradiction—a tolerance that would seem unusual in anyone, during any era, but that strikes us as all the more stunning in a not-terribly-well-educated Spanish Catholic woman living at a time when the Inquisition had done so much to advance the cause of the vengeful, exquisitely cruel, and fanatically literal-minded.

This tolerance for conflict and for the apparently irreconcilable would not only serve Teresa well, but also prove to be a psychic necessity, since so much of her adult life appears to have been a nest of roiling, insoluble contradictions. ("When I was in the midst of worldly pleasures, I was distressed by the remembrance of what I owed to God; when I was with God, I grew restless because of worldly affections.")

What's most amazing—and most appealing—about her is the fact that she was such a creature of opposites. She describes herself as weak-willed, vain, shallow, fond of pleasures and comforts, easily seduced and distracted ("Anyone who gave me so much as a sardine could obtain anything from me"). And yet she possessed the courage and steely determination to accomplish (more or less singlehandedly) the strenuous and controversial reform of the Carmelite Order, which, as Sackville-West describes it, had become little more than an ongoing tea party:

> Friends and relations, both feminine and masculine, might be received there. . . . Little presents changed hands, sweetmeats and oranges, jam, scent. . . . Many a sister had her little private store of provisions in reserve. . . . Gossip and the latest news circulated freely in that agreeable circle . . . and the fashionable topics of culture, philosophy, music, literature, and even, more dangerously, Platonic love, came under lively discussion during the long afternoons.

That was the situation when Teresa became a novice, and for the next quarter century or so, until, in her late forties, she undertook the task of reforming her order. Under Teresa's direction, these pleasant amusements came to an end, and the seventeen convents that she helped establish throughout Spain were rededicated to the principles of poverty, purity, obedience, and contemplation. Though nearly always in ill health, she spent the last twenty years of her life (she died at sixty-seven) traveling constantly to oversee the foundation and operation of those seventeen convents—which represented nothing less than a reproof and challenge to the laxity and self-indulgence of the sixteenth-century Spanish clergy. (Nor did she accomplish these reforms without, as one might expect, overcoming a great deal of potentially perilous intrigue and strong opposition from the clerical establishment.)

Teresa claimed to hate writing, to be unable to write; her work is full of self-doubt, of protestations that she is unequal to the task before her, of excuses for procrastination and apologies for the repetitions resulting from her lack of time to read over what she'd written. (Why is she not—for these reasons alone—the patron saint of writers?) Yet she wrote voluminously, quickly (*The Interior Castle* was written in the space of four weeks) and under impossible circumstances—in freezing cold, cramped cells, without even a table or chair. She worked while desperately ill, frequently interrupted by uncontrollable, unbidden visions and by pressing problems within her order.

She was the most practical, down-to-earth, shrewd, and sensible of souls, persuasive and skilled at dealing with the clerical hierarchy and with the political forces of her day—and at the same time a celebrated mystic, famous for the (often racking and paralyzing) transports that removed her from quotidian reality, and from ordinary consciousness. Certainly, the most striking contradiction in her life involved the disjuncture between her commitment to the active life (to the reform of her order and to the nuns in her charge) and to the more contemplative, meditative, quietist—and visionary—aspects of religious experience.

Her mystical experiences ranged from comforting intimations of the nearness of God ("I used unexpectedly to experience a consciousness of the presence of God, of such a kind that I could not doubt that He was within, or that I was wholly engulfed in him. This was in no sense a vision; I believe it is called mystical theology, the soul is suspended completely outside itself. The will loves; the memory, I think, is almost lost . . .") to horrifying visions of the devil:

"Out of his body there seemed to be coming a great flame, which was intensely bright and cast no shadow. He told me in a horrible way that I had indeed escaped out of his hands but he would get hold of me still. . . . The Lord evidently meant me to realize that this was the work of the devil, for I saw beside me the most hideous little negro, snarling as if he was in despair at having lost what he was trying to gain. . . . I have learned there is nothing like holy water to put devils to flight and prevent them from coming back again." On another occasion, God appeared to her with the gift of a jeweled rosary, which no one else could see.

No doubt the most famous of her visions was that of

the angel who pierced her heart with his burning lance "several times so that it penetrated to my entrails. When he drew it out, I thought he was drawing them out with it, and he left me completely afire with a great love for God. The pain was so sharp that it made me utter several moans; and so excessive was the sweetness caused by this intense pain that one can never wish to lose it, nor will one's soul be content with anything less than God."

It was this visitation—and her description, with its undeniably and almost comically sexual overtones—that was to inspire Richard Crashaw's overwrought verse and Bernini's graceful and equally over-the-top sculpture. Ironically, we can thank Bernini and Crashaw for the version of Teresa that has survived in the popular imagination: the swooning, hysterical female visionary, brought to the spiritual equivalent of orgasm by the overwhelming force of her religious fervor.

The reality was extremely different. Teresa was profoundly private about, and distrustful of, her visions. She tried desperately to hide her transports, which frightened and embarrassed her:

> I have lain on the ground and the sisters have come and held me down, but none the less the rapture has been observed. I besought the Lord earnestly not to grant me any more favours which had visible and exterior signs; for I was exhausted by having to endure such worries and

after all (I said) His Majesty could grant me that
favour without its becoming known.

Though she believed that her visions were coming from
God, she distrusted them, and feared that they might be
the work of the devil. Partly to ease these fears, her confessor "commanded me to make the sign of the Cross
whenever I had a vision, and to snap my fingers at it so
as to convince myself that it came from the devil. . . .
This caused me great distress."

Even her approach to prayer could hardly have been
less ecstatically passive than that of the semicomatose
woman we see in Bernini's masterpiece. What's striking
(and, in a way, hardest for the modern reader to comprehend) about her devotional writing is the cool precision
with which she outlines the steps, stages, and techniques
for "those who are determined to pursue this blessing
and succeed in this enterprise": "Beginners must accus-
tom themselves to pay no heed to what they see or hear,
and they must practise this during hours of prayer; they
must be alone and in their solitude think over their past
life—all of us, indeed, whether beginners or proficients,
must do this frequently."

And really, it should come as no great surprise: the
distance between the pretty, swooning saint we find in
Bernini and Crashaw and the plucky, resilient, practical,
and extremely capable middle-aged nun who braved the
Inquisition, reformed an entire order and, despite a life

of illness and hardship, somehow found the time and energy to write several of the great classics of contemplative literature. One image fits—and feeds—every reductive cliché about the nature of female religiosity. The other, the historical reality, defies and expands our conventional notions of what it means to be a woman (and a sixteenth-century Spanish woman, at that) as well as a great writer, and a great saint: a soul capable of embracing a dizzying range of contradictions, of keeping an unwavering focus on the nearness and grace of God without losing her humor, her common sense—and her ironic double vision.

Proceed in Darkness

DAVID PLANTE

SOME TIME AGO, I felt that everything was going wrong for me, and especially with my writing in the world. I was alone in Italy, and, after my supper, I would sit in the garden where fireflies flashed among the dark cypresses, and suddenly one evening all my senses— sight, hearing, smell, taste, touch—became engaged, and for at least a moment I felt my anxiety go. After that moment, I realized just how anxious I had been. My senses, engaged with what was all outside me and had nothing to do with my anxiety, had taken me out of myself, and that had been a relief to me. I wanted, I told myself, to be taken more and more out of myself.

Because I have always gone to books as perhaps my greatest recourse, I looked for a book in the library of the house where I was staying. Thumbing through novels and volumes of poems, I remembered having been told by my religious teachers when I was a devout adolescent that devotional books took one out of oneself, and this was what I wanted from a book now. (Though I am no longer a believer, my past faith comes back to me in profound echoes at moments, and after the fact I realized that, in a state of acute anxiety, I did not once tell myself that I must enter into myself to find out and act on the personal reasons for my anxiety, did not tell myself that I really must seek psychological help, but, instead, told myself that I *had* to get out of myself, and could find consolation only in what was all outside myself, and this, I am sure, has everything to do with Catholicism.) With, perhaps, the sentimentality that anxiety can cause, I searched for religious devotional books, but found none.

Then I thought how, as devout as I had been when young, I had never, ever experienced what had been promised me, by my religious teachers, in my devotion. Never had my prayers to God taken me out of myself and made me, by my union with Him, indifferent to myself in the world, but they had always brought me back, as if, finally, it was my fault that I couldn't rise above myself and the world, to myself in the world. And yet, I had the inculcated *idea* of the happiness I could have if I really and truly loved God, and with that idea came the greatest longing I have ever had or will ever have. It is a longing I now believe cannot be realized in religion, not least because I do not believe in God.

In the Italian house, unable to find a book that would console me and unable to sleep, I went to a desk and wrote in my diary. I wrote, not to account for my state, but simply to describe, as accurately as I could, how, that afternoon, out in the garden, I had looked through one of the glass doors into a room and had seen, reflected on the glass but as if projected into the room, a bank of white and red roses in which the furniture—a chaise longue and chairs and bookshelves—appeared to stand. And during a pause in my writing it occurred to me that exactly what I had once expected of my religion, but which had not happened, had happened while I was writing. I realized that there is an essential difference between a person as a self-regarding ego and that same person as a writer, and that writing does *not* refer oneself as a writer back to oneself, but out to something greater. The conviction came to me, as a small revelation, that whatever it is that makes one a writer has, in the end, very little to do with oneself, but rather with something beyond oneself. All writers of worth I have spoken to about this agree with me, even those in whose work there is not the least suspicion of otherworldliness. But what *is* this something beyond one?

Before going to bed, I went, late, from room to room

to make sure the shutters were closed, and in a guest bedroom at the top of a flight of stone stairs I saw a small bookcase, and there I found the works of Saint John of the Cross in the E. Allison Peers edition of 1934.

Saint John of the Cross did not even consider himself a writer. What he wrote was incidental to his main work in the world, which was the reform of the Carmelite Order he belonged to. Yet, what he wrote—poems and long exegeses on some of the poems—is equal in mastery, in beauty and glory, in spiritual power, to anything else ever written by anyone; and one does not read it for what it says about Saint John of the Cross, but for its devotion to the highest possible level of universal love.

Saint John's father, Gonzalo de Yepes, was a minor nobleman who married an orphan, Catalina Alvarez, and for this was ostracized by his family. He died shortly after the birth of his third son, Juan (or John) de Yepes, in 1542 at Fontiveros, near Ávila, in Spain. Juan and his two older brothers, Francisco and Luis, were brought up in poverty by their widowed mother. Seeking support for her family from her dead husband's brothers, one a priest and the other a doctor, Catalina traveled from town to town, but the relatives were no help. Luis died of starvation. Catalina and Francisco and Juan, just old enough, found work weaving in the commercial city of Medina del Campo, but this didn't provide enough. Juan was sent to a boarding school for poor children, most often orphans, where he was taught Christian doctrine. He worked as a sacristan in a church, and also as a nurse in a hospital. He chose to become a novice in the Carmelite Order and went to study in Salamanca, where, in 1564, he gave a student's discourse on contemplation. Ordained a priest in 1567, he returned to Medina del Campo.

Saint Teresa of Ávila arrived in Medina del Campo at the same time. She was fifty-two, devoted to reform in the Carmelite Order, and had come to the town to found a convent of what were known as discalced nuns, as opposed to the calced, who were against reform. The calced Carmelites wore sandals—*calzos* in sixteenth-century Spanish—and the discalced did not, but went barefoot. Teresa was determined to bring the order back to what she believed to be the ancient rigor of its twelfth-century rules, not only among the nuns but also among the friars. The prior at Medina del Campo suggested John to her as a helper. They met, immediately became close, and Teresa fired John's devotion to reform. Until 1574, he worked to found reformed convents, even paving the cells, and acted as confessor and resident priest to the nuns.

Fighting to suppress the reforms, a group of calced Carmelites went so far as to arrest the discalced John and imprison him in one of their own monasteries in Medina del Campo. But the papal nuncio, in favor of the reforms, pressed for his release. (Both the discalced and calced factions of the Carmelites were appealing to the Pope,

Gregory XIII, for ratification of the one against the other.) The papal nuncio favorable to the reforms died, and, certain of the support of the next one, John was again captured by the antireformists, in 1577, and taken as a prisoner to their monastery of Carmel in Ávila. He was beaten and locked up, but managed to escape and returned to where he had lived to destroy papers that included plans for the reforms. He was yet again captured by the calced, and taken to the Carmelite monastery in Toledo.

He was locked in a small, dark cell, so cold he developed frostbite. The food he was given was bad, he was not allowed to change his clothes, he was beaten every day, and he was denied all communication with the world outside. John was told by monks speaking to him through the door that the reforms had been suppressed, and that his pretensions at being a saint had been vanity. Here, alone, he began to write his poems in his head.

After six months, his old, harsh guard was changed to a younger, gentler one, who brought him paper and quill and ink, and there, it is thought, he wrote down "The Dark Night of the Soul."

After three more months, John, with the help of his guard, escaped, and took refuge with Carmelite nuns. But even when, in 1580, the Pope ratified the separation of the calced and discalced factions, so they in effect became independent orders, John, though still active in founding monasteries and convents, and doing masonry work, was treated with disdain by many discalced in power for always taking a moderate point of view on issues of their reform. He accepted his removal from every office of influence and asked to be sent to Mexico. This was denied him, and when, instead, he was offered the appointment of superior at Segovia, he asked to go as an ordinary monk to La Penuela in Andalusia. There, he was accused of having had sexual relations with Carmelite nuns. Ill with an infection, John went on to Ubeda, where he assumed no one would know of him. But there the prior did know of him and, intolerant of his reputation for saintliness, humiliated him by assigning him to the meanest cell and by objecting to the cost of caring for him, now an invalid. He died on December 14, 1591, during the night.

Everyone who had met him said he appeared always to be in a state of delight. He was canonized in 1726.

Though it was not central to his life, what remains for us most powerfully of Saint John of the Cross is his writing. The best known of his poems is "The Dark Night of the Soul," on which he commented at length in the exegeses *The Ascent of Mount Carmel* and *The Dark Night of the Soul.* On his poem "Songs Between the Soul and the Bridegroom," he wrote the exegesis *The Spiritual Canticle.* And *The Living Flame of Love* is a commentary on a poem by the same name. But the poem that appears at the center of his work, as a gold cross suspended in the

darkness of an apse is often the center of a church, is
"The Dark Night of the Soul."

Here it is in Spanish:

> En una noche oscura,
> Con ansias en amores inflamada,
> ¡Oh dichosa ventura!
> Sali sin ser notada,
> Estando ya mi casa sosegada.

> A oscuras, y segura,
> Por la secreta escala disfrazada,
> ¡Oh dichosa ventura!
> A oscuras, y en celada,
> Estando ya mi casa sosegada.

> En la noche dichosa,
> En secreto, que nadie me veia,
> Ni yo miraba cosa,
> Sin otra luz y guia,
> Sino la que en el corazon arida.

> Aquesta me guiaba
> Mas cierto que la luz de mediodia,
> A donde me esperaba
> Que yo bien me sabia,
> En parte donde nadie parecia.

¡Oh noche, que guiaste,
Oh noche amable mas que el alborada,
Oh noche que juntaste
Amado con amada,
Amada en el Amado transformada!

En mi pecho florido,
Que entero para el solo se guardaba,
Alli quedo dormido,
Y yo le regalaba,
Y el ventalle de cerdros aire daba.

El aire de la almena,
Cuando yo sus cabellos esparcia,
Con su mano serena
En mi cuello heria,
Y todos mis sentidos suspendia.

Quedeme, y olvideme,
El rosto recline sobre el Amado,
Ceso todo, y dejeme,
Dejando mi cuidado
Entre las azucenas olvidado.

I will dare to give my own translation, which makes no attempt to follow the rhythms and rhymes of the original.

On a dark night,
Bright with longing—
Oh, the thrill of risk!—
I left, no one saw me,
My house now still.

Safe in dark,
Down the secret stairs, disguised—
Oh, the thrill of risk!—
Concealed in dark,
My house now still.

On that thrilling night,
In secret, no one to see me,
Seeing nothing,
No light guiding me
But the light that burned in me.

That light led me
More surely than noonlight
Where he waited for me—
How well I knew him—
Where no others came.

O guiding night,
O night more loved than dawn,
O night that joined
Loved one and lover,
Lover transformed into loved one.

On my blossoming breast,
All his,
He slept,
I caressed him.
The air about the cedars stirred.

In the breeze from the ramparts,
I parted his locks.
He wounded my neck
With his gentle hand,
My senses suspended.

There I remained, lost to myself.
I pressed my face to the one I loved.
All stopped, and I
Gave myself up,
My pain no longer pain
Among the lilies.

Saint John considered his commentaries inseparable from the poems, so a poem and the explanation of it were, to him, one. The commentaries *The Ascent of Mount Carmel* and *The Dark Night of the Soul* leave no doubt that this poem has to do with the soul—the poem is written from the point of view of the soul, which in Spanish is feminine—and the soul's longing to be united with God; and, moreover, that the fulfillment of its longing depends on a total denial of the body and all its senses.

When reading the commentaries, I reached a point where, I realized, I had to make a choice—to read to understand what Saint John intended or to read for what his words inspired. In my Catholic youth, I believed that if devotional work was to mean anything, its meaning had to come through the Holy Ghost to me, and the Holy Ghost assured me that I could not misunderstand because my understanding came through Him. Saint John no doubt felt the same when he was writing, but his Holy Ghost and my Holy Ghost, I saw more and more as I read, were different, and what had inspired Saint John did not, for a large part of what he wrote, inspire me. Instead, I found myself disagreeing with, even objecting to, the way the writing, so much of which read as nothing more than justification of the poem's intentions. I did not want to read the poem for what it intended, but for what it inspired, and what the poem intended and what it inspired seemed to me opposed.

To see a saint merely in terms of history is, I think, to deny him his sainthood, which is transhistorical. And yet the contradictions I found between his poem and his commentaries seemed to place Saint John at a distance from me that was explained by our belonging to different times. Not that the distance was so very great. What he wrote in his commentaries was as true to the Church in which I was born and grew up as it was of his Church of the sixteenth century. But something happened in my maturity that put the Church of my youth at the same

distance as Saint John's Church. That a poem of such
sensuality should be explained as a spiritual experience
that demands the denial of everything that is sensual, demands the *mortification* of the senses, raised in me all the
resentment I, as a youthful believer, felt when the nuns
in the parochial school and the parish priest told us, as
an article of our faith, that our union with God, which
must be our greatest desire, required our denying ourselves the desires of our bodies. We were told that the
desires of the body would lead us only to defeat and
disconsolateness and despair. One of the reasons why I
ceased to believe was that I found, more and more, that
my senses were a source to me of great happiness, the
very happiness so sensually evoked in "The Dark Night
of the Soul," the very happiness that is such a consolation in the poem, the very happiness that takes one out
of oneself. The split between Saint John's poem and his
commentaries on the poem reminded me of the Christian
split between body and soul, a wound which I, over my
adult years as a nonbeliever, have healed in myself—a
wound I now see as historical and in no way a condition
of sainthood.

Still, I persisted in my reading of Saint John's commentaries to find the transhistorical saint, as all true
saints must be, and the inspiration I wanted from him.
And it occurred to me that there is at least one desire
that has always left writers feeling defeated, disconsolate,
despairing, and this has to do with their worldly ambi-

tions as writers. Worldly ambitions have never, ever brought writers happiness. But then, why does one write?

This is what Saint John can teach us:

That as the love for God cannot be achieved through reason, but through going out into the unknown, so, too, it is with writing.

That as the striving to love God often leaves one feeling arid, even abandoned by God, so, too, does one often feel arid, even abandoned, struggling to fulfill what one is drawn to fulfill when one writes.

That as the love for God requires a dedication, and, too, a renunciation of oneself to what is immeasurably greater than oneself, so does writing, and this something greater is, like God, not subjective but entirely objective, as vast in its objectivity as all of space.

And, most important, that as God, ultimately and sublimely, can only be seen as darkness in which the soul goes out to meet the one she loves, so, too, does one write in darkness, not because one has, in one's writing, nothing to say, but because everything there is to say is as great as all of that infinitely dark space which Saint John says God is.

In his commentaries, Saint John could have had writing in mind when composing this passage:

"One who is learning further details concerning any office or art always proceeds in darkness, and receives no guidance from his early knowledge, for if he left not that behind he would get no further nor make any progress; and in the same way, when the soul is making most progress, it is traveling in darkness, knowing naught."

But a writer not only writes in darkness, trusting the darkness to know more than he can know; the writer is aware that the final object of this work is always beyond him, and the closer he is drawn to that object, to try to write about it, the more he is blinded by it.

"For the nearer the soul approaches Him, the blacker is the darkness which it feels. . . . So immense is the spiritual light of God, and so greatly does it transcend our natural understanding, that the nearer we approach it, the more it blinds and darkens us."

To write about a saint is to invoke him, and the most important reason for invoking a saint is to pray to him to intercede between oneself and God. I, as a writer, pray to Saint John of the Cross to intercede with God on my behalf for the grace to write, not about what has to do with me, but about what has to do with the great and the brilliant darkness of God.

SOURCES

The Complete Works of Saint John of the Cross, 3 vols., trans. and ed. by E. Allison Peers (London: Burns Oates & Washbourne, 1934), 452, 453.

Alain Cugno, *St. John of the Cross,* trans. by Barbara Wall (London, Burns & Oates, 1982).

Second Thoughts on Certainty: Saint Jean de Brébeuf among the Hurons

TOBIAS WOLFF

THOUGH I WAS baptized a Catholic, I did not live among practicing Catholics, or go to Catholic schools, and therefore grew up knowing very little about the lives of the saints. I'd never heard of Saint Jean de Brébeuf until I came upon him in Francis Parkman's book *The Jesuits in North America*. His life was so astonishing and so dire in its conclusion that I couldn't get it out of my head, and even appropriated part of it for a short story, "In the Garden of the North American Martyrs." That was some fifteen years ago, and I still think of Brébeuf, but as I've learned more about him my admiration has become more complicated.

First, the bare bones of the man's life. He was born in 1593 to an aristocratic family in Normandy, and arrived in what is now the province of Quebec in 1625 as a Jesuit missionary to the Huron Indians. The English forced him out in 1629, but he returned to the Hurons in 1634 and remained with them until he was killed fifteen years later.

His death came about in this way. As the Huron confederacy grew stronger, or appeared to grow stronger through its alliance with the French, the Iroquois came to regard it as an unacceptable threat to their own prosperity and set about to annihilate the Hurons. This they did, in a series of assaults and massacres culminating in the destruction of the fortified villages of St. Ignace, St. Louis, and St. Marie in 1649. Jean de Brébeuf and his fellow missionary Gabriel Lalemant knew of the impending Iroquois attack and were urged to flee, but they remained in St. Louis to minister to eighty Huron warriors who were fighting a rearguard action to cover the retreat of their people. The Hurons put up a fierce resistance but were finally overwhelmed. Those who hadn't been killed in battle were afterward, according to the custom of both sides, tortured to death. Brébeuf and Lalemant were among them.

Brébeuf was led out first. They tied him to a stake and went to work. He showed no sign of pain, but called

out encouragement to his fellow captives and threatened
the Iroquois with hellfire for their wickedness. They applied their own fire to him, and when that didn't shut
him up they cut off his lips and stuck a hot iron down
his throat. They poured boiling water over his head in
mock baptism, hung a necklace of burning hatchets
around his neck. They made him witness the torture of
Lalemant. Nothing broke him. His stoicism provoked
them to greater and greater outrages. They stripped off
his flesh and ate it in front of him. Finally, in a fury, they
cut his heart out and ate that too. By his calm fortitude
he inspired them to kill him much sooner than they'd
intended. They tortured him for less than four hours before impatiently taking his life. Lalemant's agony was
more evident, and therefore more satisfying, and they
carefully spun it out for seventeen hours.

It would be presumptuous to describe such men with
words like "faith" and "courage"; what they endured
cannot be accounted for in words. It can hardly be imagined. But what strikes deepest in me is their concern for
the Huron warriors whom they stayed behind to serve.
They laid down their lives for their friends. That is
something I can imagine. And it happened here, on
ground familiar to me, not in some distant desert. Brébeuf, especially, is an American figure—no miracle-
working monk or haloed cave dweller but a pioneer, an
explorer, at home on wild rivers and murky forest paths,
at the council fires of painted men who ate their enemies

and were not always clear as to who their enemies were. Think of it: the young heir of a proud name raised to receive the best the world had to offer, refusing it all for a life of famine and disease, solitude, arctic winters, and unrelenting danger among people whose suspicions could never be allayed, whose friendship could never be relied on, whose motives and intentions must always remain a mortal mystery.

Brébeuf did all this, and more. Through ceaseless study he became an eloquent speaker of the Huron language, and created a grammar and lexicon to help other missionaries master the tongue. As a matter of course, and regardless of personal risk, he visited the sick and dying to preach and baptize. He kept a record of his life among the Hurons that is remarkable for its anthropological detail and, at times, its poetry. Here is Brébeuf on the subject of dreams, and their importance to the Hurons:

> They hold nothing so precious that they would not readily deprive themselves of it for the sake of a dream. If they have been successful in hunting, if they bring back their canoes laden with fish, all this is at the discretion of a dream. A dream will take away from them sometimes their whole year's provisions. It prescribes their feasts, their dances, their songs, their games—in a word, the dream does everything and is in truth the principal God of the Hurons.

Every glimpse we have of Brébeuf shows us a man of unshakable certainty. Not even in his last and darkest hour does he cry out, "Father, why hast Thou forsaken me?" This certainty is the source of all that I find chastening and stirring in his life, and all that troubles me as well. His mission was to bring unbelievers to the Church, to harvest souls, and he allowed no scruple or doubt or courtesy to stand in his way. When he couldn't persuade, he threatened. His sermons were hectoring and endlessly repetitious, so much so that ridiculing him came to be a sport among the Hurons, who had to be bribed with tobacco to listen to him at all. He hoarded food, and during times of starvation rationed it out to those who made the best show of piety. He was capricious in his use of baptism; at one time he withheld it from dying children for fear of being blamed for their deaths, at another he forced it on them even against their parents' wishes.

Brébeuf had come to speak, not to hear. He offended the Hurons by treating their own beliefs with scorn. He heaped contempt on their shamans and healers, and ignored the advice they gave him concerning the medicinal properties of native plants. He made fun of their ceremonial attempts to influence nature, but did not hesitate to play the wizard himself with magnets and clocks and magnifying glasses, and with self-designed rain-making rituals; at one point he was tried for sorcery before a tribal council and barely escaped with his life. He thus gave legitimacy to Huron suspicions that Christianity was, at best, a healing society of the kind they already had, or, at worst, a bag of tricks. Baffled by his failures, he tried to persuade the Huron chieftains to coerce their people to convert, and helped institute the practice of sending children away from their parents to be educated by French priests and nuns in Quebec. (The children kept running away, and the experiment was abandoned.)

For all his transcendent purposes, Brébeuf was help-lessly a creature of his own time and culture. The Jesuits depended on support from the French government and business enterprises, and had no choice but to serve their interests; in fact, they were tolerated by the Hurons only because the French had declared the acceptance of the Jesuit missions a condition for trade. The missionaries used this arrangement for their own ends. They allowed only converts to buy muskets, and at one point threat-ened to break off all commerce unless the entire Huron nation became Christian. These policies led to many ex-pedient baptisms, and created hard feelings between Hu-ron traditionalists and those who were willing to take up the cross for the sake of trade. Brébeuf himself made mis-chief between the Hurons and their allies the Neutrals, ham-fistedly playing them off against each other until he was nearly killed for his pains.

When Brébeuf first arrived among the Hurons they were a strong and numerous people. Twenty-five years later their nation was extinct, reduced to a few starving bands seeking adoption by other tribes. The Jesuit missionaries had much to answer for in this sorry end. They'd given the Iroquois plenty of reason to suspect that their presence among the Hurons was less a revelation of apostolic zeal than of French territorial and mercantile ambitions. In promoting their faith, the same missionaries tirelessly attacked Huron rituals and beliefs and traditions of tolerance that held this diffuse people together, and thereby divided them at the moment of their greatest danger. Brébeuf, especially, was relentless in his scorn for the spirituality that gave Huron life its meaning and coherence. In the end, he helped destroy the people he had come to save.

I do not mean to judge Jean de Brébeuf. He put all his gifts on the altar. He was loyal and resolute and courageous to his last breath. He lived the faith he professed. He was willing to accept any duty, any danger, any hardship, not for his own sake but for the sake of the people he hoped to serve. Everything he did, he did with the best of intentions. And yet this is exactly what disturbs me when I consider his life among the Hurons: that with complete purity of motive and satisfaction of conscience he was able to injure their deepest beliefs, their pride, their social structure, their very humanity, by treating them as crude and expendable vessels of the souls it was his business to save. He did these things not to please himself, but in accordance with the common understandings of devout, civilized men of his time and place. He had no idea of the limits placed on those understandings by the conditions of his upbringing and nationality and language. Who does? The perspectives from which we see Brébeuf were not available to him, as the perspectives from which we will one day be seen are not available to us.

Here is the problem. Is it possible to live a life of authentic faith without the kind of headlong conviction shown by Brébeuf? What else could have sustained him in his solitude and frustration and suffering? I envy him his certainty, until I think of the arrogance and blindness that came with it. We have learned to suspect such ardor. As I write these words, men of unbending principle and purity of motive are righteously herding people into camps and planting bombs on airplanes and firing artillery shells into crowded marketplaces. Our greatest murderers have been True Believers. And so, mindful of the evils done in faith's name, we have learned to be wary of faith itself, and of the voice that speaks for any single faith. We've taught ourselves to listen for the truth in each competing voice, to extend recognition to every contender.

But how much of this tolerance can we stand, without losing our way? If all things are true, then what particular thing is worth living for, let alone worth dying for? How unsatisfactory it is to be forever open to discussion, to see the other side of every argument, to give respect in so many directions at once. I know I am not alone in my disgust with the flaccidity of spirit that comes upon us as the consequence of trying always to accommodate the justice in each claim on our sympathy and understanding. I believe that this disgust is the greatest spiritual problem of our time. In its grip we long for certainty as for the clear streams and lush fields of a childhood home we never really had. How dangerous this longing is, what terrible things it makes us do for those who promise to satisfy it.

And still I confess that I feel rebuked by such assurance as Brébeuf's, Brébeuf who never hesitated, who went to his death without a second thought. The Lord Himself didn't do that. He prayed for the cup to pass Him by. Even at the end, He doubted, for which I give thanks. His doubts are blessings. They pardon us for ours. I'd be lost without them.

SOURCES

Denys Delâge, *Bitter Feast,* tr. by Jane Brierly (Vancouver: University of British Columbia Press, 1993).

Francis Parkman, *The Jesuits in North America* (Boston: Little Brown and Co., 1900).

Reuben G. Thwaites, ed. and trans., *Jesuit Relations and Allied Documents* (Cleveland: Burrows Bros. 1886–1901).

Bruce G. Trigger, *The Children of Aataentsic: A History of the Huron People to 1660* (Kingston and Montreal: McGill-Queen's University Press, 1976).

My Left Feet

ENRIQUE FERNÁNDEZ

I'M THE PERSON you want to be lost in the desert with. Follow me and you will not die of thirst. How will I find us water? By stepping on it. You will sense we are safe from the eternal drought of the eternal sands when you notice that on my feet I am not wearing Clark's desert boots but Timberland's waterproof brogans. For I know that even in the desert there must be one puddle and that it is my fate to step on it.

Even when it hasn't rained, I step on a puddle caused

by a backed-up street sewer or splashed by an open fire hydrant or fed by the hose of a Central American refugee who is washing the curb of a Korean greengrocer. One night, one tropical night when like all tropical nights it had rained, I walked with a friend in the darkness of a Miami nightclub parking lot toward our car. Splash! He stared at me in disbelief. "It's true what they say. You step on puddles."

I also step on feet. In a nightclub parking lot I have only the shame of my wet shoes—until I discovered the waterproof brogans—but inside the club I walk with the tread of a golem in a German Expressionist movie, ruining the gloss of polished Italian loafers, destroying toes in open sandals, provoking contempt and ire. Living dangerously. My work as a Latin music journalist has taken me to salsa clubs where a) unlike, say, a hardcore scene, inflicting pain on your fellow clubgoers is not a sign of solidarity; b) being light on your feet, deft, smooth, sharp, suave is highly regarded; c) many of the patrons are tough customers, gun-packing machos who practice rough trades in the mean streets and who don't find the ruining of their Italian loafers or the destruction of their lady friends' toes simpatico.

It's a miracle I'm still alive.

When I was in college I worked as a waiter in a very small, trendy, charming Spanish restaurant. After a week of enduring toe-crushing pain, my fellow workers, who included the owner's wife, agreed I should be exempted from the dress code and allowed to, nay, ordered to, wear sneakers instead of hard-soled dress shoes.

I didn't play sports as a kid. The few times I did, one of my ankles would twist and I would be out of the game. My parents took me to a bone surgeon, who diagnosed something or other and prescribed orthopedic shoes. They hurt. Also, they did no good.

I'm feet dyslexic. I'm faultily wired. I'm clumsy.

"You better go get yourself fixed by Saint Lazarus," a fellow Cuban American told me after observing how often I tripped, stumbled, and stepped on puddles. He was a musician, conversant with the religious practices that have come out of our native country, what is known in Spanish as *santería,* the worship of saints.

Santería mixes African religion with Roman Catholicism. It was first practiced by slaves from the Yoruba nation brought in the eighteenth and nineteenth centuries from what is Nigeria today to work in Cuba's sugar plantations. The Yoruba were and are a highly sophisticated people, and they found a way of holding on to their religion without alarming their white masters. They looked for affinities between their own deities, the *orichas,* and the representations of Catholic saints. For example, a saint holding a sword, like Saint Barbara, stood in for Changó, the fierce warrior god.

In the Spanish and Portuguese colonies of the New

World, the Africans were not forbidden to play drums, as they were in the American South. When the slaves played to their gods, the masters assumed they were paying homage to the Christian saints, albeit in a very rhythmic way.

Because of its association with saints, this cultural sleight of hand was called *santería*. With time, *santería* became more than a disguise for African rites, as true elements of Christian belief and practices seeped into the mix. And with time, the new mixed religion—syncretism is the academic name for this process of cultural fusion—spread beyond Cuba's African subculture. *Santería* became so widespread everyone came to believe in it, at least enough to fear its powers. *"Con los santos no se juega,"* Cubans of all races say. "You don't mess with the saints." And *santería* kept on spreading.

The Cuban exodus prompted by the radical changes of Castro's revolution brought *santería* to the United States on a massive scale. Many other Latinos embraced it with the same enthusiasm with which they embraced Afro-Cuban music, baptized in the American barrios as "salsa." And even non-Latinos got into *santería*.

Walk into a *santero*'s house and you will find altars to the saints. Many are familiar Catholic images, like the Virgin Mary or the Baby Jesus. One popular image is that of a bearded man on crutches, wearing little more than a loincloth and exposing a body covered with sores.

He is Saint Lazarus, and the African deity he represents
is Babalú-Ayé. Remember Desi Arnaz banging on drums
and chanting, "Babaloo"? That's who he was calling.

The lame Saint Lazarus, aka Babalú-Ayé, is the patron saint of feet. Thus my compatriot's prescription to
cure my chronic stumbling, ankle-twisting, and stepping
on puddles. Like most Cubans I respect *santería,* but I
have never really practiced it. My forays into this wonderful, magical, and yet very practical and earthy religion
have been intellectual. It plays such an important part in
my home country's culture and in the culture of U.S.
Latinos that I have felt obliged to understand its basics.
I have even written articles about it, and have researched
them by going to drum ceremonies and interviewing
practicing *santeros.* But I am not an initiate. There is no
altar in my home; nor do I light candles, sacrifice chick-
ens—animal sacrifice is *santería*'s most controversial fea-
ture—or consult a *babalao* to help me order my life. So
when it was suggested that I seek Saint Lazarus's help, I
thought, Why not? But I did nothing about it. Until . . .

I was in Havana two years ago, writing a magazine
piece on what life was like in my home country these
days. Another Cuban-American journalist, also there on
assignment, suggested I go to the shrine of Saint Lazarus
during the week of his feast day: "It's a freak show."
And then I remembered how in my childhood I had seen
a photo essay in a Cuban magazine about the Saint Lazarus parade—if that's what it can be called. Like other

Catholic countries, Cuba has had a tradition of making "promises" to the saints. That is, you ask the appropriate saint to help you with some problem, like getting over an illness, and you offer to visit the saint's shrine in repayment.

Every year believers who have made promises to Saint Lazarus walk miles to his shrine. On the last stretch, about a mile and a half of a semirural road a few miles outside Havana, the march to the shrine becomes more dramatic as those who have made serious promises walk it on their knees, praying for their sins' forgiveness. At least, that's how I remembered it from the magazine article.

All of this was standard folk Catholicism. But the Cuban twist was *santería,* since, as I said, the Catholic saint and the African god were fused into one. In fact, the Catholic saint was not the guy with the crutches and the sores—along with Saint Christopher, the patron saint of travelers, and Saint George, who slew the dragon, *that* Saint Lazarus was declared pure fable many years ago by the Catholic church and banished from the company of legitimate saints. This Saint Lazarus was some early Christian bishop who stood squarely on two feet and wore proper bishop's vestments. But never mind; his name was Saint Lazarus also, and as far as *santeros* were concerned, he was Babalú-Ayé, patron saint of the lame and of those who have problems with their feet.

I went there to ask him to cure mine from their embarrassing ineptitude with puddles and the toes of gangsters' molls.

It was December, the day before the feast of Saint Lazarus, and I could see pilgrims walking alongside the road that led to the small town where the shrine was located. The shrine was outside the town, at the end of a smaller road, which was blocked to traffic so the believers could do their thing. And the things they did!

Sure enough, there were folk who walked that last mile and a half on their knees. But the ones who had made really intense promises went down on their bellies and crawled. In most cases the connection with the crippled saint was obvious. One severely disabled man, in filthy rags which had become bloodied from his crawling, had big chunks of cinder block tied to each twisted leg— an extreme form of fulfilling his promise. His body zigzagged up the road like a sidewinder's. Two young men from the town, used to this yearly procession and to seeing this one penitent every year, cheerfully announced, "*La culebra* is here!" The snake. Caribbean humor is merciless and tough. But no tougher than another crawling believer, who insisted on his macho privilege to suffer.

In front of this penitent, another man brushed away the pebbles on the road with a palm frond. It was a *santería* practice of *abrir camino,* opening the road, which usually has metaphorical and spiritual meaning, but here was carried out quite literally. The road-opener would encourage the crawler and give him instructions, acting like his spiritual personal trainer. When the tough crawler, who was not tied down by stones and showed no signs of physical disability, reached a strip of metal laid at the churchyard's gate, his road-opener told him to "kiss Oggún," that is, to kiss the metal in honor of Oggún, god of iron, and he kept on brushing away the pebbles.

The crawler did not kiss Oggún; instead, he looked up at the other man with fierce bloodshot eyes and told him to stop his road-clearing work. He wanted to feel the pebbles. He wanted to feel the pain. He wanted to bleed. The other man kept brushing until the crawler stopped, looked up again, and said, "If you don't stop, I'm going to stand up and fuck you up." The other man stopped. The crawler went inside the church, which was filling with pilgrims. He crawled up to the altar, received a priest's blessing, and then stood up, lean, muscular, able-bodied. Observing the fierceness of his promise and his obvious lack of physical handicap, a man in the church commented, "He must have done something terribly evil to feel he must pay for it like this!"

A woman I assumed to be a nun—no one wears religious habits in today's Cuba—was leading the crowd in prayer and giving them advice on religious protocol. Most of it had to do with observing Catholic instead of *santería* rites. She asked for the silence required in church—characteristically Caribbean, *santería* ceremonies can be social and informal even while being intense; that is, someone can be going into a spiritual trance at one end of a room while at the other end someone else is eating and talking. And she asked people not to give the saints anything to smoke; it's a common practice to offer a lit cigar to the images of certain saints. "This is a Catholic church," she said, "and we have rituals different from those of other religions. Please observe our rules."

I stood to one side of the procession of crawlers and walkers and genuflectors and looked at the statue of Saint Lazarus. He seemed overly dressed and overly healthy, unlike the folk of Saint Lazarus, whose life-size, sore-infested, leaning-on-crutches statues can be seen on display in the windows of religious stores on Bergenline Avenue in Union City, New Jersey, and, of course, on Miami's Little Havana strip, Calle Ocho. But if people will crawl to pray for this Saint Lazarus's help, he must be the right saint. So I prayed. Something like: *Saint Lazarus, Babalú-Ayé, please help me walk straight without tripping, stumbling, twisting my ankle, stepping on feet, or splashing on puddles.* And then, I turned around and went back up the road to the car. It was getting dark.

Along the way I noticed that police officers were frisking men who had just arrived on the scene. I asked one of the cops what this was about, and he replied that some people took advantage of the crowd and the darkness to settle old scores. Some of these guys certainly looked like they should be searched. One was a virtual folk caricature of a Cuban tough guy, a *guapo*. He was a light-skinned mulatto with a thin mustache and a hard, handsome face. He wore perfectly creased jeans and a tight-fitting undershirt. He was built like a motherfucker. And by his side stood his son, no more than ten years old, dressed exactly like his father, also built like a motherfucker, staring hard and mean; absolutely frightening. He also got searched.

Others who were frisked appeared quite harmless: hippiesque student types slinging bookbags. No women were frisked. And no one—it hurts to admit it—frisked me. Too old, perhaps, too soft, too unlikely to flash a blade on the night of Saint Lazarus.

By the time I got back to my hotel it was nighttime. I stepped out of the car.

Splash.

Havana, I remembered, always had a water-drainage problem: too much rain. It also had a water-supply problem. I know all this because many years ago my father worked for the city's water department. He got to drive a white station wagon with the city's coat of arms and the words ACUEDUCTO DE LA HABANA on it, but after a few days of having rocks thrown at it when he cruised through neighborhoods where there were water shortages and/or flooded streets, he gave it back to the city. Water problems. Puddles. Splash! Saint Lazarus had not worked his magic on my feet.

I told all this to the Cuban-American musician as soon
as I was back in New York. I felt betrayed by the saint.
I had gone to his shrine, albeit not crawling. I had
prayed. I was still a clumsy idiot.

"Did you believe in the saint's power?" he asked.

"Well, I prayed, didn't I?"

"But did you believe?"

"I don't know. Yes. No. I prayed."

"If you don't believe, it doesn't work."

So that was it. The problem was not my physical
clumsiness. I was, I am, a spiritual klutz. I prayed without believing. "Words without thought do not to heaven
go." Even Claudius, that vile, incestuous, usurping mur-
derer knew this, while Hamlet, my fellow klutz, thought
Claudius was praying, so he didn't kill him for fear of
dispatching him to heaven. Spirituality has its rules. *Con
los santos no se juega.*

Anyway, what was the big deal? The Timberland
company had already solved half my problem. And by
now the gangsters and their molls were used to seeing
me stumbling around the clubs, so they just moved their
nimble feet out of my way.

I saw something else that late afternoon on the
pebble-strewn road to the shrine of Saint Lazarus. There
was a man who was crawling for the sake of his son, a
two-year old boy with a clubfoot. The man was big and
ebony-skinned, as perfectly muscled as a classical sculpture. His knees and feet and elbows were bleeding badly.

In front of him a light-skinned *santero,* dressed in white from his shoes to his hat, opened the road with a fresh palm frond, while by his side the man's wife walked, holding their son's hand. She was a high-toned mulatto, gracefully shaped in a tight satin dress and she walked on high heels. On the man's back rode his son, naked and beautiful, so beautiful his clubfoot seemed like no imperfection at all. I couldn't help but think he would grow up to be a Caribbean Lord Byron.

The man was powerful, but he had been crawling for some time and occasionally he would stop. Then, someone would come out from a neighborhood house and offer him water to drink. Thus revived he would resume his pilgrimage. The boy bounced on his father's broad back, having the time of his life, the ride of his life, smiling to the passersby; absolutely, perfectly happy. I didn't stay with them, but went on ahead toward the church, and when I walked back I missed them in the crowd.

When I later wrote about this visit to Cuba, I left out the pilgrimage to the shrine of Saint Lazarus/Babalú-Ayé. The article I eventually published was infused with politics, as have been all recent articles on Cuba. I had thought I would find politics on the road to Saint Lazarus, people praying for the fall of Fidel or for his endurance. But I found—and lost—something else instead: grace.

The image of that family fulfilling a promise was so

overpowering that it confused me. Everything was too meaningful, too symbolic: the Holy Family, the Passion of Christ, the white-clad *santero* with a palm frond moving with the grace of an Alvin Ailey dancer, the crawler built like a titan, the child with the clubfoot hanging loosely on his father's back like a Greek boy on a dolphin, the mother walking with the sass of a *mulata* in the old Cuban folk theater. Too much.

And there was my failure with the saint, which seemed like an entirely different agenda. Only now do I realize my blindness. Just as I had prayed without believing, I had seen without praying. Visions are spiritual gifts and I had seen this one with secular eyes.

That *was* Saint Lazarus. That *was* Babalú-Ayé. Who else could command so much iconography? I left him crawling, bleeding, sore-infested. What I should have done was pray right there and then for a cure for his son's disability, to give him a spiritual power charge. Maybe then the deity brought in chains to the New World, reincarnated as a false saint, surviving as a real one, summoned a thousand times in the foolish rituals of an old American TV show, crawling along a road full of penitents that December afternoon, would have shown mercy on my petty pilgrimage and blessed away the clumsiness of my two left feet.

A Family Man

PAUL BAUMANN

WE WERE LYING IN BED discussing our children, as married people sometimes do just before turning off the light and just after tossing aside in bitter and covetous disgust the real-estate transactions in the local newspaper. How can there be peace with justice if one's neighbors' property values ascend heavenward while yours languish in purgatorial suspension? But to whom does the beleaguered and undervalued property owner, fantasizing a killing on the real estate market and early retirement to pursue pious works, cry? To Saint Joseph,

another overanxious father? To Saint Joseph, the patron
saint of petit-bourgeois dutifulness and uxorious discipline ("When Joseph woke from sleep, he did as the
angel of the Lord commanded him; he took his wife, but
knew her not until she had borne a son; and he called
his name Jesus")? To Saint Joseph, the obedient taxpayer
("In those days a decree went out from Caesar Augustus
that all the world should be enrolled")? To the church's
patron of social justice (". . . Joseph, being a just man
and unwilling to put her to shame, resolved to divorce
her quietly"), harried fathers of families ("And he rose
up and took the child and his mother by night, and de-
parted to Egypt, and remained there until the death of
Herod"), and working men ("Is this not the son of the
woodworker?")? What satisfaction can one expect from
the heavenly solicitor for such notoriously undervalued
properties as Peru, Belgium, Canada, and China? Or
should I petition "Joseph the Joiner," as James Joyce im-
piously described the world's most famous carpenter,
cuckold, and foster father, "patron of the happy demise
of all unhappy marriages"?

More on that soon. But about our children, those
mites of God's clay, the fruit of our lawful embraces
(Joyce again; he was, after all, a family man if not a
property owner, and, as it turns out, a keen ruminator
on Saint Joseph's travail). Would our eldest, heir apparent and apparent visitor from Mars, ever learn to pay
attention and stop tormenting his sister? we asked each

other. Would she ever stop tormenting him—not that he didn't deserve it? Why does he act like that, anyway? It can't be sex; he's only ten. Maybe it is sex. Jesus! When will the two-year-old stop throwing her dinner dishes across the kitchen and taking off her soiled diaper in the living room? But she's only two. When will he stop spilling food on the floor? Will he learn how to pour milk? How is it that she, the eight-year-old, so delicate of complexion and ankle, so sneaky with a rabbit punch, never spills anything? Where did they come from? Is someone crying? How would Saint Joseph—spouse of the Queen of Heaven, reputed father of the King of Kings—handle this? Patiently, I know.

Ah, family life. If it didn't have a patron saint, someone would have to invent one. How did my wife and I, once vowed to perpetual procrastination, get in so deep among the pacifiers, Legos, and dollies? How did we end up back at Caldor, where once our own parents led us in solemn procession down the evil-smelling aisles and where we swore never to return? How did we come to a reconciliation with plastic and polyester, with Pampers and the color pink? How did my life end up looking more like Saint Joseph's than like that of my original role model, James Bond?

It is in the nature of things, I suppose. Turning to my overworked and underpaid, overwrought and under-Catholicized (read Jewish) wife, I put a respectful hand on her deflated belly, that omphalos of our little world.

Each of our children had kicked but more often fluttered about in utero, and I warmly remembered how uncanny and unnerving it had been to feel such palpable life inside my wife's familiar body. ("And when Elizabeth heard the greeting of Mary, the babe leaped in her womb; and Elizabeth was filled with the Holy Spirit. . . .") My wife, too, thought of that sovereign and mysterious liquid universe in which her children leapt and tumbled as numinous and as achingly wondrous as first love. An unexpected, unearned, incalculable visitation. "Yes," she said, "yes," in the manner of Joyce's expansive Molly Bloom but in shorter sentences. "For he has done great things for me," she might have said in the manner of Mary, according to Luke. What could I do but stand by at a discreet distance, seeming to tend the livestock somewhat in the manner of Saint Joseph—he who was entrusted, as tradition tells us, with the sublime secret of the Incarnation and, more prosaically, the care and guardianship of Virgin and Son?

I want to get at the curiously diffident figure of Joseph by way of Joyce, and by aligning him with the equally self-effacing figure of Leopold Bloom, the cuckolded hero of *Ulysses*. The truths of fiction and the truths of biblical religion are not unrelated. Certain aspects of reality can be captured only in narrative. Paradox and parable must in this sense be enacted or witnessed to, not analyzed away. Like liturgy, literature uses language and drama to immerse us in a re-created and revivified world.

Karl Rahner, the late German theologian, writes of the lives of saints that "the events of this earthly life are not simply gone and past, over and done with forever, but they are preparatory steps that belong to us for eternity, that belong to us as our living future."

That is not a bad way to describe what happens in Joyce's novel. In *Ulysses,* Joyce employs a variety of narrative techniques, especially parody and stream of consciousness, to present the events of one day, June 16, 1904, in Dublin. Stephen Dedalus, an aspiring writer, and Leopold Bloom and his wife, Molly, are the central characters. Mimicking the mythic structure of Homer's *Odyssey,* Joyce follows Stephen and Bloom, his Telemachus and Odysseus, or Ulysses, as they wander the city on their mundane rounds, unknowingly in search of each other. Every act, gesture, and emotion of Joyce's characters takes on an imperishable quality thanks to the intensity of his writing and the manifold allusions of the novel's plot. Joyce wants to pull back the veil before the quotidian to reveal the mythic or transcendent quality of human existence. In this regard, I think the tribute to that "insignificant man" Joseph in Rahner's collection of sermons, *The Great Church Year,* can aptly be applied to the inconspicuous Leopold Bloom: "The life of this insignificant man did have significance; it had one meaning that, in the long run, counts in each person's life: God and his incarnate grace. . . . Who can doubt that this man is a good patron for us? This man of humble, everyday routine, this man of silent performance of duty, of honest righteousness and of manly piety, this man who was charged with protecting the grace of God in its embodied life?"

Joyce, as is well known, imbued his fiction with the kind of spiritual revelations or "epiphanies" he no longer found compelling in Irish Catholicism. He created the kind of mysteries, enigmas, and signs in his fiction that he had initially found in Catholic doctrine and ritual, and he borrowed freely from Catholicism in doing so. As Malcolm Bradbury has written, Joyce's work retains the church's redemptive imagery as well as its message of love. *Ulysses'* elaborate documentation of one day in Leopold Bloom's life challenges any merely material or naturalistic accounting of human existence. "Bloomsday," as Joyce's admirers have labeled the events of *Ulysses,* is something like what Rahner calls the "one today of eternity" God has promised for those who love him.

For Joyce, artistic creativity mimics and even partakes of the mystery of creation itself. In her famous stream-of-consciousness rumination at the end of the novel, Molly Bloom, Leopold's unfaithful wife and the novel's Penelope, puts the riddle of the world this way: ". . . as for them saying theres no God I wouldn't give a snap of my two fingers for all their learning why don't they go and create something I often asked him atheists or whatever they call themselves go and wash the cobbles off themselves first then they go howling for a priest and they dying ... ah yes I know them well who was the first person in the universe before there was anybody that made it all who ah that they dont know neither do I so there you are they might as well try to stop the sun from rising tomorrow. ..."

Fatherhood, or the "mystery of paternity," in the phrase of the Joycean critic Stuart Gilbert, is emblematic of the power and paradoxes of creation. In this sense, Bloom's famous cuckoldry seems to be a sign of the essential ambiguity of all human longing and attachment. As Richard Ellmann has written, Joyce used sexual betrayal as "a parable of the dilemma of all creators, whether of books or of worlds." There is something "sado-masochistic," as Ellmann characterizes it in his essay "Becoming Exiles," in the very nature of our passions. Without desire we can achieve nothing, yet there is no desire without jealousy, no valuing one thing without spurning something or someone else. Worse, "to delight in possession is to allow the conceivability of dispossession, to rely on constancy is impossible because it can only exist as a relation to inconstancy; what is absent calls attention to what is present." Human happiness is fleeting because the desires that ignite our passions in the same motion undermine our certainty.

Who is a father and who a son is not at all easy to unravel, Joyce suggests. Stephen Dedalus, a spiritual orphan, must find his way to the childless Leopold Bloom, his mystical foster father. In the maternity-hospital scene where Stephen finally meets Bloom ("now sir Leopold that had of his body no man-child for an heir"), Joyce celebrates the mystery of new life in his commendation of a new father. "By heaven, Theodore Purefoy, thou has done a doughty deed and no botch!" Joyce rejoices. "Thou art, I vow, the remark-ablest progenitor barring none in this chaffering allin-cluding most farraginous chronicle. Astounding! In her lay a Godframed Godgiven preformed possibility which thou has fructified with thy modicum of man's work. Cleave to her! Serve! Toil on, labour like a very bandog and let scholarment and all Malthusiasts go hang. Thou art all their daddies, Theodore. Art drooping under thy load, bemoiled with butcher's bills at home and ingots (not thine!) in the countinghouse? Head up!"

Maybe it takes a Joyce to evoke without cliché the joy and nagging mystery of fatherhood—its uncertain-ties so easily distorted by the language of "family val-ues." Bemoiled with bills and drooping under a freely willed load puts the right gleeful spin on the mock-epic adventure of fatherhood and husbanding. Conceivably the angel's real words to Joseph were, "Cleave to her! Serve! Toil on, labour like a very bandog." At least that's what Joseph appears to have done.

Understanding what fatherhood's "modicum of man's work" entails is not a straightforward proposition. Joseph's fate, like Leopold Bloom's, is especially sugges-tive. You have to be given one of those heedless Godframed Godgiven preformed possibilities to appreciate how onerous and liberating custodianship can be. That paradox is compounded by the constant and eerie discovery of oneself in one's offspring. "I'm becoming my father," moans one exasperated son after another as he raises his own children. In this regard Joyce reminds us that the Virgin Mary in fact gives birth to a son who is also her own father. "Paternity may be a legal fiction," Stephen Dedalus further speculates. "Who is the father of any son that any son should love him or he any son. . . . Fatherhood . . . is a necessary evil. . . . Fatherhood in the sense of conscious begetting is unknown to man. It is a mystical estate, an apostolic succession, from only begetter to only begotten. On that mystery and not on the madonna which the cunning Italian intellect flung to the mob of Europe the church is founded and founded irremovably because founded, like the world, macro- and microcosm, upon the void."

Stephen Dedalus finds that mystical estate, that spiritual legacy, in the advertising canvasser Leopold Bloom, the uncommon common man Joyce makes the unlikely hero of his novel. In this sense, Bloom can be seen as a kind of Joseph—and perhaps Joseph as a kind of Bloom. Every new creation needs a foster father, Joyce contends. Even the incarnated God needed one.

But to return, for the moment, to my wife and me in our bourgeois bedroom. The metaphysical connotations of fatherhood alluded to above had more or less banished comparative real-estate values from my mind. So I contemplated further how those mites of God's clay had forged a bond between my wife and me that was deeper than the word "domesticity" suggests. A bond that is, in fact, as deep as the world itself—which is what I take Joyce to mean when he describes human life as "soaring imperishable impalable being." Like a good many couples, we knew each other for many years before marrying and having children. We knew the macro- and microcosm and the void, so to speak. For those years our lives revolved around—ourselves. We were, after all, urged on to self-fulfillment as a generational, even constitutional duty. But now there are (gulp) three more very Godpossibled and equally grasping souls in the picture. We somehow let scholarment and all Malthusiasts go hang. But while our world has become more crowded, I would argue that it also has become larger. "For sirs," Stephen Dedalus puts it, sounding uncannily like Pope John Paul II, ". . . our lust is brief. We are means to those small creatures within us and nature has other ends than we."

I ventured to express these aboriginal feelings to my less mystically inclined roommate.

"Children are a real bond, don't you think," I said dreamily.

"Yes, they are," she replied with a slyness of tone that should have alerted me to the banana peel ahead. "So where, exactly, do you fit in?"

My wife laughed. ("But as he considered this, be-hold, an angel of the Lord appeared to him in a dream, saying, 'Joseph, son of David, do not fear. . . .' ") Not a wicked or unfriendly laugh. More a knowing laugh. I took this teasing in the spirit in which it was intended. At least I think I took it in the spirit in which it was intended. It was, in part, a legitimate complaint about the dishes I had left unwashed in the sink. But it was more. Saint Joseph, I vaguely remember, appeared before me at that moment.

Well, maybe he didn't exactly appear. But Joseph's notorious marital forbearance did cross my mind. It was not so much that my wife was about to reveal the until then unsuspected real paternity of my children. At least I have received no hint of such a complication. No, it was rather that Saint Joseph's unique circumstances exemplify those ambiguities surrounding paternity.

My wife was asserting, in her whimsical way, a cer-tain primacy of place in regard to our offspring. I took no offense. While I don't think biology is destiny, I do think that it is, well, biology. In *Ulysses,* for example, Joyce devotes each episode to an oblique discussion of a different bodily organ. "My book is among other things the epic of the human body," he said. And the procre-ative body obviously takes center stage. The ties that bind mothers to children are physiologically irrefutable, emotionally unmistakable, and, I realize, culturally highly suspect. Nevertheless, I confess that I think motherhood is closer to the center of things, if by the center we mean the source of life. "They all write about some woman," Molly Bloom observes. Mothers and babies are literally knitted together. The attachments are multiple and unmediated, and that solidarity transcends the womb. We are linked navel to navel to Eve, not Adam.

Motherhood is an irrevocable umbilical connection. Women carry life within them as well as nurturing it with the substance of their own bodies. (That's transubstantiation for you!) Fathers, however, are physically detached, apart. Connection must be forged. Fatherhood is an artifice in a way motherhood never can be. In some sense it really is a matter of apostolic succession, a leap of faith—is that why we call God the Father Almighty? Mommy seems to come first in myth, fairy tale, and popular prejudice. *Mother* is often the last word on the lips of the dying. "Mamafesta" is what Joyce called *Finnegans Wake.* So it is not surprising that a mother comes first, at least from the human side of things, in the Christian story of redemption. Or that the man—Joseph, that is— is conspicuously shunted to the side. So Joseph's status as foster father may be worth thinking more about. Compared to the intimacy, risks, and rewards of motherhood, all fatherhood is, Joyce suggests, a kind of foster fatherhood. And if read broadly, Joseph's consternation over Mary's seeming procreative autonomy is the consternation of every man over a woman's procreative near self-sufficiency. From the only begetter to the countless begotten, every human father is a stand-in.

In this context, it is a pleasing paradox that patriarchal religion should single out as a model of fatherly duty a man who is denied any biological connection to the son for whom he is remembered, and in whose name he is venerated. Joseph, as Joyce might say, seems utterly superfluous, a necessary evil, in the central drama of the Incarnation. How we make sense of this paragon of fatherhood who yet is not a father in the strict definition of the word tells us something about the nature of God as well as that of our own destiny.

Of course Joseph was not above worldly or stereotypical masculine concerns. Scripture is determined to provide answers of a sort to the delicate questions about Joseph's and Mary's conjugal life. Learning of Mary's condition, Joseph is perplexed—as perplexed as the most incredulous New Testament reader. Understandably, he "resolved to divorce her quietly." He may have been concerned about Mary's safety, for the penalty for adultery was stoning. Happily, the problem is resolved by the intervention of an angel, to this day the most practical solution to the problem of suspected adultery. "Do not fear to take Mary your wife, for that which is conceived in her is of the Holy Spirit," goes history's most famous reassurance of a suspicious husband. Joseph is obedient. Very much like Bloom's return to the adulterous Molly, Joseph turns away from any attempt to control things. Dependency is somehow equated with humanity in both instances. In choosing faith and constancy over doubt and separation, Joseph establishes himself as the guardian of the saviour of the world and subsequently as a protector of children and virgins down through the ages. To be sure, Joseph's willingness to believe what the Holy Spirit tells him in his dreams also established him as the butt of a million jokes. As a befuddled cuckold, he became a stock figure of ridicule in story, legend, and song. Indeed, the popular imagination finds it hard to separate Joseph from the idea of cuckoldry, even if he has been cuckolded by the Progenitor of us all. In the traditional English Cherry Tree carol, Joseph emerges as a very human figure indeed.

> Joseph was an old man,
> And an old man was he,
> When he wedded Mary
> In the land of Galilee.
>
> Joseph and Mary walked
> Through an orchard good,
> Where were cherries and berries
> So red as any blood. . . .
>
> O then bespoke Mary,
> With words so meek and mild
> 'Pluck me one cherry, Joseph,
> For I am with child.'

O then bespoke Joseph,
   With answer most unkind,
'Let him pluck thee a cherry
   That brought thee now with child.'

O then bespoke the baby
   Within his mother's womb—
'Bow down then the tallest tree
   For my mother to have some.'

Then bowed down the highest tree,
   Unto his mother's hand.
Then she cried, 'See, Joseph,
   I have cherries at command.'

O then bespake Joseph—
   'I have done Mary wrong;
But now cheer up, my dearest,
   And do not be cast down.

'O eat your cherries, Mary,
   O eat your cherries now,
O eat your cherries, Mary,
   That grow upon the bough. . . .'

In religious art, at least until relatively modern times, Joseph is usually portrayed as an elderly man, at once lending credence to Jesus' otherworldly paternity and making more plausible Mary's perpetual virginity. As a heavenly patron, Joseph—Mary's chaste and holy spouse and Jesus' father—was thought to be particularly well situated to intercede on behalf of his earthly clients. Saint Francis de Sales (1567–1621) put his analogical imagination to work in suggesting that the threesome of the Holy Family was a kind of earthly counterpart to the Trinity. Mother, Father, and progeny do, after all, form the primeval triangle. The Christian story has been described as a family drama. But to a large extent, any cult of Saint Joseph lay dormant through the first millennium of Christianity. This is attributed to the problems Joseph's status as husband presents to the ideas of Mary's virginal conception and her perpetual virginity. Once those doctrines were firmly established, Joseph could emerge as a more substantial figure in his own right.

A French religious writer, Jean Gerson (1363–1429), is reputed to have been the most effective early promoter of Joseph's cult. Gerson's efforts resulted in Pope Sixtus IV's promulgation, in 1480, of March 19 as Saint Joseph's feast day. Saint Teresa of Ávila was another advocate. She attributed to Joseph the successful financial management of her burgeoning order. The Jesuits also promoted Joseph as a model of Christian fatherhood. In more recent years the "chaste spouse" shouldered significant ecclesiastical and even political responsibilities. Pius IX proclaimed him Patron of the Universal Church in 1870. Pius XI commissioned him into the church's battle against atheistic communism in 1937. In that capacity, the Catholic church established a second feast day, the Feast of Saint Joseph the Worker, on May 1, 1955. Given the subsequent demise of dialectical materialism and the collapse of the Soviet Union, Joseph's spiritual potency appears not to have diminished in the time since his fiduciary exploits among the Carmelites.

Asking what we know about the "real" Joseph is a bit like asking what we know about real sightings of Elvis. Obviously there is little we can know. Scripture, as usual, contradicts itself on many of the relevant facts. In Matthew, for example, it is Joseph, not Mary, who receives the annunciation of Jesus' birth. Joseph's gospel appearances are confined to the birth narratives in Matthew and Luke, although his status as Jesus' foster father is referred to briefly elsewhere. No actual word of Joseph's is recorded in the New Testament. Matthew tells the story of the Incarnation from Joseph's perspective. Regarded as the most "Jewish" of the evangelists, Matthew emphasizes the importance of Joseph's Davidic lineage. "Matthew's major concern," writes Biblical scholar John P. Meier in *A Marginal Jew: Rethinking the Historical Jesus*, "[is] Jesus' Davidic sonship through Joseph. We might almost sum up the message of 1:18–25 with a paradox: although Jesus is virginally conceived, nevertheless he is the Son of David through Joseph, his legal father."

According to Meier, Joseph was most likely a native

of Nazareth and an observant Jew. As such, he would
have taken a special interest in his firstborn son, and
probably passed on his occupation to him. What Joseph's
occupation was, except that he worked as a craftsman, is
uncertain. What seems certain, at least according to
scholarly consensus, is that Joseph's conspicuous absence
from the accounts of Jesus' ministry in all likelihood indi-
cates that he died before Jesus began his public life. Joseph is not with Mary at the foot of the cross.

Questions about the virgin birth and Mary's and Joseph's chaste marriage are outside the competence of
scholarly investigation, Meier winningly notes. Obviously, the virginal conception of Jesus lies at the heart
of the Christian incarnational message and of any real
understanding of Joseph. As the historian Peter Brown
writes in his seminal study, *The Body and Society: Men
Women, and Sexual Renunciation in Early Christianity*, "the
cult of the Virgin offered the luminous inversion of the
dark myth of shared fallen flesh." Mary's motherhood of
Jesus redeems "the physical bonds created between human beings by their bodies." Through Mary, Christians
have been able to embrace the full humanity of Jesus, for
in looking at Christ they "looked on the flesh of a kins-
man, taken from the tranquil human substance of the Virgin's womb."

Alongside the mystery of Mary's "yes" to God
stands the curious figure of Joseph, who was as obedient
and faithful in his way as Mary was in hers. Under the

circumstances, you might say Joseph's chaste fidelity was a miracle in its own right. "Let him pluck thee a cherry/ That brought thee now with child," the Joseph of popular imagination says, confronting his wife's apparent betrayal. Yet the Joseph of tradition miraculously soldiers on, laboring like a very bandog, searching for shelter where Mary can give birth, fleeing to Egypt to protect his young foster son, traveling to Jerusalem to have his firstborn dedicated at the Temple, returning to the Temple courtyard in search of Jesus when he was left behind as a twelve-year-old. "Son, why have you treated us so? Behold, your father and I have been looking for you anxiously," Mary reprimands her son, only to be told a mystery. "How is it that you sought me?" Jesus replies. "Did you not know that I must be in my Father's house?"

In such riddles, we are vividly reminded of Joseph's surrogate status. Yet his fidelity did not waver; not much, anyway. Doubtless that is the obvious and yet difficult point. All human constancy seems miraculous given the transitory nature of things. The faithful are vulnerable to the mockery of the world. As Joseph is. As Leopold Bloom is in his essentially chaste marriage to the adulterous Molly. Joyce even plays these two cuckolds off against each other. "Qui vous a mis dans cette fichue position?" Stephen Dedalus idly remembers a French joke. "C'est le pigeon, Joseph." Similarly, Buck Mulligan, Stephen's blaspheming companion, put the implausibility of Jesus' origins into the "Ballad of the Joking Jesus."

I'm the queerest young fellow that ever you heard.
My mother's a jew, my father's a bird.
With Joseph the joiner I cannot agree,
So here's to disciples and Calvary.

Ulysses is notoriously the chronicle of the exceedingly ordinary events of that June day in 1904 (the actual day
Joyce met his wife, Nora). Joyce's mock-epic gives to the
humblest of human activities and the humblest of lives
the solemnity of ritual. In both the novel and the story
of Joseph, what is most characteristically human depends
on memory and the tangible presence of the past. That
depth of time and experience finally depends on simple,
or not so simple, human constancy and love. In *Ulysses,*
that love is manifest in the life Bloom and Molly have
shared, and which now, despite every betrayal, is an in-
expungable part of who they are individually. Constancy,
for which Joseph is rightly remembered, is the essential
virtue. Without it—without daily human promise-
making and -keeping—we cannot hope to see ourselves
or life whole. Promise-keeping connects the past to the
future—it gives structure to the disconnected flux of
events and experience. Leopold Bloom's transcendent
virtue is this sort of dogged constancy. His dead father
and son, for example, live vividly in his memory, shaping
his every living expectation and feeling. His unfaithful
wife is still his wife. This humane steadfastness prepares
him in turn to become Stephen Dedalus's spiritual father.

Like Joseph, Bloom is a practical family man, a Jew, a
provider and protector. Like Joseph, he is a prosaic figure
yet "a just man." It is said of Joseph that into his hands
was entrusted the saviour of the world, the incarnate
Word. Bloom is also entrusted with the incarnate word
in the form of Stephen Dedalus, future author of *Ulysses,*
the word made flesh on the page. As Karl Rahner wrote
of Joseph, Bloom is very much a protector of the grace
of God in its embodied life when he allows himself to
become the lost and betrayed Stephen's guardian.

Like Joseph, Bloom is a cuckold who yet demonstrates a larger and truer loyalty, and in doing so reveals
a redemptive sense of human possibility. If Joseph must
call upon angels to assuage his doubts over Mary's miraculous conception, Bloom calls upon the angels of his
better nature to accept his wife's waywardness with loving equanimity. "By what reflections did he, a conscious
reactor against the void incertitude, justify to himself his
sentiments?" Bloom answers: ". . . the futility of triumph
or protest or vindication: the inanity of extolled virtue:
the lethargy of nescient matter: the apathy of the stars."
In other words, Bloom will trust his heart against the
logic of the calculating world. Life's betrayals cannot be
remedied through human mastery and manipulation.
Bloom, the doting family man, knows that self-
sufficiency is an illusion. Love puts an end to self-
sufficiency. According to Anthony Burgess's wonderfully
engaging study *Rejoyce,* Bloom is also entrusted with the

word, for in becoming Stephen Dedalus's guardian Bloom gives shelter to the future author of *Ulysses*. In a typical Joycean paradox, Bloom is foster father to his own creator.

Fatherhood is one way in which men live that need, and is perhaps the most seductive way in which we try to extend our imagined control over life. But for Joyce, paternity is a sign of the limited nature of our control. Bloom is the truest father because he is the least vain of men. Paternity, like any good and truly human thing, is something given to us, not something we can claim authorship of. From the only begetter to the countless begotten—from Joseph the carpenter to Leopold Bloom the advertising man—human fathers are but intermediaries.

Bloom is also, of course, married to another Mary— the famous Molly—a Mary who is very much a second Eve, an earth mother, a sign of creation and renewal, and of life itself. In *Ulysses*, Molly is the center of things, and like the Virgin Mary she sanctifies in Joyce's scheme the bonds created between human beings by their bodies. In the famous litany of affirmation with which she concludes the novel, the adulterous Molly Bloom is understood to be just as much the handmaiden of creation as her virgin prototype. Mary and Joseph, Molly and Leopold, I want to say, are two of a kind.

For Joyce, fatherhood is a powerful sign of the paradoxical nature of reality. Similarly, Karl Barth, the Protestant theologian, saw in the mystery of Jesus' birth a sign of the ultimate nature of God. What was the meaning, Barth asked in his explication of the Creed, of "the miracle of the procreation of Jesus Christ without a father"? Mary's virginal conception of Jesus was not a sexual but a pneumatological act, an act of the Holy Spirit. As in Genesis, God's breath—"the pigeon," as Joyce notes—impregnates Mary. "God himself takes the stage as the Creator and not as a partner to this Virgin," Barth writes. Yet it is within a woman's body that this new creation and ultimate self-revelation of God takes form. Joseph, as said earlier, is pointedly "excluded." What then are we to make of the "powerless figure of Joseph"?

Barth regards Joseph's exclusion as a judgment. To the extent that "the male [is understood] as the specific agent of human action and history," such perishable human accomplishment is subordinated to God's power as creator and redeemer. Joseph as representative man is a symbol of all human vanity, of "the sovereignty of human will and power and activity generally." In this sense, perhaps it is as fathers—as worldly creators— that men are most tempted to imagine themselves self-sufficient and self-perpetuating. Both Joyce and the Bible suggest that such hubris is less a temptation for women, who in giving birth to all new life have a more realistic understanding of our connection and dependence on the source of life itself. (Barth does not argue that men are innately more creative or women immune to sin.) "In

this sovereignty"—in this human longing for mastery
and autonomy—"man is not free for God's Word."
Only "when his sovereignty is excluded, he is able to
believe in the Word of God."

Or the words of Joyce. Saint Joseph, like Leopold
Bloom, remains a compelling figure because of the way
he relinquishes sovereignty where we expect him to de-
mand it most. In looking to either man, it is possible to
see that what we pride ourselves on giving to others—
our trust, fidelity, and love—is not ours to withhold; that
what we receive in return is not ours to keep. Where at
first we feel most excluded—"So where, exactly, do you
fit in?" asked my wife—we are ultimately most at home.
For, finally, we cannot make ourselves happy. Fulfillment
must come from outside—it must come as a gift. That is
the multifaceted paradox embodied in these two figures.
Joseph and Bloom participate in the transcendent by the
measure of their self-abnegation; they find reconciliation
not in retribution or even justice, but through faith and
love; they embrace human finitude as an affirmation of
mystery, not its denial. They are most fully themselves,
and their stories most open to a transcendent reality,
when they are least self-regarding. Bloom asleep alongside Molly and Joseph alongside Mary are icons of hope-
fulness. That, at least, is what this husband and father
takes away from their strikingly similar stories.

SAINT THOMAS
APOSTLE

Seen and Not Seen

PAUL ELIE

IN THE SUMMER of 1993 the Metropolitan Museum of
Art exhibited a pair of bronze sculptures by the Renaissance master Andrea del Verrocchio. Since 1483 the two
figures had stood in a cupola outside the Orsanmichele
in Florence, exposed to sun and moon, wind and rain,
chimney smoke and car exhaust, until their surfaces
were hardly visible under layers of grime. In 1988 they
were removed for restoration, and five years later they
were put on view at the Metropolitan, flanked by exhibits

that showed how they had been restored and how they had been cast in the first place, five centuries ago.

"Verrocchio's Christ and St. Thomas" was the sort of modest, unsung, scholarly exhibition that even the most ardent museum patron can miss without knowing the difference. I almost missed it myself. I had come to the museum intending to see the Magritte retrospective, but the line was a Sunday afternoon long, so I wandered into the cool dark rooms of medieval art, just looking. Here were works I knew well, shorn of wonder by their familiarity. I paid my respects and moved on. Farther in, the Lehman wing was brightly lit, and there the two figures loomed up like some medieval prophet's vision of the Renaissance beyond—Christ and Saint Thomas, a pas de deux in shining bronze. Christ's right hand was raised in blessing; his left one pulled his cloak away from his side so that Thomas, leaning toward him, might see the wound there, and touch it, and know him as the risen Lord.

I wasn't just looking anymore. Something majestic was being enacted in the next room. I went closer to see for myself—and I had an insight there, as Thomas had had in Jerusalem two thousand years before, and I remembered how he had become my patron saint when I was confirmed as a Christian once upon a time. But I am getting ahead of my story, and Saint Thomas's.

Thomas's encounter with Christ is one of the more familiar episodes in the New Testament. We have an account in chapter 20 of John's gospel. Over the centuries scholars have conjectured a great deal about the authorship of this gospel. Because it is thick with concepts from neo-Platonic philosophy, for centuries it was thought to be the gospel written last and embellished most—the gospel most remote from the experience of the apostles. But more recent scholars have argued that its idiosyncrasies mark it as "authentic Jesus material." And no one has successfully dislodged the tradition that its first author was John the apostle, an eyewitness who recounts what he saw.

John tells us that on the evening of the day when Jesus rose from the dead—the first Easter Sunday—the apostles assembled in a room and barred the doors, afraid they would be persecuted. Yet Jesus came and stood among them. "Peace be with you," he said. Then he showed them his wounds. He breathed on them, and bid them receive the Holy Spirit (the Greek word *pneuma* means both "breath" and "spirit"). As the Father had sent him, he declared, so now he was sending them and with power: as they forgave sins so sins would be forgiven, and as they retained sins so sins would be retained.

Here enters the apostle who will be known till the end of time as Doubting Thomas. We have seen him before. He appears in all four gospels, and in John's account he emerges as ardent but hesitant, like Peter but without the keys to any kingdom. When Lazarus died and Jesus made plans to go to see Lazarus's sisters in Judea even though he might be stoned there, Thomas said: "'Let us also go, that we may die with him.'" Later, when Jesus tried to explain his destiny to the apostles, Thomas didn't understand, so he pressed the point, prompting Jesus' boldest declaration about himself. "'You know the way I am going,'" Jesus said. But Thomas didn't know, and he said so. "'Lord, we do not know where you are going; how can we know the way?'" To which Jesus replied, "'I am the way, the truth, and the life.'"

This Thomas, John tells us, was absent from the group on the evening after Jesus rose from the dead. "Now Thomas, one of the twelve, called the Twin, was not with them when Jesus came." In the days afterward, the disciples told him they'd seen Jesus. But Thomas had his doubts, and he knew what it would take to dispel them. "'Unless I see in his hands the print of the nails, and place my finger in the mark of the nails, and place my hand in his side,'" he told them, "'I will not believe.'

"Eight days later," John continues, "his disciples were again in the house, and Thomas was with them." Again the doors were shut, yet again Jesus came and stood among them and offered them peace. Now Jesus' arrival might itself be a sign that he really had risen from the dead. Remember, there were bars on the doors. But Thomas still had his doubts, and rightly so, because if what he doubted (and this is what John suggests) was that the Jesus the others had seen was flesh and blood, a man walking and talking, Thomas would hardly be persuaded by a figure who was able to pass through locked doors.

Prove it to me, this Thomas insisted. Show us what you're made of.

Jesus turned to him and said, " 'Put your finger here, and see my hands; and put out your hand, and place it in my side; do not be faithless, but believing.' "

We don't know whether Thomas reached out then, whether he pressed his finger in Christ's wounded hands and felt the gash over his ribs. All we have is his reply, and it is enough.

" 'My Lord and my God,' " Thomas said.

" 'Have you believed because you have seen me?' " Christ asked Thomas. " 'Blessed are those who have not seen and yet believe.' "

In the moment Christ speaks as if to all time: his words rise from the text to address the reader directly, a line cast in a long high arc across the centuries to fall at our end of the pond. *Blessed are you, dear reader, you who have not seen me and yet believe.* But it is the visual image of the encounter, not the words, that hooks the mind and sinks in and doesn't let go. Christ reveals himself. Thomas reaches out. The other disciples look on.

John's account of Christ and Saint Thomas is read at services in the days after Easter, and in the Catholic parishes I know, it is often presented as a footnote to the Resurrection—a story on a human scale, easier for the ordinary churchgoer to understand and identify with than the astonishing and theologically packed accounts of Jesus' passion, death, and rising from the dead. The priest will note that Thomas is also called Didymus, "twin" in Greek, and he'll make this the moral of the story: Doubting Thomas is the most ordinary of believers, a twin to us all.

In Verrocchio's "Christ and St. Thomas," though, the encounter is rendered literally larger than life. Christ and Saint Thomas crowd out of the cupola that would enclose them. They are giants, with broad shoulders and deep chests, draped in cloaks that fall over them fold upon bronze fold. Thomas is the proverbial innocent of antiquity, all apple cheeks and flowing hair. And Christ—well, he looks the way a man who has died and come back to life might look: his face is lined, his eyes are hooded, his hairline has receded, and there are jagged gouges in his hands where the sculptor who created him, like the men who crucified him, must have hammered spikes through.

Seeing "Christ and St. Thomas," one can understand why Verrocchio was a favorite of the Medicis and the teacher of Leonardo and Botticelli. And yet the grandeur of the two figures seems to derive from something other than Verrocchio's way with bronze. Other artists have depicted the episode's natural climax, and shown Thomas touching Christ's wounds. Verrocchio has presented instead the moment just prior to that one, when Christ shows his wounds to Thomas. This arrangement is known in Christian iconography as "The Incredulity of St. Thomas," and it is a subtle and profound approach to the story. The moment of truth comes not when truth is confirmed, but when truth is revealed. It is open-ended, undecided, still in progress.

In Verrocchio's work this moment of truth is made incarnate with power, and the notion that Thomas is our twin is given body and soul. That day at the Met, I was struck by the way Thomas's experience of revelation resembles the experience of the person who looks at Verrocchio's sculptures. Thomas has come to see something; in a different way, so has the museum patron. As if to stress this kinship, Verrocchio has shown Thomas leaning in from the lip of the cupola, keeping a foothold in the world outside it—our world—with the huge toes of his right foot.

You don't have to be an art historian to feel that kinship in your bones. And you don't have to be a believing Christian to suppose that it finally has to do with religious experience. Thomas leans close to examine Christ, and meets his God. The art lover steps up to see the work, and encounters Christ. Christ invited Thomas to see and believe, and so has Verrocchio, in a work packed full of the implications of seeing and revealing.

I spent nearly an hour with the two figures that Sunday afternoon at the Metropolitan. I looked at them from every conceivable angle, now straight on, now from one side, now the other, now up close, now from afar, as though I hoped to make the work's solidly classical proportions fragmented and cubist. And I looked at the other people clustered around the sculptures. Most of them considered the work itself for a few moments and then moved on to the ancillary exhibits arrayed around it. In time I joined them. Glass cases displayed models of Christ and Saint Thomas—the size of G.I. Joe dolls—to demonstrate the "lost-wax" casting process. A series of photographs showed the two sculptures in their original cupola outside the Orsanmichele, their surfaces a rheumy green, and then at various stages of the restoration— hung on winches, laid on worktables, attended to by experts in lab coats and protective eyeglasses. A documentary film played over and over on a television in a far corner, filling the gallery with the narrator's coolly authoritative voice.

The side exhibits were very interesting. There was something comforting in the way the models and photographs reduced the two figures to the scale of our own time, presented them as the subjects of chemical analysis and curatorial know-how. And yet I kept returning to the figures themselves. They held their poses in the cupola, caught forever in the act of encounter. Christ pulled his

cloak away from his side. Thomas leaned toward him.
So did I. I was in the mood to wonder.

Thomas struggled to see Christ with his own eyes—as
flesh and blood, and as Lord and God. For this, the
church has recognized him as the patron saint of people
who suffer from blindness. That is wonderfully paradoxical. I would like to go further, though. I think we can
recognize Thomas as a patron or type of all those who
would reckon with Christ, and I think we can see his
encounter with Christ as a definitive example of how that
reckoning might come about.

No one today can see Christ the way Thomas did.
We cannot be present in a locked room in Jerusalem in
the first century, eating and praying and going over the
events of the past week when Christ comes by. We cannot put our finger into the wounds in Christ's hands, or
place our hand in his side. We cannot look him in the
eye and say, "My Lord and my God." Christ himself
seems to have acknowledged this when he called blessed
those who have not seen and yet believe, and the New
Testament is full of warnings to those who would see
the divine. Thus Paul, who was blinded by lightning during his conversion, called faith "the substance of things
hoped for, the evidence of things not seen," and observed that Christians must live by faith and not by sight.

Yet those who would believe in Christ must see him,

somehow, and must see him for who he is. Arguably this is the point of the Doubting Thomas story. If anyone is going to believe in Christ, he has got to reckon with him personally—see him with his own eyes. John, whose gospel is an account of what he has seen, tells how Thomas reckoned with Christ so that other would-be believers might be led to reckon with him themselves.

In itself that doesn't tell us much. For practically every passage in the gospels is a record of somebody's reckoning with Christ—as a son, a teacher, a healer, a feeder of multitudes; as a religious rebel, a threat to public order, and a convicted criminal; as a stranger on the Emmaus road, and as risen Lord and God, ascending to heaven but promising to return when the time is right.

Thomas's encounter with Christ occupies a special place in the gospels, though. Scripture scholars have proposed that John's gospel, traditionally placed last when the four are grouped, originally concluded with chapter 20, the account of Thomas and Christ being followed only by a brief coda: "Now Jesus did many other signs in the presence of the disciples, which are not written in this book; but these are written so that you may believe that Jesus is the Christ, the Son of God, and that believing you may have life in his name." Presented at the end of the gospel accounts, Christ's revelation of himself to Thomas at once sums up those signs and wonders we've read about and points toward those we can only imagine. And Thomas's response can be seen as a précis of the shape conversion might take in those who would see Christ with their own eyes. Doubt yields to faith; sight leads to insight, and then, God willing, to vision. Thomas seeks God, and in the risen Christ he finds him.

If we are latter-day twins of Doubting Thomas—as the priests tell us in church on the Sunday after Easter—we've got to wonder just how a person today might see Christ. And some of us must wonder just how we might see Christ ourselves, with our own eyes. How, how? Tell us. Show us. Let us know. Twenty centuries is a long time, and wayward history has accumulated on the figure of Christ like grime on a bronze giant; we look around us, and don't see signs and wonders but a broken world, a fractious people, and no end in sight, just length of days unfolding further and further away from the moment of truth. With Ivan Karamazov, we say: Sure, we would believe, if only we too could know Christ personally, as the apostles did, if only we could see for ourselves the miracles we're told he performed.

What must we see in order to believe? Where do we stand in relation to Christ and his contemporaries, such as Saint Thomas? Kierkegaard dwelt on these questions at length in *Philosophical Fragments,* weighing what he called "The Case of the Contemporary Disciple" against that of "The Disciple at Second Hand." As Kierkegaard saw it, the disciple who was a contemporary of Jesus (called "the God" in his text) had the great advantage of seeing him with his own eyes. "But may he also believe that this makes him a disciple? By no means. If he believes his eyes, he is deceived, for the God is not immediately knowable." For Christ is knowable only through faith, which is granted by God. Given this, the disciple who had actually seen Christ probably found it *harder* to believe as a result. "He is constantly reminded that he did not see or hear the God immediately, but merely a humble human being who said of himself that he was the God."

For the disciple at second hand, things are harder in some ways—but easier in others. Distant in time from the events in Jerusalem, he must sift through all the "gossip, chatter, rumors" and the like that have come to surround Christ, and he is insulated from the shock of Christ's appearing, which would make clear just how radical a proposition faith in Christ is. To his advantage, the notion that God walked the earth has been "naturalized" over time, and so in some ways has become easier to believe. More important, this disciple's distance from Christ in time reminds him that his stance toward Christ is founded upon faith and not mere historical evidence. Kierkegaard found a characteristically brilliant metaphor for this: "Is not Venice built over the sea, even if it became so solidly built up that a generation finally came upon the scene that did not notice it; and would it not be a sad misunderstanding if this last generation made the mistake of permitting the piles to rot and the city to sink?"

Kierkegaard's point is that "all disciples are essentially equal." The contemporary disciple and the disciple of the last generation—our generation—stand in the same relation to Christ. We become his disciples—and his contemporaries—through faith.

Kierkegaard was a Lutheran and deeply iconoclastic, and these aspects of his character help to explain his insistence that Christ can be known through faith alone. In declaring his own contemporaries equals of Christ's through their faith, he could more or less take for granted that Christ had been made known to them through the churches and through a vigorous Christian culture—art, music, liturgy, philosophy—present in Denmark and the rest of Europe at that time.

This can no longer be taken for granted. Christ is still present in our culture, but even in the churches there is doubt about whether he ought to be, and even those who would see Christ are reluctant to be seen as Christians, to make him known. And much of Christian culture today seems to dispel faith rather than call it forth.

Someone once wrote that the church is Christ made visible. Here and now such a thought seems smug and dishonest, an echo from a presumptuous age. Yet if it can't be said that the church is Christ made visible, it can't be denied that the church should make Christ visible. That is its work in the world. And in these circumstances, the Doubting Thomas story makes clear that the act of seeing Christ is intimately connected with the act of making him visible. Witnessing and bearing witness are two parts of the same encounter, and one encounter with Christ gives rise to another.

That's the way it was in the church's beginning, with Christ's first disciples. Once they had seen Christ, so they were compelled to make him visible to others. John explained this in the opening passage of his first letter, in words that call to mind Thomas's encounter with Christ: "That which was from the beginning, which we have heard, which we have seen with our eyes, which we have looked upon and touched with our hands, concerning the word of life—the life was made manifest, and we saw it, and testify to it . . . that which we have seen and heard, we proclaim also to you." John made Christ visible by telling about him in his gospel, and through his account, Thomas's struggle to see Christ has become a way for others to see Christ for themselves.

We can see this in the Doubting Thomas story. After his rising Christ came by. The apostles saw him. They told Thomas. Thomas doubted. Then he came and saw him too. John was there. He saw it. And he let the world know.

Thomas himself went on to make Christ known to others as a missionary, according to the Christian tradition. He is said to have brought the gospel to parts of Persia, Syria, and India, where Christians on the Malabar coast have long called themselves "Christians of Saint Thomas." Tradition has it that he was martyred there, speared to death by an enemy of the gospel. His relics, according to Butler's *Lives of the Saints* (1759), have had a complicated journey: they were brought from Malabar to Edessa in Mesopotamia to the Aegean isle of Khios to Ortona, in the Abruzzi region of Italy, where they were still venerated in Butler's time.

The legends told of Saint Thomas are collected in works such as the third-century *Acts of Thomas,* which Saint Augustine dismissed as apocryphal, and *The Golden Legend,* a medieval collection of readings on the saints. In these legends, as in John's gospel, Thomas is ardent but hesitant. One tells how the apostles divided up the parts of the known world as destinations for their missionary work. India fell to Thomas, but he was reluctant to go there even after Christ appeared to him in a vision. "Send me anywhere but India," Thomas begged. Christ then appeared to an Indian king, Gundafor, and sold Thomas to him as a slave. (Christ as a slave trader? Clearly Thomas was to be a slave to the gospel.) When Thomas arrived in India the king asked him his trade, and learning that he was a carpenter, commissioned him to build a new palace. But while the king was away Thomas preached and taught instead, and gave the building funds to the poor.

From this point Butler's telling cannot be improved upon. "On his return Gundafor asked to be shown his new palace. 'You cannot see it now, but only when you have left this world,' replied Thomas. Whereupon the king cast him into prison and purposed to flay him alive. But just then Gundafor's brother died, and being shown in heaven the palace that Thomas's good works had prepared for Gundafor, he was allowed to come back to earth and offer to buy it from the king for himself. Gundafor declined to sell, and in admiration released Thomas and received baptism together with his brother and many of his subjects."

Here we have Thomas seen through the eyes of medieval Christendom. He balks about his work in the world, but in his faith he is sure. Once, he had to see for himself before believing; now, his eyes are on heaven, his claim in things not seen.

Thomas appears more characteristically in a legend of the Virgin Mary's Assumption. It is believed that upon her death Mary was assumed into heaven, body and soul. As the story goes, Thomas wasn't present at the bedside when Mary died, and when the other apostles told him what had happened to her, how she had gone, he doubted it. But an angel appeared to him and dropped into his hands the girdle Mary had worn; then, and only then, did he believe.

It seems obvious that this legend is the Doubting Thomas story clearly adapted to suit a different miracle. Even so, the legend suggests a religious truth: that even after he had seen the risen Christ, Thomas had fits of unbelief. At the Cloisters one afternoon I came upon a fifteenth-century German wood carving of the legend which presents his predicament in splendid miniature. The other apostles—dressed like burghers—are shown gathered around Mary's deathbed, and through an open door the absent Thomas is seen scrambling up a rock precipice to where the angel dangles Mary's girdle above him. For Thomas, faith is an uphill climb; the signs are before his eyes but just out of reach.

Apocryphal, incredible, contrived to support a point of Marian doctrine, with Christ absent and an angel appearing at the moment of truth, the legend of Thomas and the girdle displays all the qualities that made the Protestant reformers suspicious of the saints, and that make us suspicious of them today. But the biblical account on which it is based suggests why the saints are vital to Christian belief in any age. Thomas's experience one Sunday in a locked room in Jerusalem presents in bold relief the would-be Christian's encounter with Christ. Thomas doubts, yes, but he seeks. He sees Christ for himself. He recognizes him as God. And once he has seen Christ, he makes Him known to others.

These are the essentials of the life of a saint, really any one. For whatever else they are, the lives of the saints are records of personal encounters with Christ from his time down to ours. In them we can see the great variety of ways people have seen Christ with their own eyes, then gone on to make him known.

How unfortunate, then, that in an effort to emphasize the need for a personal encounter with Christ the church has come to doubt the usefulness of the saints. John Paul II has canonized prolifically, but the church in North America is unsure and even embarrassed about the saints. Saints are present to us as statues or the occasion for feast days, as symbols of ethnic solidarity or the stuff of theological quandaries, but they generally are not seen as people who sought God and in Christ found him made known.

So it was that when it came time for me to be confirmed as a Catholic Christian a dozen years ago, I knew almost nothing about the saints. I was sixteen, and my family belonged to a suburban parish that seemed determined to symbolize American Catholics' emancipation from the urban, ethnic, tradition-soaked enclaves typical of the church earlier in the century. The parish church, dedicated in 1963, was named not for a saint but for a doctrine—the Assumption, which had been promulgated only in 1950 (five hundred years after that German artist depicted Saint Thomas scrambling up a rock face for Mary's veil). It was (and is) built of red brick and shaped like a seashell, the pews fanned out around the altar; in the windows, pieces of stained glass had been cut into triangles and diamonds and trapezoids and then combined to form abstracted figures of Christ and the apostles. The pastor and his associates were decent, genial, no-nonsense men who made the effort to make the gospel relevant to the parishioners' lives, and to leave out the sticky accretions of history and culture, of Latin and plainchant and scholastic theology—all the bars of the cage from which, due to the Second Vatican Council, the church and its people had just been sprung.

One priest who had worked in the parish was now the bishop of the diocese, and he would return in the spring to confirm several dozen of us in our faith. During the winter we prepared for confirmation in weekly classes organized around a workbook called *Making Moral Decisions,* and in a retreat during which we were asked to lie in the pews and pray. Then, one evening a month before the date of the rite, we were told to return the next week having picked a confirmation name, that of the saint who would be the patron of our adult lives in faith.

My father was waiting in the parking lot in his green '74 Valiant, and as we drove home I explained the assignment. There was a problem, I told him. I didn't know about any saints.

"Well," he said. "There's Saint Francis of Assisi, and Saint Francis Xavier, the missionary, and Saint Bonaventure, the medieval theologian—the college in Buffalo is named for him. There's Saint John, and there's Paul—but you already have his name. And there's Saint Thomas—

Thomas Aquinas, the philosopher, and Thomas More, he was a martyr, and the apostle Thomas. Doubting Thomas."

"Right, right." He was naming the greatest saints, the most intellectual ones, I could tell, appealing to my exalted sense of myself. I appreciated the effort. He was missing the point, though, and I told him so. Here I was, supposedly ready to be confirmed, and I didn't know anything about those saints except what he told me. Wasn't it wrong to be confirmed in a faith I really didn't understand or even know much about? Wasn't that shallow and hypocritical, exactly what Jesus wouldn't want?

We were almost home. He turned down our road. The headlights flashed on the siding of the house on the corner.

"Maybe you're right," he said. "Maybe you're not ready to be confirmed after all." And then: "Maybe you don't believe."

"Maybe not," I said. "Maybe I never will."

"May be."

He pulled the car into the driveway and we went inside, and right away I called Eileen. She was my best friend, and I was in love with her—in love with the way she abandoned chemistry-lab procedures in favor of spontaneous public readings from *Look Homeward, Angel* and the *Norton Anthology of Poetry*.

I asked her if she knew what her confirmation name would be.

"Thomas," she said. "For Thomas Wolfe, because he's my saint, isn't he? It's supposed to be meaningful, the name is supposed to mean something to you. I don't care what they say. I'm going to be confirmed and my patron is going to be Thomas."

It was decided. I was going to be confirmed and my patron was going to be Thomas.

We were confirmed in our seashell church a month later, dozens of us, all with new names of obscure provenance. Eileen delivered the first reading, I, the second. After the gospel, the bishop performed the rite itself. He sat in a chair in front of the altar. We stepped up, one at a time. Eileen had learned that he disliked the prospect of confirming a girl in the name of Thomas, but she went right ahead, and so did he, etching the sign of the cross on our foreheads with his right hand.

What about the crisis of faith that had struck me as my father and I rode home from church in the green Valiant that evening? I hadn't resolved it. In a sense I never have, and don't fully expect to. But my father had told me what I needed to know. While he couldn't give me a crash course in the lives of the saints, he made clear that confirmation was an authentic sounding of my experience of Christ as I surged toward adulthood. My doubts were my own. My faith was my own. I was free to see Christ for myself, and it was up to me to reckon with him in the encounter. Thomas the apostle was my patron saint after all.

And what a patron. He is the patron saint of doubters, of those of us who find that belief and disbelief trade places in the soul like watchmen taking shifts; he is the patron saint of those who suffer from blindness, who try as we might can't see as we ought. I want to go further, though, to claim more. Thomas is the patron of all of us who would try to see Christ for ourselves, who would dare to draw close, to reach out and touch him and know him as Lord. Thomas is our twin, yes—but more than that he is Christ's twin, the human person Christ came to make himself known for. One is of God, the other is one of us, yet they are figures cast from the same bronze, forever joined in an encounter, the end of the story still waiting to be told.

Between "Point Vierge" and the "Usual Spring"

KATHLEEN NORRIS

For the birds there is not a time that they tell, but the *point vierge* between darkness and light, between nonbeing and being. You can tell yourself the time by their waking, if you are experienced. But that is your folly, not theirs.

—Thomas Merton, *Conjectures of a Guilty Bystander*

I FIRST CAME TO the virgin martyrs as an adult, and from a thoroughly Protestant background, which may explain why I have little trouble taking them seriously. I find them relevant, even important, but many Catholics I know so resent the way they were taught about these saints that they've shoved them to the back of the closet. "Why are you writing about the virgin martyrs?" one Benedictine sister asked me, incredulous and angry: "They set women back! As if in order to be holy, you had to be a virgin, preferably a martyr. And that's not

where most women are." Another friend relates, "In parochial school, we were taught things like, 'She sacrificed
her life to preserve her virginity,' and we thought, well,
why didn't she just give it to him—like a handbag? The
nuns never explained to us what virginity *was*. They
didn't want you to know exactly *what* you weren't supposed to give up, so you were regularly confused by
these cryptic narratives."

The women who provoke such irritation and puzzle-
ment, identified in the church's liturgical calendar as "virgin and martyr," were among the first women revered
by Christians as saints. Most date from the persecution
of Christians under the Roman Emperors Decius and Di-
ocletian in the third and fourth centuries, but they range
from second-century Rome to sixth-century Persia,
where Christians were persecuted by both Persian emperors and Jewish kings. They were a source of inspiration to Christians through the Middle Ages, but today
they are maddeningly elusive. There is no entry for "virgin martyr" in *The Catholic Encyclopedia,* and one can
search entries there, and in *The Encyclopedia of Early Christianity,* on both "virginity" and "martyrdom" without
getting a picture of these women or their importance in
church history. A secular reference, the *Women's Studies
Encyclopedia,* reveals that while the tales of early women
saints and martyrs (some of them virgins) have largely
been dismissed as legendary, historical sources do exist,
notably the *Ecclesiastical History* of Eusebius, written early

in the fourth century, and the third-century *Passion of Perpetua and Felicitas,* which is especially valuable because Perpetua's diary—our main source for the episode—is also one of the only examples of women's writing to come down to us from antiquity.

Growing up a Methodist, I envied Catholic girls their name days, holy cards, medals, and stories of women saints. I had few female images of holiness, except for the silent Mary of the crèche, and "girls of the Bible" stories sanitized for middle-class consumption. It was a far less textured and ambiguous world than that of a Benedictine sister I know who recalls two virgin martyrs among the many images of women in the windows of her childhood church. "There was Barbara, and Catherine, my namesake," she says, "which made me enormously proud. I found it inspiring that women could be saints. I also remember that my mother used to pray to Saint Barbara 'for a happy death,' which seemed a powerful thing." Like many girls of the 1950s, she was also invigorated by Ingrid Bergman in the film *Joan of Arc.* "After I saw that movie," she said, "I had my hair cut short, and walked around *being* Joan. I had no armor, of course. My uniform, all that summer, was a faded blue sweatshirt."

But for all their power to inspire a young girl, the virgin martyrs convey an uneasy message of power and powerlessness. They die, horribly, at the hands of imperial authorities. They are sanctified by church authorities, who eventually betray them by turning their struggle and witness into pious cliché, and even by lying about the causes of their martyrdom. It's enough to make one wonder if the virgin martyrs merely witness to a sad truth: Whatever they do, or don't do, girls can't win. A book published in the early 1960s, *My Nameday—Come for Dessert,* is a perfect expression of this heady ambiguity. Offering both recipes and religious folklore, the book defines virgin martyrs as young women "who battled to maintain their integrity and faith." But the radical nature of this assertion—that girls could have such integrity as to suffer and be canonized for it—is lost in Betty Crocker land: "St. Dorothy was racked, scourged, and beheaded in Cappadocia. Her symbols are a basket of fruit and flowers, which may be incorporated in a copper mold for her nameday dessert."

A girl named Dorothy, reading such prose, might conclude that the world (or a part of it called Cappadocia) is a very dangerous place. At least until dessert. Eventually she might discover that, more than most saints, the virgin martyrs expose a nerve, a central paradox of Christian history: While the religion has often justified the restricting of women to subservient roles, it has also inspired women to break through such restrictions, often in astonishingly radical ways. And the church, typically, has emphasized the former at the expense of the latter.

The story of Dorothy is beautiful, in a way. A young

woman who has refused a lawyer's proposal of marriage
is mocked by him as she is being led away to her execu-
tion. Her crime, as with most of the virgin martyrs, is
being a committed Christian who refuses to marry or to
worship idols as required under Roman law. The young
man calls out to Dorothy, asking her to send him fruits
from the garden of paradise. This she agrees to do.
When, after her death, an angel delivers three apples and
three roses, the young man converts to Christianity and
is also martyred. Dorothy, then, is a dangerous young
rebel, a woman with the power to change a man and to
subvert the Roman state, in which, as Gilbert Marcus has
noted in *The Radical Tradition,* "marriage and the family
were the basis of *imperium* . . . the guarantee of the gods
that Rome would continue."

Although the names of many of the young women
martyrs of the early church are known to us (Agatha,
Agnes, Barbara, Catherine, Cecilia, Dorothy, Lucy, Margaret), the political nature of their martyrdom has been
obscured by the passage of time and by church teaching
that glorifies their virginity, which we erroneously conceive of as a passive condition. For them, virginity was
anything but passive; it was a state of being, of powerful
potential, a *point vierge* from which they could act in radical resistance to authority.

The vigorous virginity of these martyrs has also been
muted by the language Church Fathers have used to describe them. Contrast an account of the sixth-century

slave Mahya—who ran through the streets of her south
Arabian town of Najran, after her owners and family
have been put to death, shouting: "Men and women,
Christians, now is the moment to pay back to Christ
what you owe him. Come out and die for Christ, just as
he died for you. . . . This is the time of battle!"—with
the words of Methodius of Sicily, in a passage still found
in the Roman Breviary for the feast of Saint Agatha:
"She wore the glow of a pure conscience and the crimson
of the Lamb's blood for her cosmetics." While this imagery may have impressed Agatha's bravery upon Methodius's original ninth-century congregation, to us it just
seems sick.

We live at the end of a century sickened by violence.
Any claim we make to an enlightened modernity must
be weighed against the fact that child prostitution is big
business on a global scale; that most marriages in the
world are arranged, as they were in ancient Rome, for
economic and/or social advantage (the most advanta-
geous being the selling of a young daughter to an older,
wealthier man); that female infanticide and genital mutilation are still commonly practiced in many cultures; that
in more civilized countries, the stalking, rape and often
the murder of young women are staples not only of the
nightly news but of dramatic entertainment. Maybe it's
time to reclaim a *point vierge,* and try to hear what the
virgin martyrs are saying.

The most recent virgin martyr to be officially sanctified by the church is Maria Goretti, a twelve-year-old who was stabbed to death during an attempted rape in 1902 by a man we would now term a "stalker." Maria Goretti was an Italian peasant from a town near Anzio, a girl in a vulnerable position, both economically and socially. Her father had died when she was ten, and, reading between the lines of the Roman Breviary ("she spent a difficult childhood assisting her mother in domestic duties"), we can assume that both child and mother were at the extreme margins of a marginal culture. For a young man to take advantage of such a situation is not unusual, nor is his resorting to violence when he is rebuffed. We understand these facts all too well, from similar events in our own day.

Maria Goretti, canonized in 1950, was the first virgin martyr declared such by the church for defending her chastity rather than her faith, and it's easy to see this development in a cynical light: a perfect expression of a sexually uptight era. Indeed, a popular pamphlet of the time, written by an American priest, dubbed her "the Cinderella Saint." But our cynicism blinds us to a deeper truth: A martyr is not a model to be imitated, but a witness, one who testifies to a new reality. And our own era's obsession with sexual "liberation" blinds us still further, making it difficult to see the true nature of Maria Goretti's witness, what it might mean for a peasant girl to "prefer death to dishonor." We may make fun of someone so foolish—a male friend recalls with shame

how he and his schoolmates snickered over Maria Goretti in the playground of his parochial school, not long
after she was canonized—but such joking is a middle-
class luxury.

For Maria Goretti, the issue was not a roll in the
hay. The loss of her virginity in a rigidly patriarchal
peasant culture could have had economic and social consequences so dire that it might well have seemed a choice
between being and nonbeing. And is it foolish for a girl
to have such a strong sense of her self that she resists its
violation, resists being asked to do, in the private spaces
of her body, what she does not want to do? When I was
fifteen, and extremely naive, I was attacked by a young
man, a college student, who I'm sure remembers the evening as a failed attempt at seduction. What I remember
is my anger, the ferocity of my determination to fight
him off. I know now that I'm lucky that I was able to
simply wear him out; another man might have beat me
unconscious and then raped me. It happens more than
we like to think, even to middle-class girls like me. But
the poor are far more vulnerable; perhaps the scandal of
Maria Goretti is the recognition that there can be bodily
integrity, honor, and even holiness among the poorest of
the poor—that even a peasant girl can claim an inner
self that no man can touch.

What we resist seeing in late-twentieth-century
America—where we are conditioned, relentlessly, by images of girls' and women's bodies as *available*—is how

fierce a young girl's sense of bodily integrity can be. Pre-pubescent and adolescent girls often express, as Robert Bolt writes of Saint Thomas More in his preface to *A Man for All Seasons,* "an adamantine sense of self." This is not necessarily a sure sense of who they are—in girls, this is still developing—but, rather, a solid respect for their physical boundaries. In the early Christian martyrs, this expressed itself as an unshakable faith in Jesus Christ, which enabled them to defy worldly authority. And, as Andrea Dworkin observes in a chapter on virginity in her book *Intercourse,* each of the virgin martyrs "viewed the integrity of her physical body as synonymous with the purity of her faith, her purpose, her self-determination, her honor."

The virgin martyrs make me wonder if the very idea of girls *having* honor is a scandal, and if this is a key to the power that their stories still have to shock us, and, even more important, to subvert authority, which now, as in the ancient world, rests largely in the hands of males. The genocidal excesses of our century have not dulled our capacity to be appalled by the brutality of the tortures inflicted on these young women. If anything, our era has made us more fully aware of the psychological dynamic of sexual violence against women that these stories express so unconsciously, in raw form.

The story of the fourth-century martyr Saint Lucy of Syracuse is typical of the genre. At the age of fourteen (the median age for marriage in a culture that expected women to bear five children on average and die young, often in childbirth), Lucy was betrothed to a young pagan nobleman. Inspired by an earlier virgin martyr, Saint Agatha, Lucy refused him and gave her goods to the poor. Both acts marked her as a Christian, and as Agnes Dunbar's *A Dictionary of Saintly Women* (1904) recounts: "The young man to whom she was betrothed denounced her as a Christian before the governor, Pascasius, who spoke insultingly to her. As she openly defied him, he ordered her to be dragged away" to a brothel, that she might be raped there, "but it was found that neither strong men with ropes nor magicians with their spells could move her an inch; so Pascasius had a fire lighted to burn her where she stood; but as the flames had no power against her, one of the servants killed her by plunging a dagger into her throat."

Other versions of Lucy's story, like so many of these tales, provide detailed accounts of the verbal give-and-take between the martyr and the governing authorities, who are both enraged and frightened by the claim of the martyrs to an inviolable, divinely grounded sense of self. Saints Barbara, Catherine, Irene, and Margaret, among others, give speeches so replete with scriptural allusions that they amount to a form of preaching. Here is Mahya again, as Sebastian Brock and Susan Ashbrook Harvey describe her in *Holy Women of the Syrian Orient,* "castigating her torturers with a mighty freedom in the Spirit. . . . Publically stripped naked at the orders of the king,

Mahya yet holds to her dignity, boldly stating, 'It is to your shame...that you have done this; I am not ashamed myself...for I am a woman—such as created by God.' Had she finished her scriptural allusion," the authors note, "Mahya would have added, 'created by God in his own image,'" both male and female. Typically, such speech angers male rulers; an account of the Syrian martyr Euphemia states that "Priscus the Proconsul was troubled in his mind that he was overcome by a woman." And typically, the more the martyrs talk back, the more they mock those in power by their allegiance to Christ and his invincible power, the more frenzied is the male response, and the more the violence escalates. It's not pleasant reading, but it is good psychology.

It should come as no surprise that the virgin martyrs are both admired and feared for their intelligence, and for their articulate tongues; Catherine of Alexandria, for example, is the patron saint of philosophers because she converted the fifty philosophers who were sent to explain to her the error of her ways. No surprise, either, that they are often tortured by having their tongues torn out; it's one way to silence a woman. But a theme of many of the stories is the martyr's miraculous ability to remain lucid, even eloquent, throughout her tortures; to retain even the capacity for worship (expressed best in these memorable words: "plunged into a cauldron of burning pitch, she lived for three days, singing praises"). While this outrages the modern consciousness, it also demonstrates that the silencing of holy women is not easily accomplished.

Accounts of virgin martyrs are so full of what one critic has termed "imaginative chaff" that they've typically been dismissed by church historians, labeled "dubious," "spurious," "a farrago of impossibilities." To appreciate the relevance of the virgin martyrs for our own time, we need to ask not whether or not the saint existed, but why it might have been necessary to invent her; we need not to get hung up on determining to what extent her story has been embellished by hagiographers, but to ask why the stories were so popular in the early church, and also to contemplate what we have lost in denigrating them. A case in point is Thecla, a virgin and, by some accounts, a martyr of the second century. Her cult was officially suppressed by the Catholic Church in 1969—she is thought never to have existed—and few people other than scholars are aware of her today. But, as Englebert's *Lives of the Saints* informs us, "there was no more famous name in Christian antiquity."

One can easily see how Thecla's story would have appealed to women in a church that had begun to consolidate power in its male clergy. Converted to Christianity by the apostle Paul, she becomes an apostle herself. When Paul refuses to baptize her, fearing that because of her youth and beauty she will not remain celibate, Thecla baptizes herself. Paul, having learned his lesson, later commissions her to preach. Thecla is one of several miracle-working women mentioned in apocryphal acts of the apostles, and as scholar Gail Paterson Corrington writes in *Women in Early Christianity,* "the equality of the female convert to the male apostle is frequently demonstrated both by her assumption of his role and functions (teaching, baptizing, preaching) and by the continuity of her apostolic work without his assistance." In studying the relevance of the virgin martyrs for our own time, we might also note that belief in their power still shows up in surprising ways. As a Benedictine historian wrote to me, "I have always been struck by the inverse ratio of historical knowledge about a saint and the oral tradition. We know nothing about Agatha other than the tradition of her death during Decius' persecution in the East coast of Sicily." The monk continues, "But when I ran across a statue of Agatha in a Chicago fire station and a year later saw people in Catania, Sicily, invoking Agatha's intercession to keep Mt. Etna's lava at bay, I had to admit to an incredibly deep and broad current of tradition at work."

Ironically, it is by taking the virgin martyr stories at face value that we can best see the kernel of meaning that they contain, their wealth of possibility. Surely it is significant that the "acts" of these young women, based on the acts of the apostles, those in turn based on the actions of Jesus in the gospels, incorporated the hopes of an embattled and vulnerable Christian minority. Their stories often strike me as Christianity of the most radical sort; these seemingly powerless girls were able to do what Jesus did, and change the world around them. Irene, for example, a first-century martyr, raises her father from the dead after his attempt to kill her (by having her dragged by wild horses—a typical grotesquerie) results in his own death. She brings back a child from the dead, and later raises *herself* from the dead, an event which results in the conversion to Christianity of many thousands.

What may be most valuable for modern people in the accounts of virgin martyrs is the depth of psychological truth they contain. An account of Saint Barbara states that her father, a wealthy man, built "a strong, two-windowed tower in which he did keep and close her so that no man should see her great beauty." When Barbara escapes his control—surreptitiously baptized a Christian, she convinces the workmen to add a third window, so that she may meditate on the Trinity—her father's rage is without bounds. It is he who betrays her to government authorities for refusing to worship pagan gods. When their tortures, including a scourging and burning, do not work, but seem only to strengthen Barbara's resolve to pray, the men beat her with hammers and lop off her breasts. Finally, it is her father who drags her up a mountain by her hair and beheads her. He is then struck dead by lightning. A dysfunctional relationship, to say the least. In our day, Barbara and her dad might end up on the front pages, fodder for the true-crime market.

And where is Barbara's power in all this? The oddly satisfying logic of hagiographical construction makes her the patron saint not only of stonemasons, architects, and prisoners, but of electricians and artillery gunners—of anyone, in fact, in danger of sudden death. Here the depth of Barbara's radical subversion is made clear. While she is most commonly depicted holding her tower, she is also one of the very few women saints who is sometimes pictured holding the eucharistic elements, a chalice and host. A person in danger of dying without receiving the last rites from a priest may pray to Barbara, and it's taken care of; she replaces the priest, and the sacrament.

One would think that Barbara's priestly attributes, or those of Petronilla, a first-century martyr, whose "usual emblem," according to the *Oxford Dictionary of Saints*, is "a set of keys, presumably borrowed from St. Peter," would make them favorites of Catholic feminists; instead, like the other virgin martyrs, they are largely forgotten, considered an embarrassment by women still smarting from the prayers of the old Roman Missal, which managed to be both sappy and insulting in giving thanks that God "didst bestow the victory of martyrdom on the weaker sex." But to forget a martyr is to put her through another martyrdom. Eric Partridge's *Origins* gives as the origins of our English word "martyr" both the Latin *memor* (mindfulness) and the Greek *martus* (witness); which suggests that when we are no longer mindful of a martyr, we lose her witness, we render her suffering meaningless.

I believe that the meaning, and the relevance, of the virgin martyrs rests in what one scholar of the early church, Francine Cardman, terms their "defiance of the conventions of female behavior," a defiance that their belief in Christ made possible. Knowing that they were loved by Christ gave them the strength to risk a way of life that was punishable by death (under Roman law, both a soldier's refusal to fight and a woman's refusal to marry and breed for the Empire were treasonous offenses). That the virgin martyrs have been betrayed by the very church that sanctified them may be clearly seen in the fact that, although they were executed for rejecting marriage, by the Victorian age, when Christianity had long been the dominant religion in the West, a scholar translating stories of the virgin martyrs could label as "unchristian" that which had made them Christian martyrs in the first place.

In a classic case of blame-the-victim, Agnes Smith Lewis, writing in 1900 on the subject of Syrian martyrs, seems shocked by their unladylike behavior, stating that they "made themselves unduly obnoxious to the heathen, and brought upon themselves and their friends a bitter persecution, not only by their steadfastness in the faith of the Christ, but also by their *unchristian* renunciation of the marriage bond; a teaching which, if successful, would have upset all respectable society, and put an end to civilization." (Italics mine.) This was exactly what the Romans had feared; what most offended their sense of family values. Lewis does express some sympathy for the martyrs, recognizing that "their alternative was to have been forced into loveless marriages with unsympathetic, and perhaps godless men."

In their stories, the virgin martyrs are usually betrayed by those closest to them: fathers, suitors, mothers. Over the centuries they have been betrayed, even sneered at, by their biographers, who turn the loveliest of their symbols into objects of derision. Take the tale of Juthwara, an English virgin martyr listed in *The Oxford Dictionary of Saints*. A young girl becomes gravely ill when her beloved father dies; she is duped by a conniving stepmother, who offers a remedy (for some no doubt thoroughly English reason, cheeses applied to the breasts) and then suggests to her son that Juthwara is pregnant. In the telescoped drama typical of these tales, when the young man finds Juthwara's underclothes moist, he immediately beheads her, and, the narrator notes, dryly, "The usual spring of water then appeared."

Juthwara patiently carries her head back to the church—the virgin martyrs are nothing if not persistent—shocking the young man into repentance. He eventually founds a monastery on a former battleground.

The narrator reports, saucily, that Juthwara's "usual emblem is a cream cheese or a sword." Once our laughter subsides, we might ask what message this tale carried to its original audience. We might look beyond the fairy-tale elements to a story of betrayal transformed into love, of a witness given that has the power to change lives, to transform a battlefield into a house of prayer.

Once again (or, as usual), a virgin martyr gives witness to a wild power in women that disrupts the power of male authority, of business as usual. Is this a *point vierge?* Do we need to speak now about the power of virginity? Current dictionary definitions of "virginity" are of little use in helping us to discover why, in legends of the Christian West, virginity has so consistently been associated with the power to heal, why the virgin spring is a place of healing.

The 1992 *American Heritage Dictionary* defines a virgin in terms of incompleteness, as "a person who has not experienced sexual intercourse." The adjective *virgin* is defined in a more revealing way, as a "pure, natural, unsullied state, unused, uncultivated, unexplored, as in virgin territory," a definition that allows for, and anticipates, use, exploration, exploitation. In *Intercourse,* Andrea Dworkin correctly sees such definitions as coming from a male frame of reference, in which "virginity is a state of passive waiting or vulnerability; it precedes and is antithetical to wholeness." But "in the woman's frame," she writes, "virginity is a fuller experience of selfhood and

is not an idle metaphor. I knew a Williams boy—no doubt destined for great things in the corporate world—who regularly solicited at Bennington for his thriving business as a pimp. And a few years ago, when the movie *Pretty Woman* was a hit, an exceptionally bright and gifted fifteen-year-old girl I know attended a school Halloween party as the "pretty woman" character—a prostitute—and her parents, teachers, and friends considered it cute, not worthy of discussion.

I am grieving now for the girl I was back in the 1960s, who struggled with cultural definitions of a woman as someone attached to a man; who had to contend with a newly "liberated" definition of sexual freedom as that which made me more available to men. My response was to fear my own sexuality: mostly, I kept to myself and read books. Other girls expressed their fear by throwing themselves at men, often throwing themselves away. I grieve for the suicides, and for the girl I knew who survived, but with badly mutilated genitals. She had cut herself with a razor blade in a desperate attempt to rid herself of an exceptionally cruel and manipulative boyfriend. It took me a long time to see that with the peculiar logic of the mad, she had done something powerful (from the Latin "to be able to do things," to achieve a desired end). By damaging the only part of herself that was valuable to her boyfriend, she managed to get rid of him, and also received the psychiatric help she needed to become her own person.

I think of this girl as a virgin martyr, though she was neither a virgin nor a martyr by the dictionary's definitions. She may represent another kind of virginity, what Dworkin has termed "the new virginity, a twentieth-century nightmare," based on the belief that "sex is freedom." Now, Dworkin writes, the blood demanded of us is "not the blood of the first time [but] the blood of every time," expressed in increasingly violent images in both pornography and the fashion industry, and in bodily mutilation as fashion.

What might it mean for a girl today to be like the early virgin martyrs, to defy the conventions of female behavior? She would presume to have a life, a body, an identity apart from male definitions of what constitutes her femininity, or her humanity. Her life would articulate the love of the community (be it a family, a religious tradition, Christian or otherwise) that had formed her, and would continue to strengthen her. And she would be virgin, in the strongest possible sense, the sense Methodius had in mind when he said of Saint Agatha: "She was a virgin, for she was born of the divine word."

What about the virgin martyrs? Do they set women back? Do they make room for the majority of women, who are not virgins but mothers? The Benedictine sister spoke of virginity as something "reserved, preserved or reclaimed for what it was made for." In reclaiming our virginity, we women can reclaim our first selves. We can allow the fierce, holy little girls we were to cast judgment

on the ways our adult lives do and do not reflect what
we were made for. If the Catholic Church chose, for its
own purposes, to suggest that a holy woman need be a
virgin, preferably a martyr, that is not our problem. As
Thomas Merton observed, birds do not tell the time.

We can reclaim our own saints—Wilgefortis (or
Uncumber), for example, a virgin martyr who just may
be an example of earthy, feminist humor. To avoid an
arranged marriage, she grew a beard (a crime for which
her father had her crucified), and since then she has
served to help married women become unencumbered of
evil husbands. All you need is a prayer and a peck of
oats. And there is Saint Perpetua, that martyr of early-
third-century Carthage, breast-feeding her child in prison
before being fed to the lions; and the aged deaconess
Apollonia, seized by a crowd that beats her, breaks her
jaw, and tears out her teeth. The issue here is not physical virginity, but the status of unprotected women whose
outrageous claim—to have been made in the image of
God—was greatly feared by governing authorities and
punished to the full extent of the law.

We can use these stories to remember the extent to
which women have always been feared by male authorities, to better recognize the ways that this fear translates
into violence against women. We can remember that no
woman is safe, or respectable, once she claims for herself
the full psychic power of virginity. The noblewoman
Ruhm responds to news of the massacre of her husband

and other Christians in her town by walking bareheaded with her daughter and granddaughter into a public square: "She, a woman whose face no one had ever seen outside the gate of her house," gives a speech so powerful that the king is shaken by it. He wants to execute all the townspeople "for letting her go on at such length and thus lead the town astray." When Ruhm refuses to deny Christ, the king has her put to death, but not before he has killed her daughter and granddaughter and poured their blood into her mouth.

That story comes from sixth-century Syria; a witness to a horror closer to us may be found in a *New Yorker* article by Mark Danner about a massacre that occurred in December of 1981 in El Salvador, in the hamlet of El Mozote. Most of the peasants killed were evangelical Christians, and among the stories the soldiers told, years later, was that of a young girl, a story remarkably similar to accounts of the virgin martyrs:

> There was one in particular the soldiers talked about that evening (she is mentioned in the Tutela Legal report as well), a girl on La Cruz whom they had raped many times during the course of the afternoon, and through it all, while the other women of El Mozote had screamed and cried . . . this girl had sung hymns, strange evangelical songs, and she had kept right on singing, even after they had done what had to be done,

and shot her in the chest. She had lain there on
La Cruz with the blood flowing from her chest,
and had kept on singing—a bit weaker than before, but still singing. And the soldiers, stupefied,
had watched and pointed. Then they had grown
tired of the game and shot her again, and she
sang still, and their wonder began to turn to
fear—until finally they had unsheathed their ma-
chetes and hacked through her neck, and at last
the singing stopped.

One wonders: will the "usual spring" appear on the site
where she died? Will this strange story of a powerless
young girl who has the power to make soldiers afraid be
embellished over the years, as the soldiers try to live
with the horror of what they have done? This nameless
girl has made her witness: it began when the soldiers'
wonder began to turn to fear; and continued as they argued afterwards about her death. She had brought them
to the *point vierge,* where conversion begins in the human heart.

"Some declared that the girl's strange power proved
that God existed," Danner writes. "And that brought
them back to the killing of the children. There were a lot
of differences among the soldiers about whether this had
been a good thing or whether they shouldn't have done
it." Sometimes it takes a death to make us see the obvious. Sometimes it is a fierce little girl who is hard to kill,

who gives witness to a mystery beyond our understanding and control. And in the wild center of that young girl's heart, we glimpse love stronger than death, a love that shames us all.

Good Friday, 1994

SOURCES

Brock, Sebastian P. and Susan Ashbrook Harvey, *Holy Women of the Syrian Orient* (Berkeley: University of California Press, 1987).

Brown, Peter, *The Body and Society: Men, Women and Sexual Renunciation in Early Christianity* (New York: Columbia University Press, 1988).

Cardman, Francine, "Acts of the Women Martyrs," Gail Paterson Corrington, "The Divine Woman," and other essays by JoAnn McNamara, Elizabeth Clark, Ross Kraemer in Everett Ferguson, David M. Scholer, and Paul Corby Finney, *Studies in Early Christianity* (New York: Garland Publishing Co., 1993).

Clark, Elizabeth A., *Women in the Early Church* (Wilmington, DE: Michael Glazier, 1983).

Danner, Mark, "A Reporter at Large: The Truth of El Mozote," *The New Yorker,* December 6, 1993.

Dunbar, Agnes B. C., *A Dictionary of Saintly Women* (London: George Bell & Sons, 1904).

Dworkin, Andrea, *Intercourse* (New York: Free Press, 1987).

Englebert, Omer, *The Lives of the Saints* (New York: Collier Books, 1964).

Farmer, David Hugh, *The Oxford Dictionary of Saints* (Oxford: Oxford University Press, 1982).

Ferguson, Everett, ed., *Encyclopedia of Early Christianity* (New York: Garland, 1991).

Grubbs, Susan Evans, "Saints and Martyrs (Women) in Early Christianity," in *Women's Studies Encyclopedia,* vol. III, *History, Philosophy, Religion* (New York: Greenwood Press, 1991).

Lewis, Agnes Smith, trans., *Studia Sinaitica No. X: Select Narratives of Holy Women from the Syro-Antiochene or Sinai Palimpsest* (London: C. J. Clay and Sons, 1900).

McLoughlin, Helen, *My Nameday—Come for Dessert* (Collegeville, MN: The Liturgical Press, 1962).

McNamara, Jo Ann, *A New Song: Celibate Women in the First Three Christian Centuries* (Binghamton, NY: Harrington Park Press, 1985).

Marcus, Gilbert, *The Radical Tradition: Revolutionary Saints in the Battle for Justice and Human Rights* (New York: Doubleday, 1993).

New Catholic Encyclopedia (Washington, D.C.: Catholic University, 1967).

Our Patron Saints. With Prayers and Indulgences (New York: John Crawley & Co., 1963).

The Roman Martyrology (Baltimore: John Murphy Co., 1916).

Our Lady of Guadalupe and the Soup

NANCY MAIRS

TAKING AN UNFAMILIAR SHORTCUT through a residential neighborhood on Tucson's west side, my husband screeches to a halt and throws the van into reverse, bobbing me around like one of those dashboard puppies in my wheelchair in the back. "Look at that!" George cries, pulling up beside a mural depicting La Virgen de Guadalupe painted on a hole-in-the-wall grocery, La Tiendita, at the corner of two empty streets. "Isn't that wonderful!" Such wall art is common here, especially in the barrios, and it often features La Guadalupana, as do

jewelry, scarves, and other articles of clothing, and even
the hoods of automobiles. This is a relatively crude pro-
duction, not signed: the figure faces the wrong direction,
and most of the significant details are missing. But she
stands upon the head of a truly glorious fanged serpent,
painted a violet so intense that it shivers in the opales-
cent light of an overcast winter day in the desert, surrounded by scowling brown pre-Colombian heads. The
overall effect is exuberant and, indeed, wonderful, a treasure stumbled upon in haste.

Perhaps because we're in a hurry, it doesn't occur to
me until hours later, as I settle in to begin this essay, that
I am, both aesthetically and spiritually, not the woman I
used to be. I was certainly brought up to know that the
colors in that mural clashed. Except the brown, of
course—but oh! those hideous lowering profiles with
their huge noses and pendulous lips! And besides, images
of saints, even those painted in the most delicate pastels,
though marginally tolerable in museums, simply weren't
to be put on display in the everyday world. The Mary
on the Half Shell decorating a front lawn, the pale plastic
statue on a dashboard ("I don't care if it rains or freezes,
'long as I got my plastic Jesus . . ."), the Saint Christopher medal around a traveler's neck: revolting! And now
here I am admiring a garish Virgin painted on a public
wall. I guess that shows what Catholicism—even a relatively late conversion—can do to you.

On the whole, I do not regret my Protestant girlhood. With advancing age and accelerating physical debility, I have gotten out of the habit of regret. The alternative, I am afraid, would drive me mad, and I no longer wish to go mad, a state I endured with horror during my Protestant youth, not ever again. And anyway, the memories of Catholic girlhood I've read and listened to suggest that although I missed a great deal, most of it wasn't the sort of experience to be coveted. I've known woman after woman of my generation who still seethes about some elements of her religious upbringing: obtuse and even abusive nuns and priests who wielded church doctrine along with yardsticks or birch switches to intimidate their young charge, inculcating superstition and self-hatred so poisonous that, even after decades at a safe distance, she still can't speak of those dreary years without a frisson of revulsion. In the long run, Congregationalism left me a little flat, all the mystery scrubbed out of it by a vigorous and slightly vinegary reason, but hardly furious.

All the same, I do wish (and in this I may be more curious than rueful) that it had offered me the Blessed Virgin Mary. Or any feminine figure, for that matter. It may not have been altogether wholesome for a girl to grow up venerating women who leaped out of coffins and soared to the rafters to escape the stench of human flesh, like Saint Christina the Astonishing, or in response to compliments on their beauty rubbed pepper on their faces and lime on their hands, like Saint Rose of Lima.

But another kind of soul-sickness, even more enervating in its way, arises in those deprived of any sense of identity with the divine. In Congregationalism I encountered a rather abstract but unequivocally masculine God and, of course, His Son, as well as a Holy Ghost, suitably attenuated and untainted by any association with Sophia. No saints, except the guys who composed the Christian Scriptures. And no holy representatives on earth, except maybe the minister, who was invariably—and without question—a man.

Prayer, within such a structure, was always to an Other, who could be counted on to judge but not always to understand, if you had your period, say, and needed the cramps to stop, or if you were crazy in love with your boyfriend and wanted more than life itself to go all the way and had no idea where you were going to find the strength to say no. This latter situation was especially troublesome, since in Congregationalism the loss of one's virginity was strictly prohibited without any notably spiritual point being put upon the matter. Since the King James Version, like others, reproduced the mistranslation *parthenos,* "virgin," for the Semitic term for a young unmarried woman, we referred to Jesus' mother as the Virgin Mary when we referred to her at all, which wasn't all that often, but no one ever suggested to me that I should preserve my virginity in order to emulate her chastity and obedience to God. No, mine was being "saved" for the husband I would inevitably have (though it wasn't until I discovered feminist theory twenty years later that I figured out why society thought it important enough to save). Not just her virginity, however, but also her motherhood would have provided a valuable model, in my struggles as a daughter and, not many years later, a mother myself.

Because I sensed a mysterious element here for which the utter virility of the Congregationalist godhead failed to account, from early adolescence onward I coveted the saints, what little I could gather about them from books and films, having no Catholic friends, and especially Mary, whose multiplicity—maiden and mother intertwined—authenticated the personal mysteries I was destined to experience yet feared to endure without guidance. Her presence, if I could make it real in my life, could create spiritual space not for the encounter of God and man but for the bond between the holy and me.

Sometimes when alone I'd cross myself and murmur a Hail Mary, which I must have learned young from hearing the Rosary prayed as I twiddled the radio dial, and this habit persisted as I grew older. I did not pray to the Madonnas I studied in art class in college, but I contemplated their images—the severe dark skinny Byzantines, the luminous Italians—until they became a permanent part of my interior furnishings. Although I later named my daughter for my mother, I knew that the name Anne had belonged to Mary's mother, too. At last, I began to walk boldly into Catholic churches, forbidden me in my youth, staring—amused, awed, appalled—at painted statues got up in silk and stiff lace with browning bridal bouquets at their feet. In these ways, I suppose, I was preparing myself for the conversion I would eventually choose, whereby I claimed her for my own.

I don't know whether I'd have become a Roman Catholic had I remained in New England. But if I had, I feel certain that I would never have developed a devotion to Our Lady of Guadalupe. In fact, I'd probably never even have heard of her. In the area around Boston where I grew up, Catholic parishes tended to be identified ethnically. The Irish who went to St. Jude's would never have strayed into the Italian—or Portuguese or Polish or French-Canadian—Sacred Heart across town. Even though Pope Pius XII designated Our Lady of Guadalupe "Empress of the Americas"—from Eagle, Alaska, to Tierra del Fuego, North, Central, and South—in 1945, only a church attended by Mexicans or Mexican Americans would likely be dedicated to her. And certainly none would be in Enon, Massachusetts. (Of the 106 such churches in the United States as of 1980,[1] I doubt that any are in Massachusetts.) To find her, I really did have to move to the Southwest.

This matter of ethnicity has been a tangled one, right from the moment of her first apparition, on December 9, 1531, a decade or so after the Spanish conquistadores came to this continent, a long enough span for the native people who had greeted them as gods to figure out that they were human beings, and rapacious ones at that. In this bitter context, on Tepeyac Hill, at the edge of what is now Mexico City (a site already sacred to Tonantzin, snake woman and mother of gods[2]), an early convert to Catholicism, a Nahua named Juan Diego, was waylaid on his way to Mass by the sound of sublime music, perhaps birdsong. A young woman appeared and addressed him, using the affectionate diminutive "Juanito," little John. She was, she told him, the Virgin Mary, Mother of the True God, and she wanted a sanctuary to be built on that spot. He must take her message to the bishop of Mexico, Fray Juan de Zumárraga.

The bishop was polite enough, but skeptical, Juan Diego reported back to the Virgin, begging her to replace him with someone more eminent, and therefore more credible, than a peasant; but she wouldn't hear of it, and so he dutifully trudged back the next day to try again. This time Fray Zumárraga, still polite, asked for a sign, which the Lady promised to give Juan Diego the following day. Juan Diego's uncle fell ill, however, and Juan Diego stayed at home to care for him. On December 12, as he set out to fetch a priest to administer the last rites to his uncle, now dying, he was so chagrined to have missed his appointment that he tried to sneak around another way, but the Lady appeared nevertheless. Promising that his uncle would live (and indeed she

appeared to the sick man and raised him from his deathbed), she sent Juan Diego up the barren hill to pick
roses. These he bundled into his tilma, a cloak woven of
fiber from the maguey plant, and carried to the bishop.
When he unfolded the tilma, letting the roses tumble at
Fray Zumárraga's feet, imprinted on it was an image,
four feet eight inches high, of the Lady whom Juan
Diego and his uncle had seen. The astonished bishop did
as he'd been asked.

Despite the fragility of cactus fiber, the tilma still exists—preserved after 1647 under glass, though it hung
open to candle smoke and the lips and fingers of wor-
shipers until then—in the Basilica of Our Lady of Guadalupe, second only to Rome as a center of pilgrimage
in the Catholic world,[3] in northern Mexico City. The image it bears has been associated with miracles, beginning
with the healing of Juan Diego's uncle and including the
end of a flood in 1629 and of a plague in 1736.[4] In modern times, the artifact has received scientific scrutiny. In-
frared photography, one biophysicist claims, reveals an
original and quite simple image that is, in terms of the
media used, "unexplainable as a human work,"[5] overlaid
by later additions, perhaps to repair damage from the
1629 flood. Five ophthalmologists signed a certificate
stating that, on examining the portrait's eyes with their
instruments, they found themselves "looking into a human eye."[6] Even more astounding, those eyes have been

found to contain the reflected images of Juan Diego, as he appears in a contemporary painting, together with his interpreter and an unidentified third person.[7]

Thanks perhaps to a persistent Protestant intractability, I have an uneasy relationship with the miraculous. In fact, the notion of a miracle as an act of God for my benefit, which seems to underlie the use of the word by the devout, embarrasses the hell out of me. When a woman tells me that she has just escaped death because, at the last moment, God deflected an onrushing car off the road and into the desert, I wonder how she accounts for all the collisions that do take place. Does God find those people unworthy of rescue? Or does God blink? Even though my joyous life is made possible by a miracle, George having survived metastatic melanoma for some years now, and even though the wailing infant in me petitions constantly *Dear God please please don't ever let him die and leave me,* I prefer not to look on his good health as a special favor from the Almighty lest I should, at remission's end, be forced to believe myself personally abandoned.

And so my mind scuttles away from flood and pestilence and La Guadalupana's mysterious eyes. With the political features of her manifestation, however, I can engage quite comfortably. In *indigenista* terms, her image and message clearly inform the issues of social justice that first drew me into Catholic practice and, against all

odds, sustain me there. The figure, according to this in-
terpretation, encodes the concepts necessary to effect the
conversion of eight million Indians in the seven years
following the apparition.[8] (The desirability of becoming
a Catholic is a moot point, I recognize, today as four
centuries ago, but I won't get into it here. What's done
is done.) To begin with, "Guadalupe" is probably a mistranslation, influenced by the shrine in Spain, of the
name she spoke when she appeared to Juan Diego's uncle; she might more accurately be referred to as Our
Lady of Tepeyac. Several Náhuatl alternatives have been
suggested, the most widely accepted being "Coatlaxopeuh," that is, "she who crushed the serpent's head"[9]
which suggests the overpowering of the native gods by
Christianity.

The icon itself reinforces this idea. It represents a
woman with dark skin and hair (La Morenita, she is
therefore sometimes called), her eyes downcast, in contrast to the straightforward gaze of Indian gods, and her
hands raised before her in an Indian offertory gesture.
She wears a rose-colored shift filigreed in gold, and over
it a cloak of blue-green, a color reserved for the chief
god Omecihuatl, or Ome-Téotl, scattered with gold stars
auguring a new age. The black maternity band at her
waist signifies someone yet to come, and below it, over
her womb, may appear the powerful Mesoamerican cross
to suggest just how mighty that Someone will be. The
rays surrounding her form show her eclipsing the Sun

Lord Tonatiuh; and the blackened crescent beneath her feet may be a phase of Venus, associated with Quetzalcóatl, the sacred Plumed Serpent. Hence the appropriateness of the name Coatlaxopeuh. She is borne by an intermediary "angel," the carrier of time and thus of a new era.[10]

Some of these signs seem hardly less fanciful than do miraculous remedies and mysterious ocular reflections, but that's not really their point. Their power lies in the suggestion that the Virgin appeared, long before the establishment of political boundaries in the "New World," to indigenous people whose old world had begun to crumble even before the Spanish invasion; she may thus signify both the "liberation and salvation" their prophets had predicted and the new spirit early Christian missionaries hoped to find here.[11] In this sense, she is a thoroughly American[12] saint, and her relegation by U.S. Catholics to Mexico and the Southwest, identifying her dark-skinned image with "an economically and socially unsuccessful and, hence, unacceptable ethnic group,"[13] probably does reflect bias against a minority woefully underrepresented among the clergy.

Ironically, however, this possibility strengthens her appeal for those of us, whether of Mexican heritage or not, who believe, as Virgilio Elizondo puts it, that "the role of the powerless is to evangelize the powerful."[14] A reviewer of one of my books once took me to task for accepting the tenets of feminist and liberation theology merely on faith, as though one could not possibly, after long contemplation and appraisal, continue to affirm them. But God's preferential option for the poor—expressed at least as far back as Isaiah's cry for the protection of widows and fatherless children—rings true to my understanding of the Christian ethos. I must accept it, both on faith and on reflection, and act upon it if I am to carry out God's will. And in the tale of a dark-skinned peasant carrying to the conquistadores for their veneration the image of a dark-skinned Lady who promised her compassion to all humanity (even, I must suppose, the conquistadores) lies a model of the care I am, I believe, required to give.

She entered our urban, white, middle-class lives slowly. George and I had converted to Catholicism not for its saints but in spite of them; and not knowing quite what to do with them, we politely ignored them, the way you might some atavistic eccentricity in an otherwise sophisticated friend. This is rather hard to do if, every week of your life, you ask Blessed Mary Ever Virgin, all the angels and saints, and your brothers and sisters to pray for you to God. Clearly these holy figures were integral to spiritual health in a way we didn't quite fathom. Still don't, I might add, and probably never will. When I hear my elderly friends talk about Our Blessed Mother, I suspect you may have to be brought up Catholic to fully apprehend the role of an intercessor in devotional life. I

identity. In the male frame, virginity is virtually synonymous with ignorance; in the woman's frame, it is recov-
ery of the capacity to know by direct experience of the
world."

We so seldom hear virginity defined from a woman's
point of view that it is shocking, and difficult for us to
fathom. Here are the words of a Benedictine sister, star-
tled to be asked about the power of virginity. This is
"something I carry very deep within," she writes, "that I
carry very secretly ... virginity is centered in the heart
and could be named 'singleness of heart.'" Now we are
far indeed from our dictionary definition, and hearing virginity described not in terms of physicality but as a state
of being. The sister continues, "Virginity is a state that
returns to God in wholeness. This wholeness is not that
of having experienced all experiences, but of something
reserved, preserved or reclaimed for what it was made
for. Virginity is the ability to stay centered, with oneness
of purpose."

And now I am doing what I've often longed to do,
what my education and cultural conditioning have
trained me *not* to do: to bring the virgin and the whore
together, only to find that they agree. The designation
might seem brutal: Andrea Dworkin is not a whore, nor
am I. But we were both formed sexually in the mael-
strom of the 1960s, at Bennington College, and the point
I am making is that the great lie (or lay) of sexual liberation expected us, conditioned us, to play the whore. This

still tend to talk to God directly, a habit fixed by the time I was thirteen, and probably nowhere near as courteously as Our Blessed Mother would do for me.

Rather than a repository of prayer, Our Lady of Guadalupe was initially for me an exhorter to social action. In order to avoid being shut down by resentful neighbors, Casa María, the Catholic Worker house of hospitality in Tucson, was consecrated to her. The kitchen there is known as Our Lady of Guadalupe Chapel and Free Kitchen, and any tramp in the city can probably direct you to "Guadalupe's," identifiable by a brilliant painting of her on the wall beside the front door, where a sack lunch with soup is offered every day and Mass on Monday mornings. As George and I became increasingly involved in the community there, we began to think of her as the guardian of the thousand and more *pobrecitos* who lined up each day to be fed. And so it seemed natural, when our daughter left us to live in Africa, to light a candle in the lady chapel of our church after Mass each week and ask her to watch over Anne as her human parents could no longer do.

For my birthday one year George gave me a framed poster of her image. "What on earth will Mother say?" I wondered as we hung this icon on the bedroom wall. "Next thing you know, we'll be getting statues!" Sure enough. Above me as a write, in a niche formed by an old cooler duct, stands a porcelain Virgen (too white, but

I was politically ignorant all those years ago when I bought her) surrounded by two garish plastic flowers made at a local senior center and the likenesses of the Dalai Lama, Dorothy Day, and the deep-blue Medicine Buddha. Now she is everywhere in our lives: on the painted tiles outside the front door; on a plaque enameled by Salvadoran refugees in Guatemala, where the hill she stands on is dotted with animals, including a fat armadillo; as a crude little figure carved out of wood, the rays around her formed out of yellow toothpicks. I even have her likeness hand-painted on a T-shirt by a Casa María worker, holding a soup ladle and a white Styrofoam cup. Nuestra Señora del Caldo, I call her. Our Lady of the Soup. Glimpses of these images each day as I move from task to task serve to remind me to be grateful for the gift of roses in midwinter and to pray for the protection of us all.

Now I wonder how I can locate the painter of that Lady and her resplendent serpent outside La Tiendita. I have this wide blank cream-colored wall to the right of my studio door. . . .

NOTES

1. Philip E. Lampe, "Our Lady of Guadalupe: Victim of Prejudice or Ignorance?," *Listening: Journal of Religion and Culture* 21 (1): 9.
2. James E. Fiedler, reprint from the *Denver Catholic Register*, December 7, 1977.

3. J. T. Meehan, S.J., *Guadalupe Our Mother* (Washington, NJ: Blue Army of Our Lady, 1970), 5.
4. Robert Feeney, *Mary, Mother of the Americas* (Ligouri, MO: Liguori Publications, 1984), 19.
5. Ibid., 21.
6. Harold J. Rahm, S.J., "Our Lady of Guadalupe," pamphlet, no publishing information.
7. Meehan, 7–11.
8. According to Rahm's pamphlet.
9. Miguel Leatham, "*Indigenista* Hermeneutics and the Historical Meaning of Our Lady of Guadalupe of Mexico," *Folklore Forum* 22 (1/2), 30.
10. I have extracted these details from Fiedler and Leatham.
11. Fiedler.
12. A term only residents of the United States would arrogate exclusively to themselves.
13. Lampe, 11, 12.
14. Quoted by Fiedler.

The Exemplar

MARTIN E. MARTY

"SAINT DOROTHY, hear our prayer and pray for us!"
One might expect to hear such an utterance in a largely
African-American parish church on South Eberhart Avenue in Chicago. One expects to hear saints evoked by
name at parishes named after them, and this one is Saint
Dorothy's. Yet Saint Dorothy is not a household name,
and may not even be at the church named for her. In this
case, as so often, Catholics have a teaching opportunity
when someone asks a question. So we picture a child in
that church asking "Who is Saint Dorothy?"

A teacher, priest, nun, or informed parent could answer: Dorothy lived long ago—sixteen hundred years—
and far away from Africa or America, in Cappadocia. Her
legend says that she would not bring an offering to the
gods. The governor therefore had her tortured and sent
her off to be executed.

On the way to her death Dorothy, "gift of God,"
met Theophilus, "friend of God," who made fun of her.
She had said she was going to a beautiful garden. Scorn-
fully he asked if she would send him some fruit from it.
Dorothy did: while she was kneeling to be killed, she
prayed. An angel brought three roses and three apples.
The martyr-to-be sent these to Theophilus, saying she
would meet him in the garden. He was converted.
Wouldn't anyone have been? And she was canonized and
received her day, February 6.

The child hears of Dorothy through a story that even
the keepers of the books on saints call "apocryphal." She
stores it in her mind along with all the other fairy tales
and goes back to play, entertained, unmoved, ready fig-
uratively to cross her fingers when she next prays. No
roses, no apples for her.

Try another Dorothy. "Saint" Dorothy Day. Picture
a church named after her in a poor section of any city.
New York or Chicago, Detroit or Los Angeles would
do. Tell the child that this Dorothy has a day, November
8, her birthday. She also comes from long ago, having
been born in 1897. Day died in 1980, which in the mind

of the historyless urban young might as well have been
303, the presumed death date for the other Dorothy.

All saints are "other," and we tend to like them and
stories about them because of their difference from our
world and ways. Saints always come from far away, usually in time and space but also in their achievements. The
African-American child, or any child of today for that
matter, would need to use one kind of imagination to
grasp the world of the old Saint Dorothy, the kind children use when television presents them with stories of
wonder and fantasy. The new Saint Dorothy, were she
to be canonized, belongs almost to our time and lived in
cities like our own, but she also is "other," different, and
in many ways distant.

The legend of the new Dorothy needs no roses and
apples, though Miss Day helped plenty of hungry people
who stood in lines selling apples during the Depression,
or waiting for soup at one of the Houses of Hospitality
she helped set up and run. This legend needs no miraculous angels, though the survival of her Houses suggests
that some must have been near. The odds were always
against all of Dorothy Day's projects.

The modern Dorothy never had to kneel for execu-
tion, though she was capable of making good enemies.
She was a prophet—she would have cringed at the word
"prophetess," and abhorred prophetic tags—but nowadays, as they say, we do not stone the prophets. We
invite them to dinner, and dull their rough edges to do-

mesticate them. We try to make them like us, or likable to us. We even do see some of them canonized as saints. No martyr, our new Dorothy died peacefully in her sleep, her fifty-three-year-old daughter, Tamar Teresa, mother of six, at her side. If Miss Day had a grief at her hour of death, it resulted, says the new legend, from the fact that her Catholic faith meant little to her descendants. Whether she converted any Theophiluses, to compensate for their drift away, is known only to her God.

Back to the urban child who is being given an answer to her question "Who is Saint Dorothy Day?" We could answer in very flat prose or in a somewhat more oblique way, a way she would have found congenial.

First, the flat and straight way. The answer would be: Saint Dorothy Day, aka Miss Day, started her career as a journalist and never stopped publishing, particularly in the paper she founded in 1933, *The Catholic Worker*. After a wayward young life, she converted to Catholicism in 1927 and never stopped putting her Catholic faith to work. She helped invent Houses of Hospitality in her chosen New York and in many other cities, and got involved in direct action for and advocacy of the poor, the homeless, the victims of the Depression. In World War II and ever after she supported pacifism, a move that made her unpopular with many who admired her other positions and actions.

By this point, the child's eyes would be glazing over, and we would try a second answer to the question "Who

is Saint Dorothy Day?" This time we could say: Dorothy
Day is very different, she is "other," as saints are supposed to be. But she knew your world, child. The people
not far from your neighborhood did not choose to be
poor, but she chose poverty, at least of a relative sort.
She lived in cities, and could write of a Depression day
in New York:

> It was a beautiful clear summer in 1932. . . . I was
> able to walk home and savor the beauty of the
> city and of the day. For there is a beauty of the
> city, of the wide avenues, of the clean houses on
> orderly streets, of trees and little porches, and
> there were streets I loved and walks I loved . . .[1]

Such a city, to the child in a Catholic school not far from
the ghetto, would seem as remote as Cappadocia. But the
listening child would hear the rest of the sentence that
Day set in motion with the phrase "there were streets I
loved and walks I loved"; she ended it with "that were
not in the slums where I was living." As she hears this,
the child at St. Dorothy's has new reasons for identifying
with the Dorothy of this century. Dorothy Day can set
her to dreaming, to envisioning the future:

> One can conceive of a city with art and culture
> and music and architecture, and the flowering of
> all good things, as the image of the heavenly

city. Heaven is pictured as a city, the heavenly
Jerusalem.

"Saint Dorothy, hear our prayer and pray for us and
send us roses and apples from such a dreamed-of city!"
Still, no roses, no apples: only a story of Dorothy Day
sustains the listening child in an area Chicagoans call
Chatham, where this noted African-American parish—
never built beyond basement height, thanks to Depres-
sion-era financial setbacks—is an attraction in the ordinary neighborhood. This child, like millions of others
around the nation and the world, lives in the mixed pattern of shadow and sunshine described by poet Rainer
Maria Rilke the city, "is beguiling to beasts and infants
alike." The child knows the beasts. She hears of an almost infantlike simplicity in her Dorothy Day, who
chose the city, the slum, the poor places, and the poor.
Day had to leave behind some of her love of "art and
culture and music and architecture."

Dorothy Day, we would tell the urban child,
dreamed of and worked for governable cities with econo-
mies that were fair. Call that Utopian, so foolish does it
seem even thus to conceive of futures today. Day, we
would further tell the child, was a pacifist, inconveniently
for her legend—she might as well have offered her head
on the block during "the last good war," in the 1940s, as
to protest it—but conveniently for those who in more
recent wars needed her kind of signals for peace. The

world of which she dreamed and for which she worked would not experience shattered Sarajevos and Belfasts. The cities would not be bombed and the children need not be terrified. Call that paradisiacal, which means insanely remote today. Still, the story of a search for justice and peace might move the child as the story of apples and roses would not.

A new Saint Dorothy? No one should count on it. To be a fully registered saint one has to be canonized. A whole sequence of bureaucrats have to busy themselves going over the records and collecting the money. They have to look past surface piety to find the flaws in a potential saint's character and career. Day would have snorted disdainfully to throw such employed advocates off: simply ask her enemies, ask her friends, and they will tell you how "difficult" she could be. Or simply ask her, by consulting her autobiographical writings, for she never hid her way of life in her younger days. From the details Day herself provided, one has no trouble deducing that because of her bohemianism and her early ideology, many of the sanitized saints of old would shrug off her story or even blush and refuse to listen. And if she sometimes seemed saintly to those who allied with her in an enterprise called the Catholic Worker, she did not find them sanctified. Her holiness must not have rubbed off. As Stanley Vishnewski, who looked in on the Houses, put it: "The Catholic Worker consists of saints and martyrs, and the martyrs are those who have to live with the saints."[2] The saints appear as "other" and "different" and have to be kept at some distance if we are to paint them on icons, light candles at their shrines, or put them on pedestals.

Pedestals are precisely not the places for the likes of Day. She knew that, and so do her grandchildren, most of whom do not answer mail when the folks at *Salt* magazine, who would like to see her canonized, ask them about it. According to Kenneth L. Woodward, who knows and tells as much as anyone from the outside can about the cost and claptrap of canonization, of making saints, granddaughter Maggie Hennessy, then age thirty-four, wrote to *Salt*'s editors, who would have understood and anticipated her critique:

> I am one of Dorothy's granddaughters and I wanted to let you know how sick your canonization movement is. You have completely missed her beliefs and what she lived for if you are trying to stick her on a pedestal. She was a humble person, living as she felt the best way to improve on the world's ills. Take all your monies and energies that are being put into her canonization and give it to the poor. That is how you would show your love and respect to her.[3]

"Don't dismiss me so easily," Day is reported to have said, according to Woodward, when someone once

mentioned her sanctity. Equally discouraging to cam-
paigners for canonization was one of her better and bet-
ter-known friends, Father Daniel Berrigan, S.J., who
offered mass and suffered scrapes with her in the days of
protest against the Vietnam War. He spoke of the "wonderful suggestion about canonizing Dorothy":

> Abandon all thought of this expensive, overly ju-
> ridical process. Let those so minded keep a photo
> of Dorothy some place given to prayer or wor-
> ship. In such a place, implore her intercession for
> peace in the world, and bread for the multitudes.
> ... Dorothy is a people's saint, she was careful
> and proud of her dignity as layperson. Her pov-
> erty of spirit, a great gift to our age, would for-
> bid the expensive puffing of baroque sainthood.
> Today her spirit haunts us in the violated faces
> of the homeless of New York. Can you imagine
> her portrait, all gussied up, unfurled from above
> the high altar of St. Peter's? I say, let them go
> on canonizing canons and such. We have here a
> saint whose soul ought not be stolen from her
> people—the wretched of the earth.[4]

So, dear urban child, if you can still be listening, canonization and sainthood have come to this: sickness, pedes-
taling, easy dismissal, juridicism, gussied-upness, and

stealing from you. People who care may work for canonization, but immediately Dorothy Day must be yours.

This your Protestant friend, who does not pray to or
through or for or around saints, can cut a way past all
the canons and canonizations and is able to predict that
tomorrow we shall be less sure than once people were
about what a canon is and whether it is to be treasured
and how one canonizes. The lines between saints and
nonsaints become ever more blurred. The papal endorse-
ment does not mean enough in a divided Catholic church
and an ecumenical world, wherein the Catholic Day may
be closer to many Protestants and non-Christians (both
of which Day had been—baptized as a Christian by
Episcopalians, tutored in college years by skeptics, and
attracted soon after by leftists who were attracted to
Communism) than to many of those who put canonized
saints on Catholic pedestals. With all the rights and priv-
ileges given any human in general and a baptized Christian in particular, I hereby authorize you at Saint
Dorothy's to have *two* Dorothys in mind. Take your
choice between their legends, and we know which you
will choose.

What, then, does a modern saint mean to people in
canonizing and noncanonizing traditions alike? While
prayers to and through saints go on in some cases, in
others we seek exemplars and examples. The mazes of
contemporary life confuse all thoughtful people, beguiled

as we are in both our beastly cunning and our infantlike innocence. A Dorothy Day, for all the appearances of otherness and signs of difference that separate her ordinary life from our ordinary lives, is an example.

The medieval dictionaries related the word *exemplum,* something "cut out," to a clearing in the woods. Those who think about the *exemplum* say that it gives definition to the woods. Without it, there is no beginning and end to the thickness of the thicket, the darkness of its plotless, pathless ways. One cannot see the forest for the forest, so someone cuts out some trees and creates a clearing. Here the woods momentarily end and thus we define them; they become "*the* woods." Further, a clearing is the place where light falls, cultivation occurs, a cabin beckons hospitably.

So it is with exemplars. They by their living "cut out" a clearing in the woods of complex living. They give definition—in Day's case to poverty and food, war and peace, faith and unfaith—and provide a place on the Eberhart Avenues, in the St. Dorothy's churches, the Houses of Hospitality, and the companies of those who would counter the money-grabbers and war-makers. At these dark places, light falls, cultivation of the virtues occurs, hospitality calls, thanks to lives lived in particular ways—among others, too few others, in Day's ways.

Pedestaled saints like the original Dorothy come complete with legends that make them look nothing but saintly. Today ambiguity surrounds anyone nominated for sainthood, whether canonically or in the hearts of the people. Today the thirst for reading about scandal or seeing heroines and heroes exposed and pulled down, the taste for journalistic invasions of privacy and trial by headline and tube, leaves no one intact. Were there "good old days"?

The main difference between the good old days of sainthood and our time is that back then they had not yet invented the tape recorder and the camera. Today all the gossip gets recorded, the warts are displayed, the fallibilities revealed, the virtues tainted. That there were no good old days, however, is clear from what almost all the saints who left diaries or confessions tell about themselves. Of course, they had an impulse to exaggerate the flaws from the time before they were converted, just as authors of "born again" autobiographies invent lurid pasts to make the grace they found later look richer. But we know enough about autobiographies and confessions to know that often they reveal one set of vices to obscure from view another set more damaging.

Exemplar Dorothy Day in her autobiographies does indeed reveal how far from grace she had been. She had lived a post-conversion life so open to scrutiny that she gave evidence to others that her "clearing in the woods" was not all cultivated, all free from brambles. But for the beginnings, she can be an exemplar because she was more than ordinary like the rest of us; she was extraordinarily capable of finding trouble. She tells us, through

sequences in which we run out of commas to place between listed vices before she runs out of vices and sins
to register:

About the fact that she had affairs, lived with men to
whom she was not married, married a real loser who set
out to set records for number of marriages, had an abor-
tion, a common-law marriage, a child people of her day
would have called illegitimate, an early career of con-
sorting with bohemians and Communists who would
have shocked the Church in which she found a home—
in short, the kind of life in the woods and thickets that
would hold the most bored confessor's attention.

Find a home in the Church she did, however. Somewhere along the way, after Tamar was born, and in connection with her baptism, Miss Day recognized the
stirring of grace and pointings to a Truth that would begin to satisfy her intellectual longings and her search for
a base for community. She was baptized, thus gaining
grace and losing the father of her child, a committed
atheist.

Six years after these events she met Peter Maurin, as
disheveled a swinger of axes as one could hope to find
when it came time to create a moral "clearing in the
woods." Her exemplar was a French visitor whose ideal
was communal living in the countryside, and his farm
world tantalized her. She learned from Maurin, even
though he was a very unsystematic thinker. She also was
drawn to a school of French "personalists" led by Eman-

uel Mounier, most of whom were on the political left. They set out to revitalize Catholicism for the modern world by stressing personality as the basic principle of explanation and, as supernaturalists, focused on both the divine and the human personality.

But Day took this personalism and followed her vocation to the city. In both locales, Peter and Dorothy and their small company would exemplify the search for justice and peace and, they hoped, would spread justice and help promote peace.

Dorothy Day was an accomplished writer and journalist by then. She wrote, and then wished to forget, a novel, *The Eleventh Virgin,* which was semiautobiographical, just as most of her writings were somehow autobiographical. Exemplars may be humble, but they recognize in the events of their life and the interpretations they give these the base for helping others live theirs. Day combined her writing talents and her social passions and on May Day, 1933, in New York's Union Square, started selling *The Catholic Worker,* then as through the years for a penny a copy. If she must be canonized, it could be as much for what she did to encourage reading among workers and the unemployed, the masses and the massgoers, as for anything else. The letter, in her case, giveth life.

The Maurin and Day programs were less important than are their personalism and persons. Those who track the fashions and fads in movements for social justice

between 1933 and 1980 would never find Dorothy Day
"in" with the voguish or "out" with those who are beside the point. She was simply her complicated self, prag-
matic enough to adjust to changes and idealistic enough
to go against the trends of any time: that may be one
reason she seems so "other," so "different," so likely to
last after the movement people on tracks parallel to hers
have lost their followings, pedestals, and places among
historians' footnotes.

The program did include the founding of *The Catholic
Worker* as a paper and the Catholic Worker as a movement; the invention of the Houses of Hospitality, where
community and Communion, bread and Bread were
available. It included sponsoring a woodland camp where
conscientious objectors of many sorts could work—a
camp based on a Catholic impulse, though everyone except Day knew that Catholicism did not engender or encourage pacifism. The program fostered cooperative
farms that stood no more chance of altering the American economy than did the Catholic Worker of upsetting
Western capitalism. No matter: the exemplar cuts a clearing in the woods so that the thicket gets defined, the
light falls, and there are both cultivation and hospitality.

Now and then Day phased into the world where re-
porters looked in and whence headlines issued. One remembers photographs of her aging visage—a beauty,
she reminded some of Garbo when young—in the tents
of the farmworkers when their leader Cesar Chavez mo-

mentarily was allowed to emerge. Civil-rights workers gravitated toward her. The Catholic left found her Houses of Hospitality hospitable, good forums for refining their positions, sometimes with ideologies she did not need to accept because she found it sufficient to trust the vision and the hearts of people named Berrigan and their spiritual kin. She allowed for conversation with the likes of Robert Coles,[5] and allowed in photographers of note so long as they did not interrupt her meditation or talk or work.

Exemplar Day looks best in black-and-white photographs, and one pictures her world in black and white and gray. That world captures the shadows of the city, the bleakness that surrounds visions of human need, the darkness of the lonely heart, the brightness that falls from God into the figurative clearings in the rather literal jungles we call the city. As exemplar, here described as a misfit in her time and any time, as someone expressing "otherness" and "difference," she knew the source of that light.

One cannot turn the pages and close the books of Day biographies and autobiographies, or let memories of her photographs be imprinted as icons in the mind's eye, without seeing what exemplar Day recognized as that source of light. A worldly, eros-minded (in the good senses of what that connotes), "difficult," sinful, limited person, she did what saints do. She directed her thoughts and all inquiries past herself to the One who interrupted

The Long Loneliness with Presence. Like so many people
called activist, she was profoundly spiritual, an exemplar
who shames by contrast the airheaded "I'm-not-a-mem-
ber-or-religious-or-a-believer-but-I'm-*so*-spiritual"   sorts
who write bestsellers. Her epigrams, columns, and prayers will outlast by centuries the witness of today's self-
engrossed spirituality mongers.

She *was* a church member; she *was* religious, a believer, whose "pre-Vatican II piety," as we like to tab it,
served to guide her to find company with "post-Vatican
II" sorts. She used the deeper reaches toward the deepest
particular Catholicism to reach people of other faiths and
no faith, to find communion with them. Her exemplarity
was specifically Christian. She liked to quote William
Gauchat: "There is no love without the cross, and no
cross without a victim. And whether there be on the
cross or beneath it weeping, there is Christ, and sorrow
shall be turned to joy." The Christic and Christlike both
profit from her place under that cross, and from the simple love that issued from her complex, *so* complex person
and being.

Dear child of the city of today, whose attention I
have lost by now, I leave you with this: Exemplar, then,
if not or not yet Saint Dorothy Day, also liked to quote
Leon Bloy: "There is only one unhappiness, and that is
not to be one of the Saints." Since Day came to know at
least certain kinds of happiness, she must have been one
of the saints, if not of the canonical sort. And, though I

have no right to speak for her, I have a confident hunch that she would have no difficulty at all, and would express nothing but joy, if at St. Dorothy's Church on South Eberhart you today left an apple for a teacher, a rose for a friend, and a prayer to the God of both Dorothys.

NOTES

1. Dorothy Day, *The Long Loneliness,* paperback (San Francisco: Harper and Row, 1981), 159.
2. Quoted from "Days of Action" in the Catholic Worker papers, in Mel Piehl, *Breaking Bread: The Catholic Worker and the Origin of Catholic Radicalism in America* (Philadelphia: Temple University Press, 1982), 108.
3. Quoted in Kenneth L. Woodward, *Making Saints* (New York: Simon & Schuster, 1990), 32.
4. Quoted by Woodward, *op. cit.,* 35.
5. Coles has better credentials than I to write this essay, having written a biographical reflection on Dorothy Day.

The Communion of Saints

LAWRENCE JOSEPH

I.

A TIME OF INNOCENCE. That time before I was awakened to choice. Everything about the Shrine of the Little Flower made an impression. The chapel with the alabaster statue of Saint Theresa, green and gold light fused through stained-glass windows, dozens of red roses and orchids. The side altars to Saints Mary, Sebastian, Perpetua, Jude, and Joseph. Saint Jude, Saint of the Impossible, to whom my mother prayed novenas. Saint Joseph, one of two saints whose name I have. A patron saint by historical chance. Around 1910, my grandfather emigrated from the Chouf mountains in the Ottoman province of Lebanon. When asked his name by an immigration official at Ellis Island, he replied, "Joseph," his father's first name, as he would have in Lebanon. By an act of the U.S. government, Alexander Nahed (baptized Maronite Catholic, into a rite named after a one-eyed monk who lived near the Orontes River in the sixth century) became Alexander Joseph. His family's name in America would be Joseph.

Joseph would be my father's first name, too. My father, like my mother, was born in Detroit at the end of World War I. My grandmother used to explain that she went into labor on March 19, the feast of Saint Joseph, two days before my father's birth. Because she had lost two infants, she prayed to Saint Joseph. If her child lived, she would name her Josephine, or, if a boy, Joseph. Joseph Joseph.

I was nine or ten years old when I discovered my other patron saint, Saint Lawrence. The children of the Little Flower School used to attend daily Mass. Everyone had a *Saint Joseph Daily Missal,* "The Official Prayers of the Catholic Church for Celebration of Daily Mass."(I still have it: not mine, but my mother's, which my brother and I bought for her, dated, in my mother's handwriting, "Mother's Day, May 12, 1957.") Its longest section was the "Proper of the Saints." August 10 was the feast of Saint Lawrence, Martyr. Beside a small picture, words once known by heart:

In 257 Pope Sixtus II ordained Saint Lawrence to the diaconate. Though Saint Lawrence was still young, the same Pope appointed him as one of the seven deacons of the Roman Church. Summoned by the Prefect of Rome to surrender the treasury of the Church, Saint Lawrence instead distributed it among the poor. According to tradition, Saint Lawrence was roasted to death on a red-hot gridiron over a slow fire.

My father and uncle, for reasons beyond them, were owners of a failing grocery store among Detroit's poor; Saint Lawrence's distribution of the Church's treasury took hold of my imagination. Roasted to death on a gridiron over a slow fire—I had to know more. In my grandparents' attic I found an answer in a small, worn book, *Lives of the Great Saints*. (I still have this, too.) Lawrence presented "the aged, the decrepit, the blind, the lame, the maimed, the lepers, widows, and young orphans"—to whom he had distributed the Church's wealth—to the Roman Prefect, saying "Here is the Church's treasure." "You mock me," the Prefect shouted, insane with rage. "I'll see that you die a bitter death." Lawrence was bound with chains on a large gridiron over a slow fire ("an angel was seen wiping his face"). While his flesh broiled, he looked at the Prefect and smiled: "Turn me over now, I'm done on this side."

A sense of recognition, a common sense of irony.

That's what I felt about Saint Lawrence then, and what I feel about him now. A sense of detachment from total physical destruction, by the power of language transposed somewhere—into something—else. Not the duplicitous, hypocritical language of power which wrecks what is human, but a deeper language, forced into meaning, which reveals, you might say, the other side of our bodies and our souls.

Not long ago, after talking about Saint Lawrence over dinner one evening, I learned that he is also the patron saint of cooks. Those of us at the table baptized Catholic roared with laughter.

II.

I think of my saints.

Of Saint Augustine, born in that part of Africa now Algeria, the intensity of his language pitched to a clear and abstract fervor. *Magna vis est memoriae, nescio quid horrendum, deus meus, profunda et infinita multiplicitas; et hoc animus est, et hoc ego ipse sum:* "The force of memory, so immense, my God, an awesome thing, infinitely deep in its multiplicity; this thing that is the mind; this is who I am." The will, the spirit, like fire; memory and thought, mysterious and light, beautiful and dark.

And Saint Joan, visionary warrior of great skill and intelligence, burned alive as a heretic because—Mary Daly is right about it—she embodied an escape from patriarchy, a saint because of who she is, her being, which is the witch that burns within our true selves.

Or that other saint of fire, Ignatius of Loyola—a very important part of this puzzle—for whom God is revealed in what we sense, alive in the mind, seen through memory by the most disciplined will.

I think of Saint Thomas Aquinas, heavy and sad, who actually envisioned his *Summa Theologica*'s conflict between existence and essence, and who wrote the most beautiful poem in Latin of his time, the "Tantum Ergo," which we sang as children at the Benediction of the Blessed Sacrament.

> *Et antiquum documentum*
>
> *Novo cedat ritui;*
> *Praestet fides supplementum*
> *Sensuum defectui.*

"The ancient forms replaced by something new, and faith where the senses fail."

And, always, Saint Anne, of the church in Detroit in the shadow of the Bridge to Canada surrounded by a few wooden houses of the poor, where, at a side altar, before her statue and a statue of her daughter, Saint Mary, large candles burn in blue, white, and yellow glass consecrated with vows (a million vows), body braces, crutches, letters describing miracles in a corner, and that man over

there, who genuflects on both knees, who bows his head
to the floor and kisses it.

III.

I spoke to a good friend, a Catholic priest, who knows
his theology. I wanted to refresh my memory about the
Church's position on saints.

"So, what comes to your mind when you think about
saints?" I asked him.

"What do you mean, what comes to mind? A lot of
things come to mind."

"Theologically," I said.

"Theologically? Well, first of all, I suppose, is the
question of what a saint is. The word, of course, comes
from the Latin, *sanctus*. Holy. A saint is holy."

"But what does it mean, theologically, to be holy?"

"One can only be holy theologically. Holiness is a
religious idea. It has to do with God. 'A saint is one who
belongs to God . . .' "

"That's it?"

"No, that's not all of it. If you're Christian . . ."

"Let's stay with Catholic."

"All right, if you're Catholic—if you're Christian,
too—God is revealed through Christ. Don't forget your
Christology. Christ is of two natures, human and divine."

"So, there certainly can't be, as Camus once posited, 'a saint without God.'"

"I've been intrigued by that, too. But, no, not strictly speaking—you can't be a saint without God. If you're Christian—sorry, if you're Catholic—there's not even such a thing as a saint without Christ. Look, holiness properly belongs only to God. 'Holy, holy, holy, Lord God of Hosts,' remember? Holiness mirrors God, and, remember, God exists in Christ, who is completely human and completely God, God incarnate. The Word made flesh."

"But that only begs the question of what God is."

"Everything begs the question of what God is. Saint Irenaeus said it. I was reading Merton the other night, *Conjectures of a Guilty Bystander.* He quoted the Latin. *Gloria Dei vivens homo.* The glory of God is the human person fully alive. I know what you're going to say: It still begs the question. What does it mean, a human person fully alive? Love. God is love. That's what it means. It's irreducible. Eternal, a mystery. God is love, and love is human and divine. We don't know what it is, except what we know by the incarnation, by the Gospel."

"We're getting off track."

"Off your track, maybe."

"Let's get back to the saints. One need not be canonized to be a saint, right?"

"Well, that's an interesting history. Saint Paul in his

letters—Romans, I remember in particular—addresses the faithful as saints. In one sense, a saint is anyone alive who lives his life fully in Christ. Then, of course, anyone who dies in the state of grace is a saint."

"The state of grace?"

"If you're Catholic, there's no grace without Christ. Anyone who has lived a life according to the Gospel— life fully lived in Christ—is a saint. You don't have to be recognized by the Church; the Feast of All Saints attests to that. During the first centuries after Christ, different communities, or their bishops, canonized their own saints. After the twelfth century—the saints were probably used as a pretext for an ecclesiastical power play— permission for public veneration could be granted only by the Pope. Sometime in the seventeenth century, I think, the process we have now began. Its procedures were bureaucraticized during the Council of Trent. Now the process goes through three long stages—Venerable, Blessed, and Saint. To be declared blessed, there have to be two miracles; to be called a saint, there have to be two more. Canonization is an official declaration by the Church that a person is already in heaven and worthy of public veneration. I think canonization is considered infallible, but I'm not sure."

We paused. "Blessed Martin de Porres," I said. "My father had a statue of him, made by the husband of a woman who worked at the store. He's had it on his

dresser for more than forty years. Blessed Elizabeth Se-
ton, too, founder of the Sisters of Charity, who taught
me in grade school . . ."

"She's a saint now."

"I know. We used to pray for her canonization.
Somewhere in my memory I remember praying for one
more miracle."

"You also remember, don't you, the difference between adoration and veneration?"

"Vaguely," I said.

"You're not supposed to worship the saints. You
worship God. Toward the saints you show veneration.
It's an old issue in the Church—one of the doctrinal
fights during the Reformation. At the time of the Council
of Trent it surfaced again. The church had gotten very
defensive about saints. There was a lot of what looked
like saint-worship at the time, the adoration of saints'
relics, statues, and images, which was seen as an affront
to Christ. The problem is that most people imagine God,
even in Christ, too, as not human. Saints are human.
They are close to God. So people pray to the saints, by-
passing Christ. That makes the Church nervous. Christ's
humanity is diminished."

"The saints act as intercessors, then."

"Yes. The Church recognizes that. But it also
emphasizes the Christology of intercession. A saint is
able to intercede with God—the Vulgate word is *interpel-
lare,* to appeal to, to petition—because, to paraphrase

Irenaeus, a saint has lived a fully human life in Christ.
Saint Thomas said that prayer can be offered in different
ways. One way is by yourself, directly to God, or Christ,
alone; another is by praying to the angels and the saints
to pray to God for you."

"This is all beginning to make more sense to me," I
said. "The doctrine about the saints that has always attracted me is the communion of saints. 'I believe in the
communion of saints'—it's part of the Apostles' Creed,
isn't it?"

"You're right; it is."

"The communion of saints—the union of the faithful
on earth, the blessed in heaven, and the souls in purgatory . . ."

"Through Christ. The Council of Trent added the
notion of the Mystical Body of Christ. The faithful in
heaven, on earth, and in purgatory are one mystical
body, with Christ as their head. What affects one part
affects the others."

"But," I said, "what if you take Christ out of it—or,
at least, take out the Christological language. What do
you have then? A deep union, a common being—you
can visualize it. There are the saints on earth—'saint' in
the sense Saint Paul used it—who, to use your Saint
Irenaeus again, live fully human lives, who know love.
Technically, they're saints, right?"

"Right."

"Then there are those who have died, whose souls

are eternally alive, in purgatory or in heaven, because they lived lives fully human, that is to say, they lived lives of love. Clearly saints, right?"

"Right."

"And what affects one part of this common being, this union, this communion of saints, affects another. And what binds them together? Love, yes. But how? 'The Word made flesh,' if you want a Christology. But, Christology aside, what is 'the Word made flesh?' Language. A form of love. And when you have the language of love between the living and the dead you have that form of language called prayer."

IV.

My mother's father was a Melkite Catholic, another small Eastern rite of the Church, Orthodox until the eighteenth century, when it joined with Rome. When we were children, we went to the Melkite church, Our Lady of Redemption, in an old part of Detroit, each Palm Sunday. The Melkites stayed close to the Orthodox; the vestments, the liturgy, the Palm Sunday procession in which we held candles in one hand, palms in the other, were Byzantine. So was the church. While Father Riashi swung the censor, chanting a language I had never heard before, incense smoke piercing the musty, shadowy air, I remember, behind the altar, the faces of each of the twelve apostles painted around the apse. Saints. But

these icons, bright with color, slightly abstracted, I recognized. They resembled the people around me. The
presence of God, in that Melkite church, I don't remember. God and Christ were somewhere else. The saints
were close and real. You could look into their eyes.

After Joseph's Market could no longer support two
families, Joseph Joseph went to work as a meat cutter for
the Great Atlantic & Pacific Tea Company. Around the
time the international oil cartel forced Detroit's economy
into depression, he was told he would be laid off unless
he worked at a store in Port Huron, a two-hour drive
away. So, close to sixty years old, he woke every morning at five, and my mother did, too. She took three buses
crosstown to the Middle East Gourmet Shop on the city's
east side, where she cooked with her aunt and two cous-
ins. One late Saturday afternoon—what was I doing
there? did my brother tell me she might be there?—I saw
her by herself, kneeling before the side altar of Saint Jude
in the Shrine. I watched her. Small and alone in the
brown and gold shadows, praying to the saint of impossible desires. Now I realize what she prayed for that afternoon (I've never told anyone, not even now).

My grandpa Joseph died of arteriosclerosis when I
was four. Before he died his legs were amputated. My
grandma used to take me to the cemetery with her—a
long drive into the city, past the factories, the small tool-
and-die shops. There, she'd take my hand and we would
walk to the grave. "Pray to Grandpa," she said. Not for

him. Grandpa, she said, had suffered on earth, now he
was in heaven; no, pray to him. For what? Whatever I
wanted my grandpa to pray to God for. Though I must
have felt words, I remember a strange silence saturating
my mind, and that was enough. I felt my grandpa was
talking and listening to me the same way, too.

Colin Thubron observes in *The Hills of Adonis* that in
Lebanon every Melkite, Maronite, Orthodox, or Greek
Catholic village has its saint's tomb. "Sometimes," he
says, "they belong to mad or holy men or women who
actually lived, but, more often, the villagers know nothing of their origin." " 'A great prophet is buried there,'
they say, or 'a famous lady who died long ago'; or sometimes, embarrassed by the absence of any grave, they declare that a holy man or woman passed that way and so
the place is sacred."

I come back to one of Eugenio Montale's last poems,
"Clizia Nel '34" (Clizia in '34); notice its shape, like a
small object:

> Still lounging
> on the chaise longue
> of the veranda
> facing the garden
> a book in hand, perhaps already then
> the lives of half-unheard-of saints
> and baroque poets of scant reputation

this wasn't love
then as now it was always
veneration.

Clizia, Montale's Beatrice—what is the nature of that
beauty? You can build an entire world on a memory. But
how do you say something to someone who is no longer
here, but whose presence is imminent? "The lives of
half-unheard-of saints"—yet one half is still heard of,
still known. "This wasn't love," the poet says, but look
again at the repercussions of his language, refracted and
deepening—ironic. Then, as now, veneration is always
love.

Two years before my mother died of her terrible illness, my father asked me to make a pilgrimage to Carey,
Ohio, to the Shrine of Our Lady of Consolation. Our
family used to visit it when we were children, but I had
not been there in over thirty years. My recollections were
immediate, almost everything was the same—the side
altar with its statue of Our Lady of Consolation, where
I prayed as a child, and, where, I remembered, we would
kiss the statue's feet. I prayed for my mother before the
statue of Our Lady of Consolation, as my father had
asked me to do. I was alone in the church that February
afternoon, except for a man in the back, weeping. Down-
stairs, in the old church, I read letters of those seeking the intercession of miracles. Outside, there was the

holy-water font where, when I was six, my mother washed my fingers, crushed in an accident, so that they would heal, as they did.

"One may really indeed say that that is the essence of genius, of being most intensely alive, that is being one who is at the same time talking and listening," Gertrude Stein said. (Did you know she wrote about Saint Ignatius of Loyola?) "Of being most intensely alive"—*Gloria Dei vivens homo.* One who is at the same time talking and listening—is that that pure silence I remember from those times with Grandma when I prayed to Grandpa to pray for me?

Shortly before my mother died, when, because of her illness, she could not know it, my father placed beside her bed a picture of a Capuchin priest, Father Solanus Casey, who devoted his life to the poor in Detroit. The picture, shaped like a scapular, enclosed in plastic, included a scrap from a piece of clothing worn by the priest when he was alive. There is in Detroit a Cause of Father Solanus, a petition to initiate the process of beatification and canonization. The church in which Father Solanus is buried, Saint Bonaventure's, has since the Great Depression been a place in Detroit where the hungry come to receive food. But not only the poor come to Saint Bonaventure's; there are pilgrims, too, who come to this place where a holy man, who many believe is a saint, lies in the church's north transept.

"Let me show you this picture," my father said one time after we visited my mother. "It's a photograph of the dinner celebrating the opening of Our Lady of Redemption in 1927. Look closely. Here's Grandma and Grandpa Francis at one table, Grandpa and Grandma Joseph at another. And, at the head table, is Father Solanus Casey."

"What's he there for?" I asked.

"Our Lady of Redemption was located only a mile or so from Saint Bonaventure's. Father Solanus was close to the Maronites and Melkites. I've had a copy of this made, and presented it to the Capuchins. It's one of the few photographs of Father Solanus from that time."

When my mother died, the heaviness of her absence all around us, my sister said—I think she was crying— "Now, at least, I'll be able to talk with her again."

"And ask her help," I said.

"Yes, and ask her help, and listen to her, too." The resurrection of the body, I thought. And, I thought, the communion of saints.

Notes on Contributors

PAUL BAUMANN is the associate editor of *Commonweal* magazine. A graduate of Wesleyan University and the Yale Divinity School, he is a columnist for the Religious News Service and has written for the *New York Times* and *Newsday,* among other publications. He lives in Noank, Connecticut, with his wife and their three children.

RICHARD BAUSCH is the author of six novels, most recently *Rebel Powers,* and three volumes of short stories, including *Rare and Endangered Species.* His stories have appeared in the *Atlantic Monthly, Esquire, Harper's,* and the *New Yorker,* and in the *O. Henry Prize* and *Best American Stories* annual collections.

BRUCE BAWER is an Episcopalian and lives in New York. He is the author of several books of criticism, most recently *The Aspect of Eternity;* of a collection of poems, *Coast to Coast;* and of *A Place at the Table: The Gay Individual in American Society.*

SUSAN BERGMAN'S memoir, *Anonymity,* was published in 1994. Her essays and poetry have appeared in *Antaeus, North American Review, Ploughshares,* and other magazines. She lives outside Chicago with her husband and their children.

ROBERT COLES is the author of more than fifty books, including the Children of Crisis series, for which he won the Pulitzer Prize, and the Inner Life of Children series, which concluded with the best-selling *The Spiritual Life of Children.* A child psychiatrist who teaches at Harvard University, he lives in Concord, Massachusetts.

REV. AVERY DULLES, S.J. is the Laurence J. McGinley Professor of Religion and Society at Fordham University and Professor Emeritus at the Catholic University of America, and has written seventeen books and more than 600 articles on theological topics. Past president of both the Catholic Theological Society of America and the American Theological Society, Father Dulles serves on the International Theological Commission and as a consultor to the Committee on Doctrine of the National Conference of Catholic Bishops, and is a member of the United States Lutheran–Catholic dialogue.

PAUL ELIE, an editor with Farrar, Straus and Giroux in New York, has written for *Lingua Franca,* the *New Republic,* and *Commonweal,* to which he is a regular contributor. He was born in upstate New York and now lives in Manhattan.

ENRIQUE FERNANDEZ, a columnist for the *New York Daily News,* is writing a book about Latino culture.

RON HANSEN'S books include *Mariette in Ecstasy, Desperadoes, The Assassination of Jesse James by the Coward Robert Ford,* and the short-story collection *Nebraska,* for which he received an award in Literature from the American Academy and Institute of Arts and Letters. He teaches at the University of California, Santa Cruz, from which he is on leave on a Lyndhurst Foundation fellowship.

KATHRYN HARRISON attended Stanford University and the University of Iowa Writers' Workshop, and in 1983 was awarded a James Michener Fellowship. She is the author of two novels, *Thicker Than Water* and *Expo-*

sure; her third, *Poison,* is forthcoming. She lives in Brooklyn, New York, with her husband, writer Colin Harrison, and their two children.

LAWRENCE JOSEPH is the author of three books of poetry, *Shouting at No One, Curriculum Vitae,* and *Before Our Eyes.* He is married to the painter Nancy Van Goethem and lives in New York, where he is professor of Law at St. John's University School of Law.

NANCY MAIRS is the author of a spiritual autobiography, *Ordinary Time;* a memoir, *Remembering the Bone House: An Erotics of Place and Space;* two collections of essays, *Plaintext* and *Carnal Acts;* and a volume of poetry, *In All the Rooms of the Yellow House.* Her most recent book is *Voice Lessons: On Becoming a (Woman) Writer.* She and her husband, George, live in Tucson, Arizona, where they are active in the peace and justice community.

MARTIN E. MARTY is the Fairfax M. Cone Distinguished Service Professor at the University of Chicago, senior editor of *The Christian Century,* the George B. Caldwell senior scholar-in-residence at the Park Ridge Center for the Study of Health, Faith, and Ethics, and the author of many books on American religion. He is one of the few Christian writer-activists of his generation who never claims to have met Dorothy Day.

KATHLEEN NORRIS   is the author of *Dakota: A Spiritual Geography,* and several books of poetry, including *Little Girls in Church.* She serves on the editorial boards of the *American Benedictine Review* and *Hungry Mind Review,* and has lived since 1984 in western South Dakota.

DAVID PLANTE   was born in Rhode Island and is the author of fourteen books, most recently the novel *Annunciation.* He is also a frequent contributor to the *New Yorker.* He has received a Guggenheim fellowship and awards from the American Academy and Institute of Arts and Letters, and is the first Westerner to have taught at the Gorky Institute of Literature in Moscow. He lives in London.

FRANCINE PROSE   is the author of eight novels, including *Primitive People* and *Household Saints,* and two volumes of short stories, *Women and Children First* and *The Peaceable Kingdom.* Her essays, reviews, and stories have appeared in many magazines and journals, including the *Atlantic Monthly,* the *Yale Review,* and the *New York Times.* She lives near Woodstock, New York.

PAUL WATKINS   is the author of the novels *Night Over Day Over Night, Calm at Sunset, Calm at Dawn* (winner of the Encore Prize), *In the Blue Light of African Dreams,* and *The Promise of Light,* and the memoir *Stand Before Your*

God, a bestseller in England. He was born in California and now lives in New Jersey, where he is writer-in-residence at the Peddie School as well as visiting scholar at the Lawrenceville School.

TOBIAS WOLFF is the author of the memoir *This Boy's Life* and the story collections *In the Garden of the North American Martyrs*, *The Barracks Thief*, and *Back in the World*. He is the editor of the *Vintage Book of Contemporary American Short Stories* and *Best American Short Stories 1994*. *In Pharaoh's Army*, a memoir of his time in Vietnam, is forthcoming. He lives in upstate New York and teaches at Syracuse University.

Permissions and Credits